A Treasury of Great Christians' Correspondence

VOLUME 1

Letters OF Faith

THROUGH
THE

Seasons

James M. Houston

HONOR HB BOOKS

Inspiration and Motivation for the Seasons of Life

COOK COMMUNICATIONS MINISTRIES
Colorado Springs, Colorado • Paris, Ontario
KINGSWAY COMMUNICATIONS LTD
Eastbourne, England

Honor® is an imprint of
Cook Communications Ministries, Colorado Springs, CO 80918
Cook Communications, Paris, Ontario
Kingsway Communications, Eastbourne, England

LETTERS OF FAITH THROUGH THE SEASONS VOL. 1
© 2006 by James M. Houston, Editor

First Printing, 2006
Printed in the United States of America

1 2 3 4 5 6 7 8 9 10 Printing/Year 10 09 08 07 06

[Editor's comments appear in brackets throughout text.]

ISBN-13: 978-1-56292-749-3
ISBN-10: 1-56292-749-3

LCCN: 2006929567

To Barbara Priddy in admiration of her lifelong ministry among women in Washington D.C. and her selfless dedication to Jesus Christ, her Savior and Lord

CONTENTS

LETTER FROM THE EDITOR

*If you were to realize that the calendar is the great,
honorable institution by which you are introduced to
your humanity, you would not confuse the evenings
off for plays with the great holidays
of the human race. Easter is not
a day for entertainment.*

— *Eugen Rosenstock-Huessy*

$\mathcal{D}$ear Reader,

Since you are being introduced into the world of personal letters, it is appropriate that I address you in this more intimate form. Actually I am writing you on September 11, two years after the terrorist attacks in the United States. Since then, the impersonal use of "god-talk" has made us nervous, if such crimes can be motivated by "religion." For as you think about it, fanaticism, as with many other forms of prejudice, arises from making generalizations, whether it be about gender, color, race, religion, politics, social status, and much else. In contrast, the act of receiving and sending personal letters is a counter to all forms of abstraction in thought and attitudes. Perhaps it is the next best thing to presence and oral communication. As John Donne observed, "Our letters are ourselves." They are prosopographical (*prosopon*, Greek for what is personal). Letter writing then, is the informal genre we use to respond spontaneously, to promote intimacy, to sustain friendships, and to deepen relationships. I have just received a letter from someone from whom I have been alienated for the past twenty years, now saying, "I'm sorry, please forgive me." Suddenly a bridge is built over what once seemed to be an ocean apart.

Seneca, tutor of the Roman emperor Nero, was one of the most distinguished letter writers of the Roman world. He lived in a world where people only survived the tyranny of despotism by their diplomatic networking of friendships. He cites ninety-two uses of the epistolary genre for human communication! Biography and letters are traceable over the last five millennia of human history as an instrument of becoming civilized. It was the conjunction of Roman roads, political and literary unification, and the cultivation of a culture of friendship that facilitated this first great period of letter writing, as evidenced in the letters of Cicero, Seneca, Pliny, the Christian Apostles, and the fathers of the church. There are extant today over nine thousand letters of the early Christian Fathers. Nor can we forget that twenty-one of the twenty-nine books of the New Testament are letters. The whole book of Revelation is one letter, within which there are seven other letters written to specific home church situations. As Stanley K. Stowers has observed, "Something about the nature of early Christianity made it a movement of letter writers," as indeed our first letter from Gregory Nazianzen tells us.

When monastic friendships were promoted in the eleventh and twelfth centuries, letters between monks stimulated a new era of friendship. Then the Renaissance, the Reformation, and the Counter-Reformation followed as markedly epistolary cultures, from both Stoic and biblical inspiration. The subsequent Roman Catholic and Protestant pastoral interests in spiritual direction and other personal ministries further promoted new traditions of letter writing, which still continue today. The establishment of postal services at the end of the seventeenth century facilitated the great "Augustan era" of *belle-lettres* by Neo-Stoics such as Horace Walpole. Christian writers such as John Newton saw letter writing as a distinct, personal calling as well as having an eye to their publication!

Today, there is a renewed interest in letters because of the paradigmatic shift in our postmodern culture. Seeking freedom from the "iron cage of rationalism," from traditions, conventions, and institutions, Christianity, embedded in all these social expressions of religion, is now faced with new challenges for renewed intimacy of faith. Indeed, we can speak of a crisis in the transmission of the faith today because of the promotion of mass culture, secular and religious. Technology generates it all into "pop culture" of both varieties. Instead of valuing theory and abstraction, the individual is on a spiritual quest for more space through a fuller sense of life, embodiment, and personal experience.

Private lives have always been more interesting than public personae. And letters help reorientate us from generalizations to particulars, from conventions to specific actions, from theory to practice, and indeed from the profession of faith to the pulsating, living, inner, intimate expressions and experiences of walking with God, of being open before God. So Søren Kierkegaard interpreted the Bible as God's love-letter to us. Likewise, our letters can communicate our Christian faith appropriately, expressing our personal relatedness to God. They can help us open, enlarge, and share our hearts, inspire our spirits, and enrich our very being, since we are now entering and sharing "the communion of saints," throughout the last two millennia of Christianity.

But this letter is already too long, so let me tell you what we mean by calling this collection of letters, "a lectionary of letters." Perhaps for the liturgist this sounds like a misnomer. A lectionary is a collection of Scripture readings rather than a collection of letters. Since the fourth century, biblical passages have been read in public. Three annual cycles of readings, for the moveable feasts of the church calendar, have been developed to correspond to the respective use of readings of the three gospels, Matthew, Mark and Luke, while John's gospel has been incorporated in annual readings. The integration of readings from the Old and New Testaments has also developed, except for the Pascal season of Easter, when only the New Testament has been read to highlight the distinctive of Christian from Jewish faith. But as we have noted, so much of the New Testament is written in the genre of the letter, reminding us that we can never be personal enough before the triune grace of God, as three persons in one Godhead, engaged eternally in expressions of divine love. Perhaps then, the genre of the letter is not only permissible in a lectionary, but it can positively enlarge and enrich our Christian faith. This is our intent, and for which we pray as you open this book, to read these letters in the context of the daily reading of Scripture, of a thought for the day, and of praying ecumenically with many of the saints, past and present.

We start these letters with the beginning of December, because in the church's calendar this is the inception of the Advent season. Sundays have always been recognized as the feast days of the church, commemorating both creation and redemption, as the gracious acts of God from which he rested in their glorious accomplishment. Advent Sunday may be either the last Sunday of November, or the first Sunday of December, according to the annual cycle.

In commemorating the Incarnation, it is a time of personal challenge, celebrant of God breaking into human affairs by the birth of His Son, Jesus Christ. Taken seriously, it can be shattering of our own world-building enterprises. With Christmas day we celebrate the nativity of our Lord, leading into the season of the Epiphany, after the second Sunday after Christmas. Epiphany refers to the "appearance of our Lord upon earth," celebrated by the seven subsequent Sundays. Depending on the astronomical date of Easter, there may be as many as four Sundays of Lent, beginning with Ash Wednesday prior to the first Sunday of Lent. It is the season of contrition, repentance, fasting, and prayer as one faces temptation and as our Lord also enters the wilderness and anticipates his passion and death. Passion week follows to prepare us for Palm Sunday and the sequence of Holy Week, including Holy Thursday—when Jesus institutes the Last Supper; Good Friday—Jesus is crucified; Holy Saturday when Jesus enters hell; and then Sunday of the Resurrection, or Easter Day. Easter week then celebrates the risen appearances of Jesus, followed by a sequence of four Sundays after Easter. The fifth is commonly called Rogation Sunday, leading up to Ascension Day, when Christ ascends up on high. Fifty days after Easter Sunday is the Feast of Pentecost, commonly called Whitsunday, in celebration of the Holy Spirit. The following Sunday celebrates the Feast of the most Holy Trinity, together with Corpus Christ on the following Thursday. Twenty-five Sundays after Trinity then bring to a close the Western church's calendar. However, since Easter is a moveable feast, we have added more letters, in order to commemorate these special days of the church calendar for the ongoing use of this lectionary from year to year.

The selection of letters from December to May have been determined by the church's calendar, to focus on how our Christian faith has been unfolded to us and taught by the Fathers in the context of the church councils. These letters emphasize that our faith is a historic faith within the life of the whole church, as expressive of the birth, life, death, resurrection, and ascension of Christ and of the receiving of the Holy Spirit. In the second half of the year we shall read letters expressing the challenge and hostile confirmation to Christianity, either with the Roman world at its inception or in our modern world. Central to all Christian letter writing is the range of New Testament letters to which responses still go on being made, whether by scholars or by ordinary Christians. Letters, too, express the challenges Christians face within their personal sufferings—changing in character with the society we live in as well as of our witness within our professions. The Christian has always a wider perspective than any profession can ever have, forcing us to have a divine as well as human perspective. Thus the Christian's walk with God in a life of prayer, spiritual growth, and the ever-growing and enlarging inner perceptions of God in our life continue to require pastoral counseling, spiritual direction, and personal mentoring in every age of the church. It is still required on an ongoing basis, year by year.

This lectionary is intended then to serve a wide range of Christian concerns: for church members seeking to be more familiarized with the church's calendar; for the historical inquirer seeking more reference to the history of the church; for the spiritual seeker hungry to be fed more devotionally in a living faith; for the serious student perhaps in seminary training desirous of further Christian formation to teach others; and indeed for all who desire to be mentored more personally by the communion of saints. But the end result is that God alone can disciple us after our baptism, "in the name of the Father, the Son, and the Holy Spirit."

Thank you for reading this introductory letter. Now it is time to invite you to enter into the Christian world of letters, past and present, and perhaps spend time daily with them.

8003

P.S. Perhaps before you send off your own batch of cryptic e-mail messages, allow Augustine of Hippo, Leo the Great, Francois Fenelon, John Newton, or even a contemporary e-mail letter within this collection to peer over your shoulder and challenge you to write more meaningful letters in future; they might just change your life and also help you enter into more meaningful relationships!

ACKNOWLEDGMENTS

I am indebted to my editor, Craig Bubeck, who shared the vision to publish this anthology of letters and completed the process of bringing this manuscript to press. I am grateful to David Dobson and David Chao, earlier editors who gave the initial help to launch the project. Anita Palmer assisted in the early editing and her enthusiasm encouraged the task ahead. I owe warm thanks to two assistants, Diane Krusemark and Paul Philatreau, who collected and typed out some of the letters, while Paul Fiber nobly established a system for obtaining copyright permissions. My family—Christopher, Lydele, Claire, and Penelope—cheered me on with the overall shaping of the anthology, while my wife Rita endured with infinite patience my immersion in the task, which proved far greater than I had originally anticipated. Above all my warmest thanks go to the many correspondents whose letters give strong and profoundly honest, contemporary perspectives to balance the widely historical and ecumenical approaches selected. For me this has been a wonderful experience of the communion of saints.

SEASON OF ADVENT

*A*dvent is the season for human confrontation and challenge, a time in which to shift from human to divine perspectives. For it announces God's entry into human affairs. For it is not humankind that has become godlike, so that God might become human, but God who has become human so that we should become godly, in humility and love. It is, then, a season both of judgment upon human affairs as well as of promise and joy. It is the season embracing the four Sundays of Advent, as well as the Christmas season beginning with December 25 through the next two Sundays into early January.

The Advent season is deeply rooted in the biblical world, prefiguring the advent of the Messiah. Jews, when celebrating the Passover feast, still leave an empty seat at the table for his arrival. Christians, however, celebrate the historical reality of God's advent in Jesus Christ, as he invites us to his table. For Jesus is described as "he who comes," or "the coming One," with reference to both his first coming and his promised second coming (Matthew 21:9; Luke 7:19).

The technical term applied to the season, *parousia,* was used originally for the physical advent and presence of the emperor visiting a Roman city, which was often commemorated by the erection of a new monument or by special coins being struck. The Christian Advent season is a far greater event, for it announces God's entry into our world and it is thus a challenge to our secular, exclusive human mind-set with its self-focused attitudes.

THE INTIMACY OF LETTERS

*Gregory of Nazianzen (329–389) was one of the three great Cappadocian
Fathers, whose preaching led to the final acceptance of the Nicene, Trinitarian
Creed of the church by the Council of Constantinople in 381. In this letter to
his friend Nicobulus, he outlines the laconic and simple style of letter-writing
which was praised by his circle of Christian friends, in contrast with the
rhetorical finery of pagan letters.*

Since you have raised the question—letter-writers are of two kinds,
some too lengthy, some too brief. Both are equally wide of the perfect
mean, like archers who send their shafts now short of the mark, now
beyond it: both are equally at fault, though from opposite causes. The test
of a letter is its utility; we should not be long-winded when there is little
to be said, nor too brief when there is much. Why should we? ... Should
we write to such little purpose that we might as well never have written
at all? Are we to imitate a noonday shadow ... visible only by glimpses,
mere impressions of expressions? So we must avoid either extreme, to
concentrate on achieving the perfect mean ... so much for brevity.

As for the method of expression, the rhetorical is clearly to be
avoided, and the simple and natural preferred; in short, the best kind of
letter will convince both the uneducated and the learned alike, both in
popularity and yet also in profundity. To do both, lucidity is essential, for
it is annoying to have to guess a riddle and puzzle over what the letter is
trying to communicate.

The third quality in a letter is its charm. So we must take care not to
write baldly and ungrammatically, and yet also to lighten it with sugges-
tive pithy statements, proverbs, bon mots, and other sweeteners of style.
But we must avoid also using them to excess; for if their absence suggests
we are unlettered, their excess shows intemperance....

I once heard a wise man observe about the eagle, that when the birds
were setting about to elect a king, each coming decked in his different
finery, the best thing about the eagle was that it did not need to set up
looking distinguished. This is also true of letter-writing, for it is essential

to be natural, to get as close to the truth as it is possible. So much for letters—though when I am challenged what I think are more important matters, I don't always keep to the rules myself!

Scripture Meditation

We always thank God for all of you, mentioning you in our prayers. We continually remember before our God and Father your work produced by faith, your labor prompted by love, and your endurance inspired by hope in our Lord Jesus Christ.
— I THESSALONIANS I: 2–3

Thought for the Day

What a way to begin to write a letter, as the apostle Paul began his first letter to the community in Thessalonica, with many more to follow! Perhaps such faith, love, and hope will prompt us to write letters like Paul.

Prayer

The grace of our Lord Jesus Christ be with you.
— I THESSALONIANS 5:28

DECEMBER 2: THE CLASSICAL WORLD
EXCELLED IN LETTERS OF FRIENDSHIP

Seneca (ca. AD 4–65), imbued with Stoic thought, was the leading Roman intellectual of the first century. Tutor of the Emperor Nero, he was a contemporary of the apostle Paul. The idea of "paraenetic letters," guiding a

student's character by means of letters, goes back at least to Epicurus. It is
following the pattern of relating precepts and reasons for precepts to living
examples of idealized behavior. This is illustrated in this letter Seneca writes to
a younger friend, Lucilius, Procurator or Governor of Sicily, about AD 62.
Seneca is fully aware that to mentor others, one has to go on learning oneself.

*T*o his own Lucilius, Greeting!

I feel my dear Lucilius, that I am being not only reformed, but transformed. I do not yet, however, assure myself, or indulge in the hope that there are no elements left in me that need to be changed. Of course there are many that should be more integrated, or made sparser, or be brought into greater prominence. And indeed this very fact is proof that my spirit is altered into something better—than it can see its own faults of which it was previously ignorant. In certain cases sick men are congratulated because they themselves have perceived that they are sick. I wish therefore to inform you of this sudden change in myself; I should then begin to place a surer trust in our friendship—the true friendship, which I hope neither fear nor self-interest can ever sever, the friendship in which and for the sake of which people meet death. I can show you many who have lacked—not friends—but a (true) friendship; this, however, cannot possibly happen when souls are drawn together by identical inclinations into an alliance of honorable desires. And why did it not happen? Because in such cases people know that they have all things in common, especially their troubles.

You cannot conceive what distinct progress I notice that each day brings to me. And when you say "Give me also a share in these gifts which you have found so helpful," I reply that I am anxious to heap all these privileges upon you, and that I am anxious to learn in order that I may mentor. Nothing else will ever please me, no matter how excellent or beneficial, if I must keep this knowledge to myself. And if wisdom were given me under the express condition that it must be kept hidden and not expressed, I should refuse it. Nothing good is pleasant to possess, without having friends to share it.

I shall therefore send you the specific books I referred; and in order that you may waste no time in searching here and there for profitable topics, I shall quote the exact passages, so that you can turn at once to those whom I approve and admire. Of course, however, the living voice and the intimacy of a common life will help you more than the written word. So you must go to the scene of action for yourself.… Meanwhile, I owe you my daily little contribution: you shall be told what pleased me today in the writings of Hecato; it is these words: "What progress, you ask, have I made? I have begun to be a friend to myself." That indeed was a great benefit; such a person can never be alone. You may be sure that such a man is a friend to all mankind. Farewell.

Scripture for Meditation

I have called you friends, for everything that I learned from my Father I have made known to you.
—JOHN 15:15

Thought for the Day

Jesus teaches us that friendship comes ultimately from God's love.

Prayer

Father … I have revealed you to those whom you gave me out of the world.… Now they know that everything you have given me comes from you.
—JOHN 17:6–7

DECEMBER 3: THE ABUSE OF TIME ILL-SPENT

Jerome (342–420) who translated the Bible from its original languages into Latin and wrote prodigiously many commentaries of the Scriptures, never wasted a moment. He writes to a friend, Marcella, whose mother Albina was "like his own mother" in his affection for her.

$\mathcal{A}$mbrose, whose generous supplies of paper, money, and copyists enabled that "Adamanius" or "Iron Man," our Origen, to write his innumerable books, records the following in a letter to Origen from Athens. They never sat down to a meal together without something being read aloud to them, and that they never went to bed without one of the brethren to read the Scriptures aloud. Thus it was both day and night, prayer followed reading and reading, prayer [this is still a monastic custom]. Have we ever done like that? ... A couple of hours of reading finds us beginning to yawn, we pass the hand over the face, we try to repress our boredom, and if wearied without much toil, we beguile ourselves again to worldly pursuits....

I am ashamed to mention the habit of morning calls, ... where the conversation gradually gets under way, becomes regular gossip, the absent torn to pieces, other people's lives discussed, devouring each one until no one has a shred of character left. Thus when the guests are gone, we make up our accounts, and these are sure to make us either anxious or angry....

Clothing too, is less for necessity than for elegant display. For wherever our interest lies, our foot is swift, our tongue apt, our ears attentive ... and the gain of a penny fills us with joy, the loss of a halfpenny with sorrow. Made in God's image, what diverse characters, in the corruption of our hearts, do we assume! As in the theater a single actor can impersonate sometimes a robust Hercules, at others a melting Venus, or a trembling Cybele, so we whom the world would hate if we were not of the world, can play as many roles as there are sins to commit....

Let Rome keep her noise, the arena its atrocities, the circus its follies, the theater its revels.... For us it is good to cleave unto the Lord, and to place our hope in him. And one day, when Heaven has transformed our poverty, we shall exclaim, "What does heaven hold for me, and what have I required on earth, only thee, O Lord?" When heaven promises us such good, shall we grieve over the trivial and paltry things of earth?

Scripture Meditation

Let us behave decently, as in the daytime, ... clothe yourselves with the Lord Jesus Christ.
—ROMANS 13:13–14

Thought for the Day

Shall we, today, continue to stir out our lives with coffee spoons, our only monument lost golf balls?

—T. S. ELIOT

Prayer

Almighty and everlasting God, from whom comes every good and perfect gift, mercifully grant that the frequent meditation of your infinite goodness may make us love thee above all things.... Amen.

—THE BOOK OF HOURS

DECEMBER 4: THE LOST ART OF LETTER WRITING

Even at the beginning of the twentieth century, Joel Chandler Harris (1848–1908), the author of the Uncle Remus *children's books, deplored the lost art of letter writing, as he writes to his son on April 5, 1900.*

Dear Evelyn:

Your letter was waiting for me when I came home, but was not the less interesting because I had seen you in the meantime. We usually say more in a letter than we do in conversation, the reason being that, in a letter, we feel we are shielded from the indifference or enthusiasm that our remarks may meet with or arouse. We commit our thoughts, as it were, to the winds. Whereas in conversation, we are constantly watching or noting the effect of what we are saying and when the relations are intimate, we shrink from being taken too seriously on the one hand, and on the other, not seriously enough.

But people no longer write letters. Lacking the leisure and for the most part, the ability, they dictate dispatches and scribble messages.

When you are in the humor, you should take a peep at some of the letters written by people who lived long ago, especially the letters of women. There is a charm about them impossible to describe, the charm of unconsciousness and the sweetness of real sincerity. But in these days, we have neither the artlessness nor the freedom of our forbears. We know too little about ourselves. Constraint covers us like a curtain. Not being very sure of our feelings, we are in a fog about the feelings of others. And it is really too bad that it should be so. I fear I am pretty nearly the only one who is willing to put his thoughts freely on paper even when writing to his own children. This is the result, as you may say, of pure accident. I am really as remote from the activities of the world and from the commotions that take place on the stage of events as any of the ancients were. It is the accident of temperament, for I am very sure that the temperament has been molded by circumstances and surroundings. All that goes has a profound significance for me, but I seem to be out of the way, a sort of dreamy spectator who must sometimes close his eyes on the perpetual struggle that is going on....

— Your loving Daddy

Scripture Meditation

He had to be made like his brothers in every way, in order that he might become a merciful and faithful high priest in service to God.
—HEBREWS 2:17

Thought for the Day

Can we recover the discipline of letter writing to promote a more personalized expression of shared faith?

Prayer

Thou art a God near unto every one of us. And not alone do you hear that which we speak: that which we think sounds in your ear; and that which we feel and that which lies fallow both of thought

and feeling are perfectly known to you. Accept not only our thought and feeling, but all those unmeasured elements from which spring both thought and feeling.
—HENRY WARD

DECEMBER 5: LEARN TO READ SCRIPTURE AS GOD'S LETTER TO US

Pope Gregory the Great (ca. 540–604) was a pastoral theologian of integrity who, after the Patriarch of Constantinople assumed the title "ecumenical/universal patriarch" in 595, responded with the title "servant of the servants of God," a title still used by popes. Soon after this event Gregory, author of nearly one thousand letters, wrote to Theodore, the Patriarch's physician.

Since God loves most those who most rest in his love, I have a complaint to make against the gracious mind of my most glorious son, the Lord Theodore. He has received from the Holy Trinity the gift of intellect, of wealth, of mercy and love, and yet he is wholly absorbed in secular affairs. He is fully occupied with the constant ceremonies of the court, and he completely neglects the daily reading of his Savior's words.

Yet what is Scripture but God's letter to his creatures? Now, if you were somewhere abroad and received a letter from your earthly emperor, you would doubtless not pause a moment, you would not rest, you would not sleep, until you had opened it and learned what this earthly emperor had written to you.

The emperor of heaven, the Lord of men and of angels, has sent you his Letters for the saving of your life, and yet, my glorious son, you do not read them diligently. Study them, I beg of you, meditate daily on your creator's words. Learn from God's words to know God's heart, that you may long ever more ardently for the things eternal, that your mind may become inflamed with greater longing for the joys of heaven. For your soul will rejoice in a deeper rest hereafter in proportion as it now knows no rest from the love of God. To be able to do this, then, may almighty God pour upon you his spirit of consolation. May he fill you with his presence, and so relieve you of all care.

Scripture Meditation

Do not let this Book of the Law depart from your mouth; meditate on it day and night, so that you may be careful to do everything written in it. Then you will be prosperous and successful.
—JOSHUA 1:8

Thought for the Day

How to live the fullest Christian life was Gregory's great desire. Is it also your desire?

As Gregory the Great said, "For spiritual warfare we are not armed by secular, but by spiritual letters."

Prayer

Lord, let me "deny myself," by beginning to be what I am not, and cease to be what I have been.
—GREGORY THE GREAT

ENTERING INTO THE SPIRIT OF ADVENT

DECEMBER 6: LIVING THROUGH THE SEASONS OF THE YEAR

*Francis de Sales (1567–1622) worked tirelessly as the Catholic Bishop of
Geneva, writing an immense number of letters, full of wise and loving
counsel. His base was Annecy, where he founded with Madame Jane Frances
Fremyot de Chantal the Order of Visitation. His ministry focused on
laypersons who were caught up in the busy life of the world.
He writes on February 11, 1607 to Madame de Chantal.*

My very dear Daughter,

I can see that all the seasons of the year meet to give their distinctive
challenges to your soul. The winter you feel as being the season of steril-
ity, distractions, disgust, and even boredom. Then comes the month of
May with the roses in bloom, and so too are the perfumes of the spiritual
flowers released by holy desires to please our good God. Then comes the
autumn season, when you complain you do not see plentiful fruits. So be
it, because it often happens that in thrashing the wheat and pressing the
grapes, one finds more blessing in the harvesting and *vendage* than one
would have expected. For it is natural to expect everything to happen in
the spring and summer of life, but no, my dear daughter, one needs to
face the inner difficulties and problems of one's inner life, as well as the
apparent successes of outward appearances.

Ultimately, all our seasonal circumstances have to be faced in the
reality of our heavenly destiny. There only will all be all and in all. The
spring may express the beauty of the Christian life, while the autumn
may bring forth joy. So what then of the winter? The winter is needed
to exercise self-denial, and to exercise in a thousand small ways the
struggles we go through to live devotionally. It is a climate of spiritual
dryness, perhaps, yet little by little we endure it, provided we have
godliness and are determined not to get discouraged, but persist in the
fortitude of faith....

Let us then live joyously and courageously, my dear daughter. There is
absolutely no doubt whatsoever of the reality that Jesus Christ is our life.

Scripture Meditation

*Let us not become weary in doing good, for at the proper time we
will reap a harvest if we do not give up.*
—GALATIANS 6:9

Thought for the Day

Christian growth requires us to go through all the vicissitudes of life as
reflected in the church's calendar of the annual seasons.

Prayer

O God, make me truly to be a child of innocence and simplicity!
—FRANCIS DE SALES

DECEMBER 7: THE CHALLENGE OF ADVENT

---

*After a radical change in his own life, Jean-Jacques Olier (1608–1657),
companion of Vincent de Paul, founded the Society of St. Sulpice in Paris. He
devoted himself to spiritual direction through which he deeply influenced
many of the aristocracy. Here he discusses with a young lady appropriate
attitudes for the celebration of Advent.*

*M*y dear Daughter,

You know, Advent is a season of penitence when gratitude, and
above all humility, should mark our experience of this holy season. It is
one of gratitude as we compare our situation with that of the Old
Testament, without 'the consolation of Israel' that the advent of the

Son of God has brought into our Christian world. So in order that we enter into the spirit and attitudes of the church's calendar, we must continually be amazed in wonder at the advent of the Word of God, in his descent into our own hearts.

My dear daughter, how can you be loveless and indifferent if you realize the Word dwelling in his glory, enthroned in majesty, has actually stooped to be loved by us, in our creaturely limitations? Reposing eternally in the Father's bosom, he descended into Mary's womb to share our limitations. Dwelling eternally adored in the effulgent glory of the other two divine persons of the most Holy Trinity, he was born in the midst of the animals, as an abandoned pauper. It is not just that two natures were integrated, but rather he laid aside his eternal glory, and embraced the opposite of what he was as God … God as Creator of time entered this temporal reality. The Word became flesh. The Infinite became limited. The All-Powerful became weak. The wise became a child. The King became a slave. The source of all grace, "became sin for us" (2 Cor. 5:21), in suffering all its consequences on our behalf. So all our efforts to be humble still remain limited as a human being, in contrast to the infinite contrast of his divine humiliation.…

So where is your heart in the midst of such reflections of the Advent season? Should we not desire to love him, even as he exposes our own contrary attitudes of pride and selfishness? For it is the purpose of the eternal Word not only to become incarnate within Mary, and not only to be united with one particular person, but to unite in love all his beloved creatures. His gracious presence enthralls our hearts, and compels us to be responsive to such a Presence amongst us, as we are reminded of in the very holy Sacrament [i.e. of bread and wine].

This then is the season, my very dear daughter, when we open our hearts fully to his advent, to discover he comes like a divine deluge, indeed as a fire-storm into the midst of our culture and urban life. For Jesus says: "I have come to bring fire on earth, and how I wish it were already kindled!" (Luke 12:49).… It is then the time to judge everything, to become detached, to surrender everything, and to purify our loves that all are motivated by his love alone.…

Scripture Meditation

I have come to bring fire upon the earth.
—LUKE 12:49

Thought for the Day

We prepare for the Advent season by opening and cleansing our hearts to, and by, his love alone.

Prayer

O Lord, the day when the babe came down in the midst of the stall, the watchers descended and proclaimed peace. May that peace be in all our streets for all our children.

—Ephrem the Syrian

December 8: A Simple Test Whether Christ Truly Dwells within Us

John of the Cross (1542–1591), or John de Yepes, was born a weaver's son in Castile, Spain, and was perhaps the greatest lyricist of the Spanish language, who joined Teresa of Avila in establishing the reformed or discalced Order of Carmelites. He is one of the greatest mystical writers of the church, but as he shows in this letter to an unknown nun, his spiritual expectations of those falsely claiming to be indwelt by Christ could be communicated harshly.

In the practice of prayer exhibited by this person, I cannot consider her spirit to be good. The first observation I see is that she has a great fondness for her own way: while a true spirit practices great detachment from all self-desire. The second is that she is too self-confident, and has too little fear of self-delusions; while the Spirit of God is never without fear, in order—as the wise man says—to keep a soul from sin. The third is that she wishes to impress others that she is in such a good and exalted state: but this is not the fruit of the Spirit.

Rather this would exhibit the wish to be lightly esteemed, even despised, and in fact is self-deprecating. The fourth and key issue is that the fruits of humility are not evidenced. For when the graces she talks about are really there, they result in the soul's experience of inner abasement in true humility. If these had truly affected her, she would not fail to say a good deal about them. For these fruits of humility would be the most obvious change of her life. For humility can never be absent whenever we experience union with God. And because a soul is humbled before it is exalted, as Proverbs 18:12 states, we can truly exclaim: "It is good for me to be afflicted so that I learn your decrees." So the fifth and final observation is that the style and language she uses does not seem to me that of the spirit she refers to. For that spirit teaches us a simple style, free from affectation and exaggeration. Such is not what I see in her. So when she claims: "God spoke to me" and "I spoke to God" all that seems nonsense.

I advise her superiors not to take her boastful claims too seriously. Don't let her talk or write on these matters ... such discipline may seem severe, but without it, she will never possess that true gentleness of soul, in which great graces have been wrought.

Scripture Meditation

Before his downfall a man's heart is proud, but humility comes before honor.
—PROVERBS 18:12

Thought for the Day

Just as there was no room for Mary and Joseph in the inn, what shuts out Christ from our hearts at this Advent season?

Prayer

O Eternal God, make my body and soul a holy temple, purified for the habitation of Thy Holy Spirit.
—JEREMY TAYLOR

DECEMBER 9: CHRISTIAN FAITH IS LIFE, NOT A PHILOSOPHICAL SYSTEM

*Alexander Elchaninov (1881–1934) was descended from a distinguished
Russian military family and a friend of many of Russia's cultural leaders prior
to the Russian Revolution. I resided in Oxford for seven years with one of his
pupils, Mrs. Militsa Zernov, and her husband, Nicholas, who introduced me to
Elchaninov's writings. This letter is to his students from Tiflis, Georgia, where
he taught and was the school principal.*

*D*ear students,

Allow me to say something about your reading. All that you have
read until now was for the development and strengthening of your
Christian thought, your Christian outlook. But this is not enough. Not
only is it not enough, but such kind of reading should decidedly become
secondary. Christianity is not a philosophical system. It is life, a special
way of life, and this must be studied cautiously—literally every day.

There are masters of this divine life who started with the first steps
and who attained such lofty heights that one does not always understand them when they speak about these summits. You must read
them. They are of course the Holy Fathers, the ascetics, heroes, giants
in their faith and zeal for life in God: Anthony the Great (251–256),
Ephrem the Syrian (d. 373), Abba Dorotheus, John of the Ladder, ...
Theophan the Recluse, John of Kronstadt.... [They] are steeped in the
spirit of the Desert Fathers, but express it to the conditions of our life
... which for the present may remain invisible to you, but will manifest
itself when the right time comes and perhaps will save you when you
get into in real trouble.

You complain that reading the Holy Fathers is difficult and even
bores you. But try to tell yourself that it is not they who are difficult
and boring but your soul which is not yet properly prepared to see the
light that others behold. You may object that there is too great a dis-
crepancy between the heights on which they move and the pettiness of
everyday life, which holds us imprisoned. But watch closely—it cannot
be that you always experience only difficulty and boredom. At rare
moments of life—in ordeal and sorrow, or in great joy—the soul seeks
to rise; and then, perhaps, the words that hitherto failed to touch you

will acquire a different sound. At ordinary times, on the other hand, hard work is necessary ... to arouse oneself from sloth. Rest assured — these efforts will yield their fruit, and the accumulation of spiritual riches.

Scripture Meditation

Ask the former generations and find out what their fathers learned, for we were born only yesterday and know nothing, and our days on earth are but a shadow.
—JOB 8:8–9

Thought for the Day

Neglecting Christianity's saints and historical figures can lead to the trivialization of faith today.

Prayer

O Lord my God, teach my heart where and how to seek you, where and how to find you.
—ANSELM

DECEMBER 10: THE PERSONAL RELIGION OF THE HEART
MUST BE GROUNDED IN HISTORICAL TRUTH

Baron Friedrich von Hugel (1852–1925), son of an Austrian diplomat and a Scottish mother, was a devout Roman Catholic philosopher and interested in the Christian mystics. His letters of spiritual direction are most charmingly written to his niece Gwendolen Greene.

*M*y very dear Gwen,

I hate all the notion that there is no value in anything that is past—that the only value is in what we have got now. That cuts us right off, it gives us no base, it leaves out the richness and soundness of the great traditions. I want to teach you through all those gigantic things, the martyrs, gnosticism, skepticism, that atrocious thing "the eighteenth century" (i.e. as "the Enlightenment," which fooled us to believe it "enlightened"). I want you to learn about the great souls who lived through all those tracts of time. You will learn about progress. People talk so much about "progress" nowadays. Where is all this wonderful "progress" in the human soul?

Religion to be deep and rich must be historical. I can't help it if you don't believe in religion, it's an historical fact.... The New Testament—what is it in form? It is nothing—it is not even literature—but it is the bread of life. About knowledge—so many people want to know, in order to know, and nothing else. How empty it all is! What a difference is Christianity!

Christianity is a thing of the heart, and it's that which matters. No other knowledge counts but that which feeds and strengthens the mind and soul. The spiritual world is a great world of facts, and you must learn about it, as you would learn about forests from the forester. After five or six years living among the trees you will know something about them.... You want to be truthful to find the truth, to be truthful to find God. We can't eliminate all difficulties ... nor can we know God exhaustively.... We shall never be able to explain God, though we can apprehend him more and more through the spiritual life. I want you to hold very clearly the otherness of God and the littleness of mankind. If you don't get that, you can't have adoration, and you cannot have religion without adoration.

Scripture Meditation

Ever since I heard about your faith in the Lord Jesus and your love for all the saints, ... I pray also that the eyes of your heart may be enlightened.

—EPHESIANS 1:15, 18

Thought for the Day

Entering into communication with the saints at Advent can deepen our faith in God.

Prayer

> The glorious company of the apostles: praise thee.
> The goodly company of the prophets: praise thee.
> The noble army of the martyrs: praise thee.
> The holy church throughout all the world: doth acknowledge thee.
>
> —TE DEUM LAUDAMUS

DECEMBER 11: DISTINGUISHING REALITY FROM FANTASY

Malcolm Muggeridge (1903–1989) was a British journalist, social lampoonist as editor of Punch, *and well-known television commentator. Here is a letter from March 1985 to the editor who had known Muggeridge since he began his journey of conversion to Christianity a few years earlier.*

*D*ear Jim,

I always come back to one point ... and I don't mean that's necessarily the overwhelming point ... but it is one that a person who has had my sort of life is most aware of: the contrast between reality and fantasy. Because it has been for me the access to reality that drew me really to commit myself to the Christian faith. So I can't help thinking that, in our world as it's shaping—when influences like television are so enormous on people's lives—the great service that Christianity can perform, the great need that it can meet, is for finding reality.

For never before in human history has there been so overwhelming a fantasy pressing in on people. When you think of the media, of advertising, of all the unreality of utopian politics, you will think also of all the unreality of "Kingdom-of-Heaven-on-earth faith." This amounts to a fantasy of extraordinary proportions. I've been more aware of this now than ever before in spending time with students on a university campus.... The degree to which, not just the television screen, but their very teaching, their very learning that's offered them is fantasy learning.

For we are being encouraged to believe humankind is ultimately rational, so that if only we can acquire knowledge, if only we can be sorted out ... if only we can ensure that our sex life is perfectly harmonious and regular, if only our diet is correct, etc., etc. ... with all the various things that are poured in upon us, then we will find ourselves completely at ease in our society. So we are conned to believe we live successfully when life is made perfectly clear in its purposes and in its nature. Indeed, as the fairy stories used to say, we will then "live happily ever after."

Of course, the more we are committed to such fantasies, the more we will pursue notions like the pursuit of happiness. Then inevitably we fall into confusion, contradiction, and ultimately despair....

Scripture Meditation

We know also that the Son of God has come and has given us understanding, so that we may know him who is true ... keep yourselves from idols.

—I JOHN 5:20–21

Thought for the Day

Muggeridge reflected frequently upon Blake's distinction of seeing "with the eye," and of seeing "through the eye." The one is personal fantasy as shaping the world to one's own hopes and desires, while the other is using God inspired imagination, to see "through the eye" on to the reality of the God-given world.

Prayer

> *And is it true,*
> *This most tremendous tale of all,*
> *Seen in a stained-glass window's hue,*
> *A baby in an ox's stall?*
>
> *The maker of the stars and sea*
> *Become a child on earth for me ...*
> *No love that in a family dwells,*
> *No caroling in frosty air,*
>
> *Nor all the steeple-shaking bells*
> *Can with this single Truth compare—*
> *That God was man in Palestine*
> *And lives to-day in bread and wine*
> —JOHN BETJEMAN, "CHRISTMAS"

DECEMBER 12: SEEKING SELF-PERFECTION FOR ONESELF IS THE SOURCE OF MUCH FANTASY

Francois de Salignac de la Motte Fenelon (1651–1715), exiled as
Archbishop of Cambrai and tutor for some ten years to the grandson of
Louis XIV, writes to Madame De Montberon, the governor's wife.

*M*adame,

Let me show you, my dear daughter, what I believe God is leading me to tell you frankly. The mainstay of your life is a love of fantasy, cherished in your heart since childhood. It is an exaggerated self-opinion, hidden beneath the appearance of sensitiveness and heroic generosity. No one has ever dared tell you this! You have possessed it in the world, and it remains with you in the most sacred undertakings.

I always find in you a taste for intellectual pursuits and pleasures that quite alarm me; your own fastidiousness causes you to find thorns in every condition. You are an excellent counselor of others, but you get yourself overwhelmed by the merest trifles. Everything wrings your heart; you are completely taken up with the fear of doing the wrong thing, or even with further regrets when you get it right! You exaggerate your faults by the excessive vividness of your fantasies, and it is always some triviality that drives you to despair.

You foster two things within yourself, Madame, which cause you such endless suffering: your intense scruples, rooted in you since childhood, but getting more and more exaggerated in later life; and your habit of always desiring affirmation.... These cause you to doubt yourself, make you feel so helpless, and even believe you have lost God. All this comes from a life of seeking to please everybody but yourself....

You love yourself so that you really want to be only satisfied with yourself. This is the cause of all your scruples. You wish that God as well as other people should always be pleased with you, and you should always be pleased with yourself in all that you do in "God's service." So here is the irony of your situation. You appear to be so engrossed by the claims of God and of His glory. At the same time you are always anxious, for really you think you want to glorify God but actually you want this to satisfy yourself in your own self-perfection, not God at all! Ah, what delight it would be to see you calm, simple, freed from self-scrutiny, and vain fantasies about yourself!

Scripture Meditation

O LORD, *you have searched me and you know me ... you are familiar with all my ways.*
—PSALM 139:1, 3

Thought for the Day

When I allow pride to dominate my life, I become my own worst enemy.

Prayer
Grant me the grace of a humble and contrite spirit that I may
come into thy presence washed clean with tears of godly sorrow.
And let my affections be so inseparably united to thee that I may
have no carnal desires left.
—AUGUSTINE OF HIPPO

DECEMBER 13: PERFECTLY HUMAN, PERFECTLY DIVINE

C. S. Lewis (1898–1963), a don at both Oxford and Cambridge, explores the
mystery of Christ's humanity. A faithful correspondent to many admirers of
his books, he writes here to Mrs. Frank L. Jones in 1947.

The doctrine that our Lord was God and man does not mean that he
was a human body with God instead of the normal human soul. It means
that a real man [human body and human soul] was in him so united with
the second person of the trinity as to make one person: just as in you and
me, a complete anthropoid animal [animal body and animal "soul" i.e.
instincts and sensations], is so united with an immortal rational soul as to
be one person. In other words, if the divine Son had been removed from
Jesus what would have been left would have been not a corpse but a living man.

This human soul in him was unswervingly united to the God in him, in
that which makes a personality one, namely will. But it had the feelings
of any normal man: hence could be tempted, could fear, etc. Because of
these feelings he could pray: "If it be possible, let this cup pass from me."
Because of its perfect union with his divine nature it unwaveringly
answered: "Nevertheless, not my will but thine be done." The Matthew

passage and the John passage both make clear this unity of will. The Matthew one gives in addition the human feelings.

God could, had he pleased, have been incarnate in a man of iron nerves, the stoic sort who lets no sigh escape him. Of his great humility he chose to be incarnate in a man of delicate sensibilities who wept at the grave of Lazarus and sweated blood in Gethsemane. Otherwise we should have missed the great lesson that it is by his will alone that a man is good or bad, and that *feelings* are not, in themselves, of any importance. We should also have missed the all-important help of knowing that he has faced all that the weakest of us face, has shared not only the strength of our nature but every weakness of it except sin. If he had been incarnate in a man of immense natural courage, that would have been for many of us almost the same as his not being incarnate at all....

Scripture Meditation

Both the one who makes men holy and those who are made holy are of the same family. So Jesus is not ashamed to call them brothers.
—HEBREWS 2:11

Thought for the Day

If Christ shared all our humanity with us, except sin, what can we not give of ourselves to him?

Prayer

O God, raise our minds to the contemplation of thy beloved son, that, seeing his divine beauty, we may be drawn near unto him, and changed into his image, and empowered to bring every thought into obedience to Christ, into harmony with his spirit and his immortal life. Amen.
—THOMAS TREADWELL STONE

DECEMBER 14: GOD'S TRANSACTION OF GRACE

Reverend William Romaine (1714–1795), rector of St. Anne, Blackfriars,
London, was recognized as London's principal preacher. It is said people
came to London to see Garrick, the actor, but to hear Romaine, the preacher.
His grandfather emigrated from France and his father, a corn merchant, was
elected three times as mayor of London. He was a brilliant Hebraic scholar as
well as professor of astronomy at Gresham College for a period. His work
The Life, Walk, and Triumph of Faith *was a classic in its time. He writes this*
letter to a friend on December 29, 1764.

All the blessings of this good season be with my dear friend!

That man for whom Christ was born is the greatest, richest prince on earth: his revenues, his honors, his mighty allies, his everlasting kingdom are beyond all conception. Compared to what he is and has, crowns and empires are but playthings for little children.... Yet he took our flesh, that we might take his Spirit; he was born on earth, that we might have a new birth from heaven; he took our sins, that we might take his righteousness; and our miseries that we might be heirs with him in his happiness. O what an astonishing transaction is this! How full of the richest grace, flowing over with everlasting love! ...

How blest a change do they experience, when by faith they know and can say, "Unto us a child is born; unto us a son is given"? For this is the saving truth: "Jesus is the Christ"; the man is Jehovah, God and man is one in Christ; the child born is the everlasting Father—the virgin's son is Emmanuel, God with us, and her infant babe is her eternal Saviour....

Here then, my dear friend, is a matter of thankfulness to you and me, that we are taught this by God. Happy Christmas to us! Since we have lived to hear and understand the great mystery of godliness—"God manifest in the flesh." Happier still that we believe it; for whomsoever the Holy Spirit enlightens with the knowledge of this saving truth, he also gives faith to receive it, to trust in Christ as God, to depend upon him as the Almighty Savior, to rely upon his finished work, and to lay no other foundation for any grace or glory, but the life and death of this ever-blessed God-man....

—W. R.

Scripture Meditation

Beyond all question, the mystery of godliness is great.

— I TIMOTHY 3:16

Thought for the Day

Do I really want to participate in this glorious exchange of divine grace for my own self-centered condition?

Prayer

> Blessed Lord, who has caused all holy Scriptures to be written for our learning: Grant that we may in such wise hear them, read, mark, learn, and inwardly digest them, that by patience and comfort of thy holy Word, we may embrace and ever hold fast the blessed hope of everlasting life, which thou hast given us in our Savior Jesus Christ.
>
> —COLLECT FOR THE SECOND SUNDAY IN ADVENT

DECEMBER 15: THE TRUTH MAY NOT BE EMOTIONALLY ACCEPTABLE

Flannery O'Connor (1925–1964) was a short-story writer in the American South and a Roman Catholic living in a Baptist culture. Letters were important to her, for she enjoyed friendships and struggled with ill health. Here she writes to a nonbeliever "A," a pen friend for more than nine years. These are two excerpts from letters dated August 2 and September 5, 1955.

[August 2, 1955]

One of the awful things about writing when you are a Christian is that for you the ultimate reality is the Incarnation, the present reality is the Incarnation, and nobody believes in the Incarnation; that is, nobody in your audience. My audience is the people who think God is dead. At least these are the people I am conscious of writing for.

[September 5, 1955]

I can never agree with you that the Incarnation, or any truth, has to satisfy emotionally to be right. It does not satisfy emotionally for the person brought up under many forms of false intellectual discipline such as 19th century mechanism, for instance. Leaving the Incarnation aside, the very notion of God's existence is not emotionally satisfactory anymore for great numbers of people, which does not mean God ceases to exist. M. Sartre finds God emotionally unsatisfactory in the extreme, as do most of my friends of less stature than he. The truth does not change according to our ability to stomach it emotionally. A higher paradox confounds emotion as well as reason and there are long periods in the lives of all of us, and of the saints, when the truth as revealed by faith is hideous, emotionally disturbing, downright repulsive. Witness the dark night of the soul in individual saints. Right now the whole world seems to be going through a dark night of the soul.

There is a question whether faith can or is supposed to be emotionally satisfying. I must say that the thought of everyone lolling about in an emotionally satisfying faith is repugnant to me. I believe that we are ultimately directed Godward but that this journey is often impeded by emotion....

To see Christ as God and man is probably no more difficult today than it has always been, even if today there seem to be more reasons to doubt. For you it may be a matter of not being able to accept what you call a suspension of the laws of the flesh and the physical, but for my part I think that when I know what the laws of the flesh and the physical really are, then I will know what God is....

We know them as we see them, not as God sees them. For me it is the virgin birth, the Incarnation, the resurrection, which are the true laws of the flesh and the physical. Death, decay, destruction are the suspension of these laws. I am always astonished at the emphasis the

Church puts on the body. It is not the soul she says that will rise but the body, glorified.

Scripture Meditation

For everything that was written in the past was written to teach us, so that through endurance and the encouragement of the Scriptures we may have hope.... May the God of hope fill you with all joy and peace as you trust him.
—ROMANS 15:4, 13

Thought for the Day

Even when surrounded by disbelievers, my entire life should convey the Advent message.

Prayer

O Lord Jesus Christ, who at thy first coming didst send thy messengers to prepare thy way before thee: Grant that the ministers and stewards of thy mysteries may likewise so prepare and make ready thy way, by turning the hearts of the disobedient to the wisdom of the just.
—COLLECT FOR THE THIRD SUNDAY IN ADVENT

DECEMBER 16: JESUS CHRIST—IF NOT GOD, WHO?

C. S. Lewis writes on December 11, 1944, to Arthur Greeves, his lifelong friend with whom he maintained a correspondence for almost fifty years.

*M*y dear Arthur,

I was delighted to hear from you.... Your view about the divinity of Christ was an old bone of contention between us, wasn't it? But I thought when we last met you had come down on the same side as me. I don't think I can agree that the churches are empty because they teach that Jesus is God. If so, the ones that teach the opposite, i.e. the Unitarians, would be full, wouldn't they? Are they? It seems to me that the ones which teach the fullest and most dogmatic theology are precisely the ones which retain their people and make converts, while the liberalizing and modernizing ones lose ground every day.... Not of course that I would accept popularity as a test of truth: only since you introduced it, I must say that as far as it is evidence at all it points the other way; and in history also. Your doctrine, under its old name of Arianism, was given a chance: in fact a full run for its money for it officially dominated the Roman Empire at one time. But it didn't last.

I think the great difficulty is this: if he was not God, who or what was he? In Matthew 28:19 you already get the baptismal formula, "In the name of the Father, the Son, and the Holy Ghost." Who is this "Son"? Is the Holy Ghost a man? If not, does a man "send" him? (See John 15:26.) In Colossians 1:12, Christ is "before all things and by him all things consist." What sort of a man is this? I leave out the obvious place at the beginning of John's gospel. Take something much less obvious. When he weeps over Jerusalem (Matt. 23), why does he suddenly say (v. 34) "I send unto you prophets and wise men"? Who could say this but God or a lunatic? Who is this man who goes about forgiving sins? Or what about Mark 2:18–19? What man can announce that simply because he is present acts of penitence, such as fasting, are called "off"? Who can give the school a half-day holiday except the headmaster?

Scripture Meditation

[Christ] ... is the image of the invisible God, the firstborn over all creation. For by him all things were created ... all things were created by him and for him. He is before all things, and in him all things hold together.
—Colossians 1:15–17

Thought for the Day

The idea of the God-man offends monotheistic religions the most because they cannot accept God so identifying himself with humanity.

Prayer

O Incarnation, O greatest truth of all truths, uncreated and created! Wherefore are greater in number the men that scorn you, and know you not, neither believe you, than those who honor and believe you? What will you do? Will you punish so great and mortal failings? O Mercy, wherein there is so great Benignity, Love, Patience, and Humility!

—RAYMOND LULL

DECEMBER 17: WHAT'S CHRISTIANITY WITHOUT THE DIVINITY OF CHRIST?

C. S. Lewis continues his correspondence with his friend Arthur Greaves on December 11, 1944, and December 26, 1945.

Dear Arthur,

The doctrine of Christ's divinity seems to me not something stuck on which you can unstick, but something that peeps out at every point so that you'd have to unravel the whole web to get rid of it. Of course you may reject some of these passages as unauthentic, but then I could do the same to yours if I cared to play that game! When it says God can't be tempted, I take this to be an obvious truth. God, as God, can't anymore than he can die. He became man precisely to do and suffer what as God he could not do and suffer. And if you take away the Godhead of Christ, what is Christianity all about? How can the death of one man have this effect for all men, which is proclaimed throughout the New Testament?

And don't you think we should allow any weight to the fruits of these doctrines? Where are the shining examples of human holiness which ought to come from Unitarians if it is true? Where are the Unitarian "opposite numbers" to St. Francis, George Herbert, John Bunyan, George MacDonald, and even burly old Dr. Johnson? Where are the great Unitarian books of devotion? Where among them shall I find "the words of life"? Where have they helped, comforted, and strengthened us?

[December 26, 1945]

You ask me … "Surely God has always been the same loving and heavenly Father and it was the interpretation of God that Christ revealed." I see what you mean but the question is very difficult for me to answer. On the one hand, something really new did happen at Bethlehem: not an interpretation but an event. God became Man.

On the other hand there must be a sense in which God, being outside time, is changeless, and nothing ever "happens" to him. I think I should reply that the event at Bethlehem was a novelty, a change to the maximum extent to which any event is a novelty: but that all time and all events in it, if we could see them all at once and fully understand them, are a definition or a diagram of what God eternally is. But that is quite different from saying that the incarnation was simply an interpretation or a change in our knowledge.

When Pythagoras discovered that the square on the hypotenuse was equal to the sum of the squares on the other two sides, he was just discovering what had been just as true the day before, though no one knew it. But in 50 BC the proposition God is Man would not have been true in the sense in which it was true in AD 10, because though the union of God and man in Christ is a timeless fact, in 50 BC we had not yet got to that bit of time which defines it.

Scripture Meditation

When John heard in prison what Christ was doing, he sent his disciples to ask him, "Are you the one who was to come, or should

*we expect someone else?" Jesus replied.... "Blessed is the man
who does not fall away on account of me."*
—MATTHEW 11:2–4, 6

Thought for the Day

Do not let the philosophical notion of divine impassibility rob us of the
love of God towards us in Christ.

Prayer

*Almighty God, we give you thanks for the mighty yearning of the
human heart for the coming of a Savior, and the constant promise of your Word that he was to come.*
—SAMUEL OSGOOD

DECEMBER 18: LETTERS AS 'A WORD IN SEASON'

---

*Viscountess Theodosia A. Powerscourt (1800–1836) was descended from a
notable Irish family. She became a Christian at age nineteen, under the
influence of the Methodist preacher John Howell. She left some eighty
letters, of which this is the last she wrote shortly before she
died in December 1836.*

I fear you will think me very ungrateful for so long neglecting to
answer your kind letter—a word of exhortation from you always does
me good; and, indeed, we need every help to keep these heavy souls on
their way. It is a great gift to be able to speak a word in season. "How
good it is," says Solomon. "As apples of gold in pictures of silver." *Jesus*

learnt it. I believe it is by little things the children are fed. He gives us our meat *in due season.*

In this way I have often found letters special and precious means of grace, and I believe they would be more so, and no loss of time, did we more write in faith, and live more each day upon what may be prepared for us by the Spirit of God. When present with a person, *we* may try to make a thing applicable, or be tempted to do so; when absent, if their case is met, it seems more that the Lord has considered the case, and sends his message through his scribe, while it cheers the heart of the writer in passing. There is truly a secret in the ways of God with his own children, and when the Spirit finds a Mount of Olives in our hearts, to pour forth his intercessions in, we must be let into many of his secret dealings with the family of heaven....

What insignificant creatures we are, and how ridiculous we look when we clothe ourselves in robes of glory! They were never made to fit us; we cannot fill them; and yet, how self works through everything! Often a little thing discovers this to us, how we have been speaking for, and seeking self, while apparently and intentionally we have been even jealous of Jesus.... Some hint against ourselves will turn the current, and expose to our hearts our self-idolatry. I am not certain that this has ever been your experience, but I am sometimes quite disgusted with myself, to find I steal his gifts and graces to deck up this household god.... I believe, if he ever blesses us as a whole, it must be by first humbling us to submit to be blessed at any cost, and to let the Spirit take his own place within us....

Scripture Meditation

We take captive every thought to make it obedient to Christ.
—2 CORINTHIANS 10:5

Thought for the Day

Dwelling constantly upon the love of Christ will always give us a word in season to those in need.

Prayer

All that I am, all that I have,
Shall be for ever Thine.

—LADY POWERSCOURT

CONFRONTED BY THE CHRISTMAS STORY

DECEMBER 19: CHRIST AND OUR HUMANITY

Augustine (354–430), bishop of Hippo, preacher, controversialist, and teacher, has been called the most influential of all the Latin Church Fathers. In the following letter he answers the questions of a priest.

*F*irst, I want you to understand that Christian doctrine does not hold that God was infused into the human flesh in which he was born of the Virgin in such a way that he abandoned or lost the government of the universe. Nor did he transfer it to that tiny body as some kind of reduced and contracted substance. This opinion is held by people who are incapable of thinking of anything other than of physical substances.... The soul's natural constitution is very different from the body—and how much more different is that of God, who is the Creator of both soul and body! ... This is a wonder to human intelligence—which does not believe, perhaps, what it does not comprehend.

Second, you must understand the Word of God, through whom everything was made, without thinking that any part of it can pass away or change from future to past. It continues as it is, and is everywhere entire.... And so we have no reason to be afraid of the child's tiny body, lest God should seem to suffer a great diminishment in it. God's greatness is in his power, not in his bulk.... This great power, which has no difficulty in accomplishing difficult things, made the virgin's womb fruitful, from within, not from without. This power joined a reasonable soul to itself, and through it a human body too, bettering a whole human nature, and itself suffering no diminishment. It graciously took from it the title "human being" while generously giving it the title "divine being." ...

But there was thirdly a most important thing that he taught us, for our own good. For the pagans assumed they had to solicit the god's friendship through magical or heavenly powers.... For most human beings have a longing for the Divine Being. From pride not holiness, they used to suppose, and through various rituals that were not sacred but profane that they could partake of divinity.... But now that Christ has come in the flesh, people can know that God is so close to the longing they have for him—this God they were soliciting through mediating powers as if he were far from them—that he has condescended to take on human nature.

Scripture Meditation

There came a man who was sent from God; his name was John. He came as a witness to testify concerning that light, so that through him all men might believe.... The true light that gives light to every man was coming into the world.
—JOHN 1:6–7, 9

Thought for the Day

Christ's advent demands a change of human consciousness, otherwise we shall reject him.

Prayer

Look upon us, O Lord, and let all the darkness of our souls vanish before the beams of thy brightness. Fill us with thy holy love, and open us to the treasures of thy wisdom. All our desire is known unto thee, and therefore perfect what thou has begun, and what thy Spirit has awakened us to ask in prayer.
—AUGUSTINE OF HIPPO

DECEMBER 20: THE MYSTERY OF MARY'S VISITATION

Ambrose (339–393), bishop of Milan, was the mentor of Augustine during the early stages of his conversion. He was a great rhetorician. Here he is meditating on Luke 2:23, 26, 27.

s soon as Elizabeth heard Mary's greeting the child leapt in her womb and she was filled with the Holy Spirit."

Notice the choice of words and the meaning of each one. Elizabeth was the first to hear Mary's voice, but John was the first to be aware of grace. She heard with the ears of the body; he leapt for joy because of the mystery. She was aware of Mary's presence, he of the Lord's. The woman perceived the presence of a woman, the child that of the child. The women spoke of God's grace while the children gave effect to it within them, revealing to their mothers the mystery of love, and by a double miracle the mothers prophesied under the inspiration of their sons.

The child leapt in the womb; the mother was filled with the Holy Spirit. The mother was not filled before her son, but once he had been filled with the Holy Spirit he filled his mother too. John leapt for joy and so did the spirit of Mary. When John leapt, Elizabeth was filled with the Holy Spirit.... We do not learn that Mary was then filled the Holy Spirit, but only that her spirit rejoiced. Her son, who is beyond our understanding, was active in his mother in a way beyond our understanding. Elizabeth was filled with the Holy Spirit after conceiving a son; Mary was filled before. You are blessed, said Elizabeth, because you have believed.

Scripture Meditation

Rejoice in the Lord always. I will say it again: Rejoice! Let your gentleness be evident to all. The Lord is near.

—Philippians 4:4–5

Thought for the Day

We need to be as receptive of God's presence within us as Elizabeth was receptive of God's blessing.

Prayer

Come, O Lord, in much mercy down into my soul, and take possession and dwell there. A homely mansion for so glorious a majesty.

—Augustine of Hippo

DECEMBER 21: DEBATING THE IMMACULATE CONCEPTION

Bernard of Clairvaux (1096–1153), a Cistercian reformer and confidante of rulers, became the most influential leader of his century. He inspired Hildegard of Bingen and one of his pupils became Pope Eugene III. Here he writes to the canons of Lyons, France, ca. 1140, discussing his growing concern about their undue veneration of Mary, the mother of Jesus.

Among all the churches of France, the church of Lyons is well known to be pre-eminent, for its flourishing strict discipline, grave conduct, mature counsels, and imposing authority and tradition.... Because of this, I marvel ... that you should wish to tarnish your good name by introducing a new festival at this time, a rite of which the Church knows nothing, both unreasonable and which has no authority in Church tradition....

For you say the mother of the Lord should be highly honored. You are right, but the purity title you give her? The Virgin has many titles of true honor, many real marks of dignity, but she does not need any that are false. Let us honor her for the service of her body, the holiness of her life. Let us marvel at her fruitful virginity, and venerate her divine Son. Let us extol her freedom from concupiscence in conceiving, and all pain in bearing. Let us proclaim her to be reverenced by the angels, desired by the nations, foretold by the patriarchs and prophets, chosen out of all and preferred before all....

But they claim to show records, so they say, of heavenly revelations [about her immaculate conception]. How does it follow that her conception was holy because her birth was holy? ... Where did this holiness come from? ... How was it passed on? ... Can it be said she was conceived holy because she was already holy before her conception? ... Perhaps someone will argue she was herself conceived by the Holy Spirit, and not of man, but this has been unheard of until now! Rather I read that "the Holy Spirit came upon her," but not that it came with her, ... nor that she herself was conceived by the Holy Spirit; she gave birth as a virgin, but she was not born of a virgin.

Scripture Meditation

The angel answered [Mary], "The Holy Spirit will come upon you.... So the holy one to be born will be called the Son of God.... For nothing is impossible with God."
—LUKE 1:35, 37

Thought for the Day

Church practices and traditions lose their moorings when they drift from Scripture.

Prayer

O Lord, we beseech thee to keep thy church and household continually in thy religion.
—COLLECT FOR THE FIFTH SUNDAY AFTER EPIPHANY

DECEMBER 22: THE MAGNIFICAT, MARY, AND US

Letter from Adam of Perseigne (d. 1221), a Cistercian Abbot, to Andrew,
Canon of Tours. Located in Normandy, Adam was well known as a wise
counselor and was frequently called upon to handle difficult church affairs.
Much of his extensive correspondence remains unpublished.
This is from his second letter, date unknown.

I was indeed preparing to obey your command, dear one, but feeling myself quite unequal to carrying out your order, to speak without anxiety of the glorious praises of the Mother of God.... She, saluted by the angel (Luke 1:28), now made fruitful by the Holy Spirit (Luke 1:35) … honored by the leaping of the yet-unborn Jesus, commended by the prophetic words of Elizabeth (Luke 1:41–45), cries out and says: "my soul magnifies the Lord" (Luke 1:46–55)….

Mary magnifies the Lord because she herself is magnified by the Lord. Therefore she magnifies him by whom she is magnified … and the unequaled quality of her love. Many magnify him with their tongue but blaspheme him with their deeds and become persecutors through the arrogance of their hearts…. But in Mary her tongue, her life, her soul, all magnify the Lord—her tongue by proclaiming the magnificence of holiness in praise of the divine glory, her soul by her unique love, her life by grasping with mind and heart his unfathomable magnificence. "My soul," she says, "magnifies the Lord."

How do you magnify him? Do you make greater him whose magnificence has no end? Great is the Lord, says the psalmist, and greatly to be praised (Ps. 145:3). Great he is, and so great that his greatness has neither comparison nor measure. How then can you magnify one whom you cannot know from small made great, not from great made greater? You magnify because you praise, you magnify because amid the darkness of the world, being brighter than the sun, lovelier than the moon, more fragrant than the rose, whiter than the snow, you spread abroad the splendor of the knowledge of God. You magnify him therefore not by increasing his surpassing greatness but by bringing the unknown radiance of the true deity to the world's darkness.

Scripture Meditation

And Mary said: "My soul glorifies the Lord and my spirit rejoices in God my Savior, for he has been mindful of the humble state of his servant. From now all generations will call me blessed, for the Mighty One has done great things for me—holy is his name."
—LUKE 1:46–49

Thought for the Day

True adoration expresses the selflessness of the worshipper, to become fully aware of all God's benefits, as Mary was.

Prayer

O Lord, raise up thy power, and come among us, and with great might succor us.

—COLLECT FOR THE FOURTH SUNDAY OF ADVENT

DECEMBER 23: REFLECTIONS ON MY FIRST NOEL

Jerry Levine was a secular journalist with no Christian background. He narrates what happened to him in the year between Christmas Eve 1983 and 1984. As a CNN Bureau chief in Chicago, he was posted in early December to Beirut, to be bureau chief of the company in the Middle East.

The day before Christmas 1983, my first morning on the job there, I rushed out with a camera crew to cover my first story: Santa Claus and Bob Hope's visit to the Marines guarding Beirut International Airport. But on our way we came across a delegation of about fifty women carrying signs in Arabic.... I asked my driver, Fahd Anan, what was their protest about. He said quietly, "These are wives, mothers, aunts, grandmothers complaining about the kidnapping of their men. No one will help them." ... Just eleven weeks later, on March 7, 1984, Ash Wednesday, I was forced to begin an anxious experience of leading as helpless a situation as all those missing Lebanese.

Up to the time of my captivity, I had been a typically peripatetic modern man-in-motion. I was materialistic, mindlessly ambitious and unphilosophical, an emotional cynic who not surprisingly considered himself an atheist ... addicted to petulant, bullying rages, and a tendency to shut out other people's clearly visible pain. But something unexpectedly happened in the lonely isolation of solitary confinement where I was chained to a radiator that did not work, with fetters so short that I could not stand up, where I had to be blindfolded whenever a captor was near, and where there was nothing to read for the first six months.

Almost immediately, instead of worrying constantly, I began to think about myself in relation to the universe, eternity, and my fellow women and men in ways I had never done before. After ten intensely contemplative (and I know now) spirit-filled days that began April 1, 1984, I pondered my way to a respect in faith, and belief in God.... Despite my newly acquired faith, despite my enthusiasm for my new comprehensions, it was not until nine months later that I understood clearly that my journey to understanding and knowledge had only just begun....

It happened this way. On Christmas Eve 1984 at about ten or eleven o'clock one of my captors paid an unexpected late night visit to my almost freezing cold cell. I was additionally surprised when he wished me a merry Christmas and asked if there was a gift I would like. Hardly thinking about the answer, I replied immediately, "A Bible. That'll do."

I needed a Bible because, after nine months of belief that I was quite aware I had acquired without benefit of studying Scripture first hand, I was anxious to read it from start to finish. I was especially keen on knowing whether or not I had gotten it right—especially with respect to praying. To my astonishment two nights later my captor came back and gave me a brand new red pocket-sized Gideon New Testament, Psalms, Proverbs along with a ball point pen....

Scripture Meditation

In the beginning was the Word, and the Word was with God, and the Word was God ... The Word became flesh and made his dwelling among us.

—JOHN I: I, 14

Thought for the Day

Every point of time is equidistant from eternity, just as it was for the shepherds at Jesus' birth, Jerry Levin on Christmas Eve, 1984, and for you now.

Prayer

Whatever you ask for in prayer, believe that you have received it, and it will be yours.

—MARK 11:24

DECEMBER 24: CHRISTMAS EVE: RELIVING
THE VISITATION OF THE SHEPHERDS

Jerry Levine continues his narrative.

Three days later, … I had got to the part about the shepherds in Luke 2:8–20. When they had seen him, they spread the word concerning what had been told them about this child, and all who heard it were amazed at what the shepherds said to them.… I heard footsteps in the hall outside my unlit pitch-dark crypt–like room. That sound was the signal to me to pull my blindfold over my eyes, which I did.… After the man left, I pushed the blindfold above my eyes and beheld the most astonishing— or at least, unique—sight of my captivity.

On the floor, anchored in a puddle of melting wax was a flickering candle. Next to it was a bowl of fruit. And next to it a big platter and on it a "log" type of chocolate cake. In front of the cake was a very intricate and beautiful Lilliputian manger scene. Intricately carved pines stood guarding a tiny wooden barn, open to view at one end. Inside was a miniscule manger. Sitting before it was Mary holding Jesus with Joseph standing close by. There were several shepherds looking on plus cows, horses, and sheep—all carefully crafted and painted in a smaller than toy soldier scale.

The passing minutes crackled with a kind of physical and spiritual energy that seemed to be dissolving the centuries separating me from the event. I actually experienced a kind of vicarious surge when I recalled that this was happening to me not too many miles to the north of Bethlehem in a frigid room that I imagined was not any colder or less comfortable than the one in which Jesus had been born.... To relate what we witness and try to make sense for others of that long ago event is what shepherding is all about. It is, I believe, job enough to keep us all meaningfully occupied for the rest of our lives. It is a job with no end, but every day one with a new beginning, which I gladly attempt to perform.

Scripture Meditation

When [the Shepherds] had seen him, they spread the word concerning what had been told them about this child, and all who heard it were amazed at what the shepherds said to them.
—LUKE 2:17–18

Thought for the Day

To "see" the babe in Bethlehem is to guide and nurture others into faith.

Prayer

I the LORD will answer them; I, the God of Israel, will not forsake them ... so that people may see and know, may consider and understand, that the hand of the LORD has done this.
—ISAIAH 41:17, 20

SEASON OF CHRISTMAS

The nativity of our Lord is celebrated on December 25, followed by the festivals of the next two Sundays, which fall between December 26 to January 1, and January 2 and 5 respectively. The Season of Christmas is a transition between Advent, waiting on the coming of the Savior, and Epiphany, encountering the Son of God himself.

Participation in the Events of Christmas

We tend to forget that Luke's gospel is actually a letter written to his friend Theophilus (Luke 1:1–4; 2:1–21).

Many have undertaken to draw up an account of the things that have been fulfilled among us, just as they were handed down to us by those who from the first were eyewitnesses and servants of the word. Therefore, since I myself have carefully investigated everything from the beginning, it seemed good also to me to write an orderly account for you, most excellent Theophilus, so that you may know the certainty of the things you have been taught....

In those days Caesar Augustus issued a decree that a census should be taken of the entire Roman world. (This was the first census that took place while Quirinius was governor of Syria.) And everyone went to his own town to register.

So Joseph also went up from the town of Nazareth in Galilee to Judea, to Bethlehem the town of David, because he belonged to the house and line of David. He went there to register with Mary, who was pledged to be married to him and was expecting a child. While they were there, the time came for the baby to be born, and she gave birth to her firstborn, a son. She wrapped him in cloths and placed him in a manger, because there was no room for them in the inn.

And there were shepherds living out in the fields nearby, keeping watch over their flocks at night. An angel of the Lord appeared to them, and the glory of the Lord shone around about them, and they were terrified. But the angel said to them, "Do not be afraid. I bring you good news of great joy that will be for all the people. Today in the town of David a Savior has been born to you; he is Christ the Lord. This will be a sign to you: You will find a baby wrapped in cloths and lying in a manger."

Suddenly a great company of the heavenly host appeared with the angel, praising God and saying, "Glory to God in the highest, and on earth peace to men on whom his favor rests."

When the angels had left them and gone into heaven, the shepherds said to one another, "Let's go to Bethlehem and see this thing that has happened, which the Lord has told us about."

So they hurried off and found Mary and Joseph, and the baby, who was lying in the manger. When they had seen him, they spread the word concerning what had been told them about this child, and all who heard it were amazed at what the shepherds said to them. But Mary treasured up all these things and pondered them in her heart. The shepherds returned, glorifying and praising God for all the things they had heard and seen, which were just as they had been told.

On the eighth day, when it was time to circumcise him, he was named Jesus, the name the angel had given him before he had been conceived.

Scripture Meditation

She will give birth to a son, and you are to give him the name Jesus, because he will save his people from their sins.
—MATTHEW 1:21

Thought for the Day

We need the receptivity of Mary to receive these glad tidings, as well as the simplicity of the shepherds to rejoice in them.

Prayer

Dear Lord, on this day we affirm that a child is born to us, since Jesus according to our belief was this day born, a child in whom we should have joy.
—JOHN WYCLIFFE

DECEMBER 26: THE CHOICE OF CHRISTMAS DAY

Joseph Hall (1574–1656), bishop of Norwich, was a moral philosopher and a
satirist who pleaded for tolerance and unity among Christians. He also
advocated the meditative life. In this letter, penned early in the seventeenth
century, Joseph answers a gentleman who had raised questions about the
celebration of Christmas in the Christian calendar.

To an unknown Gentleman,

One would think there is every reason to celebrate these solemn Feasts [of the church's calendar] as having wonderful and unspeakable benefits, which these days serve. For instance in the Feast of the Nativity, when the Angel brought the news of the blessed Birth to the Jewish shepherds, "Behold, I bring you good tidings of great joy, which shall be to all people; for unto you is born this day a Savior." If then, the report of this blessing was the best news of the greatest joy that ever was, or ever could be that ever happened to mankind, why should its commemoration be comparable? Where we conceive of the greatest joy, what should hinder us from commemorating it as joyful indeed? But, you may argue, the day confers nothing to the blessing. Every day we should receive with equal thankfulness, as we remember all the time this inestimable benefit of the Incarnation of the Son of God. So it can be argued a set anniversary day to do this is completely unnecessary.

Know however, and consider that the All-wise God, who knew it fit that his people should every day think of the great work of the creation, as well as of the deliverance out of servitude, and should daily give honor to the Almighty Creator and Deliverer, yet ordained one day of seven for our special recognition of these marvelous works, as well knowing how apt we are to forget those duties, and so charged us to specifically remember these events....

You also argue that the exact day is debatable, or even in December at all! I agree the day is not known ... but it certainly occurred on a specific day; and no less sure we are that it was the happiest day that ever occurred in the history of the world. It is all the same to us whether it was this day or another. We content ourselves with this, that it has pleased the Church for many hundreds of years to ordain this day for the commemoration of that transcendent blessing.... Let it suffice that ever since the second century after Christ, this Feast has been ordained by the Church without contradiction, receiving many passionate reinforcements from the Church Fathers.

Among these that of Gregory Nazianzen says quite remarkably ... "Let us celebrate this Feast; not in a rhetorical but a divine way, not in a worldly but a truly spiritual manner. Not by crowning our doors with garlands, nor by leading dances, nor adorning our streets ... not with humoring our taste with dainties; not with silken and costly clothes, etc. Let us leave all these to the Pagans for their events. But we who adore the Word of the Father, let us feed on the delicacies of the Law of God and with those discourses which are particularly appropriate for this present Festival."

Scripture Meditation

And she gave birth to her firstborn, a son. She wrapped him in cloths and placed him in a manger, because there was no room for them in the inn.

—LUKE 2:7

Thought for the Day

May the festivities of this Christmas not crowd out the true celebration of the Christ child.

Prayer

Jesus is in my heart, his sacred name is deeply carved there.

—GEORGE HERBERT, *THE TEMPLE*

DECEMBER 27: THE INCARNATION OF GOD'S WORD

*Athanasius (296–373), bishop of Alexandria, was a major voice at the Council
of Nicaea and the great defender of the divinity of Christ against the Arians.
Here he writes to Epictetus prior to 372.*

To my Lord, beloved brother, and most-longed for fellow-minister,
Epictetus (bishop of Corinth), greetings in the Lord.

I thought that all vain talk of heretics, many as they may be, had
been stopped by the Synod which was held at Nicaea [the Council of
Nicaea, AD 325]. For the Faith confessed there by the Fathers according to the divine Scriptures is enough by itself to overthrow all impiety,
at once, and to establish the religious belief in Christ.... I write this
after reading the memoranda submitted by you, which I could wish had
never been written at all, so that not even a record of these things
should go down to posterity.

For who ever yet heard the like? ... That the body born of Mary is
coessential with the Godhead of the Word? ... For if the Word is coessential with the body, the commemoration and work of Mary are
superfluous, inasmuch as the body could have existed without Mary, just
as the Word also is eternal.... Or what need was there even in the Word
coming among us, to put on what was coessential with himself, or to
change his own nature and become a body? ...

But this is not so, far be the thought. For he "takes hold of the seed
of Abraham" [Heb. 2:16] unto his, as the apostle said; whence it
behooved him to be made like brethren, in all things, and take a body
like us. This is why Mary is truly presupposed, in order that he may
take it from her, and offer it for us as his own.... Gabriel is sent to
her—not simply to a virgin, but to a virgin betrothed to a man [Luke
1:27], in order that he might show that Mary was really a human being.
And for this reason Scripture also mentions her bringing forth, and
tells of her wrapping him in swaddling clothes; and therefore, too, the
breasts which he sucked were called blessed.... All these are proofs
that the Virgin brought forth.

Scripture Meditation

Since the children have flesh and blood, he too shared in their humanity.

—HEBREWS 2:14

Thought for the Day

There is nothing about our humanity we can't share with Jesus Christ who became fully human to free humanity from its bondage.

Prayer

O Lord, raise up we pray thee thy power, and come among us, and with great might succor us; that whereas, through our sins and wickedness, we are sore let and hindered in running the race that is set before us, thy bountiful grace and mercy may speedily help and deliver us; through the satisfaction of thy Son our Lord, to whom with thee and the Holy Spirit be honor and glory world without end. Amen.

—COLLECT FOR THE FOURTH SUNDAY IN ADVENT

DECEMBER 28: THE FEAST OF INNOCENTS

Cyprian (200–254), bishop of Carthage, led his people through the fierce persecution of Christians under the emperors Decius (249–251) and Valerius (253–260). His letters inspired Augustine of Hippo, who went on to face the schism of the Donatists in the same region of northern Africa. The martyrdom of Stephen, the first Christian martyr, has been celebrated on December 26. Cyprian here writes to the people of Thibaris.

*D*early Beloved Brethren,

I had thought ... to come to you ... but as we are detained here by pressing affairs ... I have sent this letter as a substitute....

You ought to realize and certainly believe that the day of persecution has begun to be over our heads; and that the end of the world and the time of Anti-Christ have drawn near. So we need to stand ready for battle, thinking of nothing else except the glory of eternal life, and the crown of confession of the Lord. So don't think the future is going to be like the past. A severer and fiercer combat is now threatening for which the soldiers of Christ ought to prepare themselves, with an indomitable faith and strong courage.... For this is what it means "to be found in Christ." This is to imitate what Christ taught and did. As the apostle John says: "He who says that he abides in Christ, ought himself also to walk, as He walked" (1 John 2:6). Likewise, the Apostle Paul exhorts and teaches, saying: "We are sons of God. But if we are sons, we are heirs of God, joint heirs with Christ, provided, however, we suffer with Him that we may be also glorified with Him" (Rom. 8:16–17)....

Do not the documents [the books of the Maccabees] testify to great virtue and to faith, and exhort us by their sufferings to the triumph of martyrdom? What of the prophets whom the Holy Spirit inspired to anticipate the knowledge of the future? What of the apostles whom the Lord chose? When the just are killed on account of justice, have they not already taught us how to die? The birth of Christ began immediately with the martyrdoms of the infants that for his name, those that were two years old and younger were killed. An age not yet fit for battle was fit for crowns! That it might appear that the innocents are they who are killed because of Christ, innocent infancy was destroyed for his name. It was thus shown that no one is free from the danger of persecution, when even such as these little ones suffered martyrdom.

How serious a cause it is then, for a Christian to be unwilling to suffer since our Lord has first suffered, or indeed, to be unwilling to suffer for our sins, since the One who had no sin, first suffered for us! The Son of God suffered that he might make us sons of God, and yet the children of men do not want to suffer in becoming a child of God!

Scripture Meditation

When Herod realized that he had been outwitted by the Magi, he was furious, and he gave orders to kill all the boys in Bethlehem and its vicinity who were two years old and under.
—Matthew 2:16

Thought for the Day

Believers' insecurities may wreak destruction on relationships but we have the identity of Christ, which gives courage even in the face of martyrdom.

Prayer

O Almighty God, who out of the mouths of babes and sucklings has ordained strength, and made infants to glorify Thee by their deaths; mortify and kill all vices in us, and so strengthen us by thy grace, that by the innocence of our lives, and constancy of our faith even unto death, we may glorify thy holy Name; through Jesus Christ our Lord. Amen.
—Collect for "Innocents Day"

December 29: The Advent Reveals God's Own Nature

The following letter to Diognetus is by an unknown writer, written about AD 124–134. Some scholars have identified Diognetus to be the code name of the Emperor Hadrian.

My Lord Diognetus,

I have noticed the deep interest you have been showing in Christianity and the close and careful inquiries you have been making about it. You would like to know more about what God Christians believe in, and what sort of cult they practice that enables them to set so little store by this world, and even to make light of death itself.... You are curious, too, about the warm fraternal affection they all feel for one another.... I salute this eagerness for knowledge on your part; and I pray God, the author of both speech and hearing, to give me such facility of speech to benefit you fully in listening to me....

The Almighty Himself, the Creator of the universe, the God whom no eye can discern, has sent down his very own Truth from heaven, His own holy and incomprehensible Word, to plant it among men and ground it in their hearts. To this end He has not, as one might imagine, sent to mankind some servant of His, some angel or prince; it is none of the great ones of the earth, nor even one of the vice-regents of heaven. It is no other than the universal Maker and Creator himself, by whose agency God made the heavens and set the seas in their bounds, whose mystic word the elements of creation submissively obey....

And was his coming, as a man might suppose, in power, in terror, and in dread? Not so; it was in gentleness and humility. As a king sending his royal son, so he sent him; as God he sent him; as Man to men he sent him; and that because he longed to save us by persuasion, and not by compulsion—for there is compulsion found in God. His mission was no pursuit or hounding us. It was in love, not in judgment that he sent him....

Before his advent, who among mankind had any notion at all of what God was like? Or do you accept the vapid and ludicrous suggestions of your own pretentious philosophers—some of whom assure us that God is fire ... some of water ... others of other various elements? Assertions of that sort are no more ... than the tricks of professional illusionists.... It is he himself who has given us the revelation of himself. But he has only revealed himself to faith, by which alone are we permitted to know God.... He bore with us, and in pity took our sins upon himself and gave his own Son as a ransom for us—the Holy for the wicked, the Sinless for sinners, the Just for the unjust.... O sweet exchange! O unsearchable working! O benefits unhoped for! ... In times past, he convinced us that our human nature by itself lacked the power of attaining to life; today he reveals to us a savior who has the power to save even the powerless.

Scripture Meditation

I am not ashamed of the gospel, because it is the power of God for the salvation of everyone who believes.
—ROMANS 1:16

Thought for Today

Christians—like the apostle—should view the Advent and Christmas seasons as opportunities to reverse the values of the world, and indeed "turn the world upside down."

Prayer

When I loved darkness I knew you not, but wandered on from night to night. But you lead me out of that blindness; you took me by the hand and called me to you, and now I can thank you, for your mighty voice has penetrated into my inmost heart. Amen.
—AUGUSTINE OF HIPPO

DECEMBER 30: THE COMFORT OF THE INCARNATION

Martin Luther (1483–1546) was both a world-shaking reformer and a pastor, writing voluminously to many troubled people. Here, in December of 1535, he addresses Prince Anhalt Joachim, who appears to have suffered from bouts of depression as well as doubts about his faith.

*O*ur dear Lord comfort Your Grace with His Incarnation!

He became incarnate to comfort and show his good will to all humanity, as the dear angels sing today, "Glory to God in the highest, and on earth peace, good will toward mankind."

I trust that Your Grace will have no doubts nor perplexities about the creed or the gospel, since Your Grace has now been well instructed in that which is the truth....

If we are satisfied with the creed and the doctrine, what does it matter even if hell and all the devils fall upon us? What can distress us—other, perhaps, than our sins and a bad conscience? Yet Christ has taken these from us, even while we sin daily. Who can terrify us except the devil? But greater than the devil is he that is in us, weak though our faith may be.... We must be weak, and are willing to be, in order that Christ's help and strength may dwell in us; as Saint Paul says, "Christ's strength is made perfect in weakness."

Your Grace has not yet betrayed or crucified the dear Lord. Even if Your Grace had, Christ nevertheless remains gracious. He prayed even for those who crucified him. Therefore, be of good cheer. In the strength of Christ resist the evil spirit, who can do no more than trouble, terrify or slay.

The dear Lord Jesus Christ, our friend and our consolation, be with Your Grace and leave not Your Grace comfortless.

Scripture Meditation

We know that we live in him and he in us, because he has given us of his Spirit. And we have seen and testify that the Father has sent his Son to be the Savior of the world.

—1 JOHN 4:13–14

Thought for the Day

Even if during this season of rejoicing we're faced with despondency and doubts, the Spirit of the incarnate Christ will strengthen and comfort us.

Prayer

Lord, I do not have a strong and firm faith. At times I doubt and am unable to trust you completely. O Lord, help me! Strengthen my faith and trust in you.

DECEMBER 31: COMMENDING THE NEW YEAR TO GOD

The Reverend Henry Venn (1724–1797), an Anglican rector, was friend of John Newton, William Wilberforce, and other evangelical leaders. His son later became chaplain to the Clapham Movement, which was concerned with social reform. Rev. Venn writes here to a widow, Mrs. Riland, on January 4, 1785.

My dear Friend,

Many uses are to be made of the times and seasons. Our dearest friends have then a more particular remembrance in our prayers. When the first day of a new year dawns, I am called to commend them who are very precious to me, to the loving protection of my God at the same time as I give him thanks for all his loving-kindness towards them in the years that are past.

Thus I have been remembering you, my dear friend, blessing, praising and thanking God for your knowledge, faith and love of him, which began so many years ago. I remember our Christmas fare, at Huddersfield; when the name of Jesus made the feast, and our souls were delighted in his riches; when the wonders of his grace, and the blessings he communicates were new, and surprising to your precious soul; a joy, spiritual and heavenly, began to be known to you. Happy times! The fruit of which we shall enjoy, together with dear Mr. Riland, will be in the world of glory.

What will you think when I tell you that this past Christmas day, in my cold church, and my few sheep around me, I had a most delightful season; and think I was never more helped in preaching in all my life, as the people listened to the subject, "God manifest in the flesh." For this great mystery is the center of all the truths. It is itself a fountain of light, like the sun. Concerning this article of faith, we may well cry out, "Blessed is the people that know the joyful sound!" This sound precisely is, "Unto us a Child is born; unto us a Son is given; who is Christ the Lord!"

I am now about to begin a series of sermons, expounding on Psalm 119, which I have never done before. Yet I am realizing there is none more profitable. For in the Psalm, the whole inner man is being delineated. And with the several changing dispositions of our poor hearts, there are also the appropriate responses and inspirations of the Holy Spirit that touch us in such an affecting way.

This is the Psalm I have often had recourse to, when I could find no spirit of prayer within my own heart, until at last the fire rekindled, and I could pray. What has been your experience of this extraordinary psalm? I know you do not read the Scripture idly, and without self-application. Have you found it pleasant and nourishing to your soul, and fastening upon your mind? All love, and all peace, to you and yours. A happy new year!

—From your affectionate pastor, H. Venn

Scripture Meditation

Direct me in the path of your commands, for there I find delight.
Turn my heart toward your statutes and not towards selfish gain.
Turn my eyes away from worthless things; preserve my life
according to your word.
—PSALM 119:35–37

Thought for the Day

A year spent meditating daily upon Psalm 119 may help you celebrate the advent of Christ within you throughout the year.

Prayer

I run in the path of your commands, for you have set my heart free.

—PSALM 119:32

JANUARY 1: IT IS THE INWARD LIFE BEFORE GOD THAT MATTERS

Søren Kierkegaard (1813–1855), the Danish Christian philosopher, writes to his cousin, Hans Peter, who was severely crippled from birth.

Dear Peter,

Happy New Year! I never go calling to offer my New Year's Greetings and send them in writing only rarely and as an exception—but you are among the exceptions. In recent years I have often thought of you, and I intend to do likewise in this one. Among the other thoughts or considerations I often have had and intend to go on having about you is this: that reconciled to your life, with patience and quiet devotion, you carry out just as important a task as the rest of us who perform on a larger or a smaller stage; engage in important business, build houses, write copious books, and God knows what. Undeniably your stage is the smallest, that of solitude and inwardness—but "vanity of vanities" as it says in the book of Ecclesiastes, when all is said and done, what matters most is inwardness—and when everything has been forgotten, it is inwardness that still matters.

I wrote this some days ago, was interrupted, and did not manage to conclude it. Today your father visited me, and that circumstance once more reminded me to complete or at least put to an end what I had begun. For there was something more I wanted to add. If I were to give you any advice about life, or taking into consideration your special circumstances, were to commend to you a rule of life, then I would say: Above all do not forget your duty to love yourself: do not permit the fact that you have been set apart from life in a way, being prevented from participating actively in it, and that you are superfluous in the obtuse eyes of a busy world. Above all do not permit this to deprive you of your idea of yourself, as if your life, if lived in inwardness, did not have as much meaning and worth as that of any other human being in the loving eyes of an all-wise Governance, and considerably more than the busy, busier, busiest haste of busyness—busy with wasting time and losing oneself.

Take care of yourself in the New Year. If you would enjoy visiting me once in a while, please do come. You are welcome.

Your cousin, S. K.

Scripture Meditation

Man looks at the outward appearance, but the LORD looks at the heart.
—I SAMUEL 16:7

Thought for the Day

We must not despise our afflictions or handicaps, since our heavenly Father knows even when a sparrow falls.

Prayer

Hear me, O God! A broken heart is my best part.
—BEN JONSON

JANUARY 2: A SURVIVOR LIVES BY NEW BEGINNINGS

*Bart Mann (b. December 29, 1933) trained as an engineer, and then
became a bush pilot in 1955. The following narrative is taken from the
January 17, 2004, entry in his pilot log books.*

*T*he beginning of a new year is very hard for my family. For it was on December 3, 1993, we received a phone call no parent wants to hear. Our dear eldest son, Keith, had died in a plane accident in the Northwest Territory. He was the only pilot and had six passengers on board. All perished. This horrific blow has changed our lives—Florence, my two sons, Michael and Dwight, and mine forever.

We had some support from church and friends but the pain never leaves. The pain is only managed differently. Many people have little or no understanding of such an untimely loss. I spent five years investigating the causes of Keith's accident, but I was thwarted at every turn. Keith was the only son who followed my own career as a pilot, but whereas I survived three crashes, our son did not survive one. Let me explain my ongoing pain.

On the night of April 11, 1957, while flying as flight engineer, we crashed on a frozen lake in Northern Quebec. We were carrying bulk fuel oil on this flight. I was the only survivor and spent the night on the lake, (soaked in diesel fuel) with my two dead partners. I was rescued the next morning and I naturally wondered *Why Me?* But being restless and wanting more challenge, I started again with Wheeler Airlines flying in the Sub Arctic and Arctic. For some time I was based at Frobisher Bay on Baffin Island.

Flying in the Arctic, and in sparsely settled areas is extremely challenging and requires a strong will to prevent disaster. One is challenged to fly in adverse weather by both owner and customer. The customer is constantly requesting greater loads to be carried than is legally allowed. While people other than the pilot seem to have great ability to forecast the weather. There is also the constant threat of unknowably flying aircraft that are not airworthy.

A second time I survived, hitting a mountain top in severe wind and down draft conditions. This was in a white out between Arctic Bay and

Pond Inlet on Baffin Island, in an Otter aircraft with a full load of passengers and mixed cargo. We escaped with significant damage to the aircraft and continued on to Pond Inlet. Again I had the feeling that God's angels had picked me up and set me safely down. During the same time period, I hit a snow-covered mound of block ice on a lake that was left unmarked. Ice blocks are cut in winter as a source of fresh water. This happened in a white out condition, which made the mound invisible. So a third time, I was picked up by angels and safely rescued. Later, flying with the Hudson's Bay Company, I covered Canada's Arctic from West to East and visited all their trading posts. In spite of these events, it was not until 1964 while flying through a pass in the beautiful Penny Highlands on Baffin Island, I was struck by the awesome greatness of creation. I realized then that I had been given the gift of extended life three times.

Then I met my wife Florence, a devout Christian and realized further the need of a more stable lifestyle, and of taking my faith much more seriously. So two years later I joined Canadian Pacific Airlines, focusing on time off more than on desirable aircraft and routes. For I really wanted to know our sons, probably because my father never knew me.

I retired on January 1, 1994. As a pilot, whether in the Bush, the Arctic and the Airline, I was always in a position to help people and I do so on a continuing basis. My concern is always with youth, since my own father never wanted to know me. I believe God has guided me in my life-long, random acts of kindness as a pilot, which have been more concentrated voluntarily for the last nine years in Red Cross prevention issues for youth, to protect them morally from disastrous consequences. For I believe my survival, physically and morally, has been granted me by God to live out 1 Corinthians 13:4–7, particularly so in my retirement.

Scripture Meditation

Love is patient, love is kind, it does not envy. It does not boast....
Love never fails.
— 1 CORINTHIANS 13:4, 8

Thought for the Day

Are we not all survivors, benefiting from God's grace?

Prayer
May God grant us the wisdom and the will to not abuse our
children physically, sexually and emotionally, nor to neglect
them, when he protects and loves us.
—BART MANN

JANUARY 3: WIDOWHOOD, THE NEW OPPORTUNITY
FOR THE CONSOLATION OF CHRIST

Jerome, the great biblical scholar, excelled in his appreciation of devout
Roman women of high rank and wealth, who left all to enter his Christian
community in Palestine. Here he writes to his friend Principia, ca. AD 412.

*P*rincipia, virgin of Christ,
You have pleaded frequently and earnestly with me, that I write an
obituary to the memory of that holy woman, Marcella. You desire that I
describe her goodness, which we have appreciated highly, so that others
may know about her and seek to emulate her character. This is my own
great desire too, so it hurts me when you go on nagging about this, and
imagine I am indifferent to the need to do so.... I praise her great devotion in forsaking both rank and wealth to seek the true nobility of
poverty and lowliness of spirit. Bereft by her father's death, she was also
deprived of her husband after only seven months of marriage. Yet young
and highborn, with remarkable beauty, she had men always around her,
but she remained remarkably self-controlled. A distinguished man of
consular rank named Cerealis courted her assiduously ... but she
rejected him firmly, convincing others that they had no hope of winning
her.

In the gospel of Luke we read the following passage: "There was Anna the prophetess, the daughter of Phanuel, of the tribe of Asher. She was of great age and had lived with her husband seven years from her virginity: she was a widow, aged eighty-four, who never left the temple, but served God with fasting and prayer night and day" [Luke 2:36, 37]. It is no wonder that she was worthy to see her Savior, whom she sought so earnestly.

So let us compare them, Anna and Marcella: the seven years with the seven months; the hope for Christ and the possession of Christ; the confession of the Christ-child at his birth with the belief in the crucified Christ; the non-denial of the child and the rejoicing in the full grown man as King. I do not draw comparisons between holy women.... Rather I conclude that those who have the same devotion should have the same reward. The skeptical chauvinist may laugh at me for dwelling so long on the praises of mere women! ... But I judge people's virtues not by their gender but by their character.

Scripture Meditation

Where you go I will go ... your God [shall be] my God.
—RUTH 1:16

Thought for the Day

Thank God for the godly women who have blessed your life so faithfully.

Prayer

Here I am, God's servant; let it be done to me, as you have said.
—CATHERINE OF SIENA

JANUARY 4: THE CIRCUMCISION OF THE CHILD JESUS
FOR A NEW WAY OF LIVING

---

*Charles de Foucauld (1858–1916) was a saint so passionately in pursuit of
Christ that he reinvented "the imitation of Christ." He did so by resigning his
position as an officer in the French army, entering the Trappist order in
Nazareth, and then moving on to create his own order in an ongoing ascetic
"descent" alone among the Tuaregs in the heart of the Sahara desert. There
he was killed, apparently in a climactic life of failure. Among his letters was
the following meditation, written in the form of a letter
from Jesus to Charles and his friends.*

My Child,

I was born, born for you, in a cave in December, in the cold, home-less, in the middle of a winter's night, in the unheard-of poverty of the extremely poor, in solitude, in an abandonment unique in this world. What, my children, do I want you to learn from my birth? *To believe in my love,* to believe that I have loved you until now. To hope in me, who have loved you so dearly.

I want to teach you to *despise the world,* which was so unimportant to me. I want to teach you *poverty, lowliness, solitude, humility, penance.* I want to teach you to love me, for I was not content with giving myself to the world in the Incarnation, sanctifying it invisibly in the Visitation; no, that did not satisfy my love. From the moment of my birth onwards, I showed myself to you, giving myself wholly to you, putting myself in your hands. From then on, you could touch me, hear me, possess me, serve me, console me. Love me now; I am so close to you....

In my circumcision, too, it was my desire to teach you obedience with humility—perfect obedience to all the commandments of the Church, whether great or small; unquestioning obedience, without discussion about the usefulness of the command, obedience for obedience's sake....

It was my desire to be called Jesus, primarily because the name is *true,* possessing that truth you ought so much to love—and also because it is profoundly tender and gentle and so wonderfully expressive of my *love* for you; finally because it is a name to inspire you to *trust* in me, to offer me your hand freely and easily, as to your Savior, so that you will always turn to me with the utmost trust, with complete abandonment. And that is what I want to see in you … that I have been a father to you. I want you, when you adore me as God, to love me as a son and a brother, with devotion and trust.

Scripture Meditation

Your attitude should be the same as that of Christ Jesus: Who … made himself nothing.

—PHILIPPIANS 2:5, 7

Thought for the Day

Christ has given so fully of himself to us that he desires so much of our love, obedience, and trust.

Prayer

O my Lord Jesus, how greatly I need direction—you loved poverty so much.

—CHARLES DE FOUCAULD

JANUARY 5: THE CIRCUMCISION OF THE HEART FOR A WHOLENESS OF LIFE

Ambrose (339–397), bishop of Milan for twenty-three years and mentor of Augustine of Hippo, wrote many letters, ninety-one of which have been preserved. Invariably, he concluded each one with the beautiful refrain of friendship: "Farewell, and love us, because we love you." He addresses this undated letter to Constantius.

*M*ost Noble Constantius,

Many persons are disturbed over the question, not by any means unimportant, why circumcision should have been made an obligation under the ruling of the Old Testament, since it was Abraham who first received the command to observe the rite of circumcision [Gen. 17:10]. Then why was it set aside as useless by the teaching of the New Testament?.... Indeed, why are infants' bodies still circumcised and imperiled at birth ... and on the eighth day ... when the mother's blood is said to be clean once more?.... It was fitting for the circumcision, commanded by the prescription of the Law, to cease after Christ came to circumcise the whole man and so fulfilled the circumcision of the Law. For who is this but he who said: "I have not come to destroy the Law but to fulfill it" [Matt. 5:17].

Yet, if you pay careful attention, the fact of the coming of the fullness of the Gentiles is the reason why circumcision of the foreskin was no longer needed. For circumcision was not enjoined on the Gentiles, but on the seed of Abraham, as you have the first promise of God: "God also said to Abraham, 'You shall keep my covenant, you and your descendants after you throughout their generations.... Every male among you shall be circumcised ... it shall be a token of the covenant between you and me.... My covenant shall be in your flesh as a perpetual covenant'" [Gen. 17:9–14].

Circumcision was but a sign until the fullness of the Gentiles should enter and all Israel should be saved through circumcision of the heart, not just a small portion of one member [of the body]. Therefore we are now excused from the rite of circumcision, and the continuance of circumcision ... is done away with [i.e. in Christ].

Scripture Meditation

Circumcision is circumcision of the heart, by the Spirit.
—ROMANS 2:29

Thought for the Day

It is much easier to perform external rites than to have a completely transformed life.

Prayer

Make us the sons of God, and heirs of eternal life … having this hope granted we may purify ourselves even as he is pure.

—COLLECT FOR SIXTH SUNDAY AFTER THE EPIPHANY

SEASON OF EPIPHANY

The season of Epiphany, from the Greek *epiphaneia* meaning "manifestation," begins on January 6 and continues for nine Sundays, then concludes with the Sunday of the Transfiguration. It commemorates the first manifestation of Jesus to the Gentiles, represented by the visit of the Magi from the East (as at Christmas we acknowledge his epiphany to the shepherds of Israel). The season goes on to encompass his baptism, followed by his first miracle at Canaan. As Advent celebrates Christ's humanity, Epiphany commemorates his divinity.

Encountered by the Mysteries of the God-Man

Jean-Jacques Olier (1608–1657) was a French aristocrat who became attracted to the renewal ministry of Paul de Vincent and then also of Cardinal Berulle. After a severe nervous breakdown, his life was spiritually transformed during the period 1639–1641. With others he established the Society of St. Sulpice in 1645, which founded seven seminaries in various parts of France. This is an extraction of the fifty-ninth letter in his collection.

I am praying to our Lord that your spirit will be filled with his holy Infancy, during this season of the church's calendar that honors this loving mystery. It is one of the graces that Christians must seek most of all, to live solely unto God. This requires, as Jesus Christ shows us in the Gospel, that we become as little children, if ever we are to enter the Kingdom of Heaven [Matt. 18:3]. This is very obvious as you write me about your anxieties and distress, when you mix your wisdom, only too human, with your natural conduct; this shows how greatly we need to be as a little child. For it is the nature of a little child of Christ, to be totally oblivious of the affairs of the world, and of its wisdom, of having a heart set on God in total detachment from the age in which we live. Thus it cannot conform to the ways of the world any longer, nor live according to its norms.

It is thus in becoming "the Child" that one relinquishes the exercise of one's own prudence and worldly wisdom to allow obedience to the movement of the Holy Spirit. The child depends upon the initiative of others. So too, the children of God are guided by the Spirit of God. They no longer conform to the ways of the world, as now not being under its tutelage. Rather they are content with the wisdom of faith, as being the wisdom of God, now given them as the rule and light for their conduct.

So they become wholly and irrevocably abandoned to his leading and guidance. So they avoid the syncretism of human and divine illumination, such as the Wise Men sought, partly astrological, partly divine, in following the star, as the light of paradise. Deprived of its clarity during their residence with Herod, when they consulted other authorities rather than faith, their motive for the quest became confused and corrupted, without having the proper spirit or right judgment. So their obedience to learn was also distorted.... In contrast, the conduct of the children of God, as possessed of the Spirit of God, while so childlike, still has a wisdom a thousand times more solid, more disciplined, and indeed more controlling, than all the world can ever give.

Moreover, this spirit of Christian childlikeness gives gentleness of spirit, as well as light, in seeking the will of God. For it is motivated by love, gentle and attractive in all its ways. For God is its perfect agent.... As a result, his august presence within us, gives us such confidence to perform all the promptings of God with amazing facility and saintly audacity. See then, sir, what blessing you will have, to possess this spirit: what peace, calmness, joy in your heart, to enter into this state of mind before God!

Scripture Meditation

See that you do not look down on one of these little ones.
—MATTHEW 18:10

Thought for the Day

Can our conception of being a "child of God" ever become deep enough?

Prayer

Lord, our God, give your children perseverance in their love towards you.
—ADRIENNE VON SPEYR

JANUARY 7: THE SON OF GOD, REVEALED PERSONALLY
IS REVEALED PARTICULARLY

John William Fletcher (1729–1785) was a Swiss pastor who immigrated to
England. He writes six pastoral letters to a member of his church at Madeley,
just north of London, to show how the Scriptures fully record the
manifestation of God in Christ to his people. This, his concluding pastoral
letter, was written in 1775.

$\mathcal{S}$ir,

According to my promise I shall now prove that the New Testament abounds, as well as the Old, with accounts of particular revelations of the Son of God.

Before his birth he manifested himself to the blessed Virgin by the overshadowing power of the Holy Ghost. She rejoiced in God her Savior, and gloried more in having him revealed as God in her soul than finding him concealed as man in her womb. Soon after Joseph, her husband, was assured in a heavenly dream that the child she bore was Emmanuel, God with us.

He revealed himself next to Elizabeth. When she heard the salutation of Mary, she was filled with the Holy Ghost, and made sensible, that the virgin was the mother of her Lord. So powerful was this manifestation that her unborn son was affected by it—for with joy the babe leaped in her womb, and even there, was filled with the Holy Ghost.

So important is a particular knowledge of Jesus that an angel directed the shepherds, and a miraculous star the wise men, to the place where he was born: and there the Holy Ghost so revealed him to their hearts that they hesitated not to worship the seemingly despicable infant as the majestic God, whom the heaven of heavens cannot contain.

Simeon, who waited for the consolation of Israel, had it revealed to him by the Holy Ghost that he should not see death before he had seen the Lord's Christ. The promise was fulfilled; and while his bodily eyes discovered nothing but a poor infant, presented without pomp in the temple, his spiritual eyes perceived him to be the light of Israel and the Salvation of God. Nor was this extraordinary favor granted only to Simeon, for it is written, all flesh shall see the Salvation of God; and St. Luke informs us, that

Anna partook of the sight with the old Israelite, gave thanks to her new born Lord, and spoke of him to all that waited for the redemption in Jerusalem.

Scripture Meditation

An account of the things … were handed down to us by those who from the first were eyewitnesses and servants of the word.
—LUKE 1:1–2

Thought for the Day

The humble in heart see more readily than the exalted of this world.

Prayer

O Lord, let our hearts be graciously enlightened by your holy radiance, that we may serve you without fear in holiness and righteousness all our lives.
—SARUM BREVIARY

JANUARY 8: CHILD BAPTISM AND REGENERATION

Augustine of Hippo writes this official Episcopal letter to Bishop Boniface in AD 408. It was a time when the church was being challenged by much confusion over the rite of baptism as it had been since the time of Cyprian in the second century. Indeed, Augustine echoes some of the letters written by Cyprian.

ou ask me whether parents do harm to their baptized infants when they try to cure them by means of sacrifices offered to demons. For if that is the nature of their credulous faith, what does their act of baptism really mean, if anything at all? My response is that the power of the sacrament is such, that when they come to real faith it acts retroactively within the Body of Christ. Thus the child cannot be caught in the bonds of another's sins, to which the child could give no real consent. "Both the soul of the father is mine, and the soul of the son is mine: the soul that sins the same shall die" [Ezek. 18:4]. The son himself does not sin, you see, when without his knowledge the parents or other persons resort to diabolical rites of worship on his behalf. On the other hand, it was from Adam that the child derived the guilt that was cancelled by the grace of the sacrament of baptism, seeing he did not then have an independent existence. He was not, so to speak, a distinct soul, to whom the above text could apply....

But the possibility of the child's being regenerated through the agency of another's will when presented for the sacred rite is the work of the Holy Spirit alone, who regenerates the child thus presented. For it is not written, "unless a person be born again of the will of her parents, or of the faith of those who offer her or who administer the rite," but rather, "unless a person be born again of water and the Holy Spirit" [John 3:5]. It is then, by water, the outward visible sign of grace, and by the Spirit who produces the inward gift of grace, which cancels the bond of sin and restores God's gift to human nature. That is to say, the human being born solely of Adam in the first place, can be reborn in Christ. Thus the Spirit who regenerates is possessed in common both by the parents who present the child and by the little one thus born again. Hence as a result of their participation in one and the same Spirit, the desire of those offer him does benefit the child.

Don't be concerned because some bring their little ones for baptism ... supposing that by this means the children will retain or recover bodily health. It will be no hindrance to their spiritual regeneration that this is not the real motive for baptism.... In fact, the infants are presented to receive spiritual grace, not so much by those in whose arms they are held ... as by the whole body of believers ... all done by the whole Church, which subsists in all the saints, because she is the Mother of each and every one.

Then you ask further: "If I set this child before you, when this child grows up, will she be a good person, or will he become evil in his ways?" You can only say, "I don't know." That is why to present the child is an act of faith.... Therefore the infant, even though she may not yet possess that faith which depends on the consent of those who exercise it, nevertheless when he grows up to man's understanding, will not repeat the sacrament, but will grasp its implications and readily adjust his mind to the truth contained in it.

Scripture Meditation

He called a little child and had him stand among them. And he said: "I tell you the truth, unless you change and become like little children, you will never enter the kingdom of heaven."
—MATTHEW 18:2–3

Thought for the Day

Family nurture should be recognized as having the whole Christian community involved supportively.

Prayer

O eternal God, Father Almighty, who gave thy only Son to be born of a woman, and to be made the Son of Man, that we might be made sons of God: grant us to be indeed your children, and be thou, now and forever, our Father, through the same Jesus Christ our Lord. Amen.
—COLLECT IN STOBART'S "BOOK OF PRIVATE PRAYER"

January 9: Is Freedom from Religion the Equivalent of Freedom from Circumcision?

Dietrich Bonhoeffer (1906–1945) was a Lutheran pastor who, as early as 1933 while a lecturer in systematic theology at Berlin University, denounced Hitler publicly. Two years later while living in England he was banned from Berlin. In 1939 just before the outbreak of World War II, against the advice of his friends, he returned from the safety of the United States to share in the sufferings of his people. He was arrested in 1943, implicated in the plot to assassinate Hitler, and hanged on Sunday, April 8, 1945. He wrote this letter from Tegel prison in Berlin on April 30, 1944, to his friend, Eberhard Bethge.

*D*ear Eberhard,

Another month gone! Do you find time flies as I do here? It often amazes me—and when will the month come when we shall meet again? Such tremendous events are taking place in the world outside, events which will have a profound effect on the course of our lives.... I am sure God is about to do something which we can only accept with wonder and amazement.... It is harder for you to go through all this alone than it is for me, so I will think of you especially, as indeed I am already doing now.... I am sorry I can't help you at all, except by thinking of you as I read the Bible every morning and evening.... They keep on telling me that I am "radiating so much peace around me," and that "I am always so cheerful." Very flattering, no doubt, but I'm afraid I don't always feel like that myself....

The thing that keeps coming back to me is: what is Christianity, and indeed what is Christ for us today? The time when men could be told everything by means of words, whether theological or simply pious, is over, and so is the time of inwardness and conscience, which is to say the time of religion as such. We are proceeding to a time of no religion at all: men as they are now simply cannot be religious any more.... What we call Christianity has always been a pattern—perhaps a true pattern—of religion.... If we reach the stage of being radically without religion—and I think this is more or less the case already—what does that mean for "Christianity"? ...

The Pauline question whether circumcision is a condition of justification is today, I consider, the question whether religion is a condition of salvation. Freedom from circumcision is at the same time freedom from religion. I often ask myself why a Christian instinct frequently draws me more to the "religionless" than to the "religious." ... For I often shrink from religious people, speaking of God by name—because that Name somehow seems to me here not to ring true, and I strike myself as rather dishonest ... (especially when others start talking religious jargon: then I dry up almost completely and feel somehow oppressed and ill at ease)— with people who have no religion I am able on occasion to speak of God quite openly and as it were naturally.

Scripture Meditation

He who loves a pure heart and whose speech is gracious will have the king for his friend.
—PROVERBS 22:11

Thought for Today

Faith has always been in danger of becoming "institutionalized," even on the personal level.

Prayer

Great is the mystery of our inheritance! The womb of a Virgin who knew not man is become the unspotted temple of God: of her he takes flesh, and to him shall all the nations come, saying Glory be to thee, O Lord.
—SECOND VESPERS, ANTIPHONY TO THE MAGNIFICAT

JANUARY 10: OUR HEAVENLY FATHER IS KNOWN BY
DETACHMENT FROM HUMAN BONDS

---

*John Tauler (1300–1361), a Dominican friar, taught nuns of his order
through his sermons and spiritual conferences. Here for the first Sunday of
Epiphany, echoing the teaching of Aelred of Rievaulx two centuries earlier,
Tauler instructs us on the significance of Jesus in the temple
at the age of twelve.*

We read in the holy gospel that when our Lord was twelve years old
he went with his parents to the temple, and that when they started home-
ward he remained there and they knew it not. Then when they missed
him on the journey and could not find him among their kinsfolk and
acquaintances, they must go back to the temple seeking him. And so they
found him.

We use this to illustrate that if you want to be a child of God you
must quit all humanity and go back to the source from which we were
created. All the natural faculties of the soul, intelligence, understanding, memory and will, lead you only into multiplicity. Therefore you
must give them all up ... and not search for your spiritual birth among
one's natural relationships....

As soon as your spirit is prepared for him, God enters in without a
moment's delay. In the Apocalypse we read our Lord's words: "Behold,
I stand at the door and knock! If anyone hears my voice and opens the
door to Me, I will come in to him and will sup with him, and he with me"
(Rev. 3:20).... The very instant your heart door is opened to him, he is
within you. If you object that you do not feel his presence, I answer that
your feelings are not what matter, for they are his to control as he sees
best, not us....

The sign of divine generation is inner freedom ... giving the soul all
the benefits of a new relationship with God. Everything now seems
related to God, to know and love nothing but God ... so that whoever
has received the gift of Divine love obtains from it more freedom from
base natural tendencies than all possible austerities and penances....
Then nothing brings you nearer to God as the sweet bond of love.
Whoever has found this way never seeks another.... The work of perfect

love is more fruitful to one's soul and to others, than all others, and gives more glory to God than all other works....

Scripture Meditation

"Why were you searching for me?" [Jesus] asked. "Didn't you know I had to be in my Father's house?"
—LUKE 2:49

Thought for the Day

Jesus promises, "If the Son sets you free, you will be free indeed" (John 8:36).

Prayer

We pray, may this captivity and freedom of divine love be granted to us, God the Father, God the Son, and God the Holy Spirit. Amen.
—JOHN TAULER

JANUARY 11: THE FAITH OF A CHILD

Baron Friedrich von Hugel (1852–1925) was viewed as a great Christian apologist in his generation. However, in this letter to his granddaughter, Gwendolen Greene, on February 22, 1921, it's clear that he saw his intellectual strength as contributing to family damage in being too forceful with his own daughter, True.

*E*ver Darling Child Mine,

I got your last letter yesterday morning, and though it was (as far as you yourself, your dispositions and affections go) as dear as ever you are, it nevertheless—through no fault of yours, but through much stupidity of my own—gave me much distress and uneasiness. You see, I have told you many a time, the biggest cross of my little old life ... was to put out my True's spiritual eyes. But shortly before she died, she showed for the first time her own initiative and freedom to ask for the Eucharist....

Now Sweet, since my True died, I do not think I have cared as much to try and serve and feed any soul as much as yours. My chief prayer has been that I might never strain, never complicate, never perplex you, and that in a Fenelon-like self-oblivion, I might just simply help and feed and carry you, if and when you required it.... So may I not have done any permanent harm to you, Child Mine! I mean: may I not have conveyed impressions so vivid that (however erroneously, they have so shaped and affected your mind) I cannot now seriously modify them? So I will now try ... to deal with your Mother's question about the Virgin Birth.

I always find it most helpful myself to dwell upon the conviction of our Lord's sinlessness, as something quite different and distinct from all and every form of human holiness. Consequently I was early convinced about the sinlessness of the Lord as the Beginning, so to speak, of a fresh creation of God. So it cannot be linked quite simply with all other human children, with at most good, but still sinful, ordinary human beings. This is doubtless the deepest reason also for all the honor paid to his Mother.

Loving old Fatherly One, H.

Scripture Meditation

See that you do not look down on one of these little ones. For I tell you that their angels in heaven always see the face of my Father in heaven.

—MATTHEW 18:10

Thought for the Day

Francois Fenelon reflected, "Jesus Christ said we must be meek and humble of heart. Meekness is the daughter of humility … only Jesus Christ can give that true humility of heart."

Prayer

> *Almighty God, through your infinite mercy you do not only receive us through your beloved Son our Lord Jesus Christ, but by who he is, we should look to you and call you Father. Amen.*
> —MARTIN LUTHER

JANUARY 12: THE WITNESS OF A CHILD

The great scholar and translator of the Bible into Latin, Jerome (342–420), writes here to a Christian mother, Laeta, about her child, Paula. This household, coming from a pagan past, symbolized the triumph of Christianity over Roman paganism.

Devoted Daughter in Christ,

You are the daughter of a mixed marriage, but as for young Paula, why, her parents are none other than yourself and my dear Toxentius. Who would ever have thought that in answer to her mother's pledge, a Christian granddaughter would have been granted to Albinus, a pagan high-priest, or that he would listen in delight to a little child babbling Christ's Alleluia, or that in his old age he would be cuddling a little one dedicated to God! Our hope is that he is already a candidate for the faith, now that he is surrounded by a crowd of Christian children and grandchildren! Yes, he may laugh and ridicule this letter, calling me an insensitive fool. But his son-in-law did exactly the same before he, too, came to the faith. One is not born a Christian, one becomes one....

When she visits her grandfather, and she gives him a hug, climbing on his knee, let her sing "Alleluia" in his ear, whether he likes it or not. When her grandmother comes to take her, her smile will show she recognizes her father, and truly is the joy of the whole family. For she destined to serve her true Sovereign, in whose army she is a young recruit, being trained to serve him ... as the bride of Jesus, and destined to reign eternally with him! ...

Nowadays, the walls of the Capitol are deserted, the pagan temples are in ruins, and people are flocking to the tombs of the martyrs. It is thus not by force, nor by might, but by the wisdom of God that people are becoming Christians. I am telling you this, Laeta, devoted daughter of Christ, so that you do not despair and give up hope for your father's salvation. The same faith which gave you a child may also win over your father. Then you will indeed be able to rejoice in having a united family in Christ. Remember the assurance of God, that "what is impossible with men, is possible with God."

Scripture Meditation

And a little child will lead them.
  —Isaiah 11:6

Thought for the Day

Reflect on the mixed marriages you know, of how the advent of the child Jesus could still make such a difference to their lives.

Prayer

Come near, O Christ! And make the Father known!
Of Thee and of the Father know we nothing—
Nothing can we know—save that which thou hast taught.
  —Avrillon

Educated to Become a Child of God

Jerome (see previous entry) continues the same letter to Laeta, showing how domestic he can be in his practical advice about education, the aim of which is to be Christlike.

*D*aughter in Christ,

I nearly forgot to answer your specific question: how to educate little Paula, who has been dedicated to Christ? Giving your first-born to the Lord is what Hannah did, or indeed Elizabeth did in the dedication of John the Baptist. Appropriately then, Samuel was nourished in the temple, and John the Baptist was prepared for his mission in the desert. So too, Laeta, you have to raise your daughter in the temple of the Lord. In her upbringing, let nothing distract her from the fear of the Lord, so that foul language and worldly songs are not heard by her. Rather she is taught the chant of the psalms.

Consequently, her nurses and teachers must not be worldly, indeed strangers to the ways of the world, and not those who adopt bad habits, or worse still then teach them to the child. Prepare her letters of the alphabet, carved in wood or ivory, placed in order, and let her memorize them in song. Putting them in order, she will then begin to recognize them by shape as well as by sound. When unsteadily she begins to write, place your hand over hers, so that she draws within the lines set for her. Begin also to encourage her in her spelling, by promising to give her a prize, and coax her with praises....

Start her study of the Bible with the Psalms, so that her heart may become enchanted with their sacred songs. Then proceed to the Proverbs of Solomon, to learn from him the science of life. The book of Ecclesiastes will accustom her to the disenchantments of the world. Job will show her admirable examples of patience and courage. What she will then learn after that, and never quit learning, is from the Gospels, which with constant reading will enter her soul, as well as the Acts of the Apostles, followed by the Epistles of the Apostles.... (Later, she will read the historical books of the Old Testament), and finally she can then read without

give them the reward of an innocent life, and they may look forward without fear to the certainty of death....

Farewell.

Scripture Meditation

Knowledge puffs up, but love builds up.

I CORINTHIANS 8:1

Thought for the Day

Do our academic institutions today need to recover the wisdom exemplified by Sir Thomas More?

Prayer

Grant, I thee pray, such heat into mine heart
That to this love of thine may be equal … and may find …
in thy lordship not as a lord, but rather
as a very tender, loving Father.

—SIR THOMAS MORE

JANUARY 15: TO NURTURE A CHRISTIAN FAMILY
CAN CREATE DOMESTIC TENSIONS

Susanna Wesley (1669–1742) was the remarkable mother of John and Charles Wesley. She had eighteen or nineteen children, only ten of whom survived infancy. A weak and foolish husband, combined with constant family sicknesses, kept her fully occupied as a disciplined housekeeper and family educator. A dispute arose in the winter of 1711–12 with her absent

*husband, the Rector, over her innovation of daily evening services at home
for her children. Because of her abilities to provide a lively educational
experience, church members began to attend also and some even withdrew
from the lackluster services of the curate, Rev. Mr. Inman. The latter
complained to her husband, and in response he roundly condemned his wife.
In this letter of February 6, 1712, Susanna replies.*

I heartily thank you for dealing so plainly and faithfully with me in a matter of no common concern. The main of your objections against our Sunday evening meetings are, firstly, that it will look particular [i.e. unusual or odd]; secondly, my sex; and lastly, your being present in a public station and character.

As to its looking particular, I grant it does; and so does almost everything that is to be performed out of the pulpit, or in the way of common conversation; because in our corrupt age the utmost care and diligence has been used to banish all discourse of God and spiritual concerns out of society, as if religion were never to appear out of the closet, and we were to be ashamed of nothing so much as of professing ourselves to be Christians.

To your second objection, I reply that I am a woman, so I am also the mistress of a large family. And though the superior charge of the souls contained in it lies upon you as head of the family and as their minister, yet in your absence I cannot but look upon every soul you leave under my care as a talent committed to me under a trust by the great Lord of all the families of heaven and earth. And if I am unfaithful to him or to you in neglecting to improve these talents, how shall I answer unto him, when he shall command me to render an account of my stewardship?

To your third objection, it was these and other such like thoughts made me at first take more than ordinary care of the souls of my children and servants; so, knowing that our most holy religion requires a strict observance of the Lord's day, and not thinking that we fully answered the end of the institution by only going to church, but that likewise we are obliged to fill up the intermediate spaces of that sacred time by other acts of piety and obligation, I thought it my duty to spend some of that day in reading and instructing my family, especially in your absence … and such time I esteemed in a way more acceptable to God than if I had retired to my own private devotions.… This was the beginning of my present practice.…

Soon after you left to go to London, Emily found in your study the account of Danish missionaries, which having never seen, I ordered her to read.... Their labours refreshed my soul beyond measure ... for several days I could speak of nothing else.... I resolved to live a more exemplary life ... and to begin with my own children.... I spend each night speaking personally with each child.... With those few neighbours who then came to me, I began to speak more freely and affectionately than before. I chose the best and most awakening sermons.... Since then our company has increased every night ... last Sunday I believe we had above two hundred, and yet many went away for want of room.... As for your proposal of letting some other man perform this, alas!, you do not consider what these people are. I do not think one man among them could read a sermon without spelling a good part of it, and how would that edify the rest? ...

Scripture Meditation

With God all things are possible.
—MATTHEW 9:23

Thought for the Day

Do many of us still live frozen ecclesiastically, instead of alive spiritually?

Prayer

Only, since God doth often make,
Of lowly matter, for high uses meet,
I throw me at his feet;
There will I lie until my Maker seek
For some mean stuff whereon to show his kill;
Then is my time.
—GEORGE HERBERT, "THE PRIESTHOOD"

JANUARY 16: DEEPENING A SON'S FAITH

*When her second child, Samuel, was away from home at Westminster school
in London, Susanna Wesley [see previous entry] kept up a flow of letters
concerned with nurturing the faith of each of her children. Her letters to
Samuel were preserved, since he copied each one he received into a letter
book. With a blend of biblical instruction and John Locke's* Essay on
Education *she writes this letter on March 11, 1704, when Samuel is fourteen
years old.*

*D*ear Sammy ...

Although the works of nature all give sufficient evidence of a deity,
and natural reason could discern him and the duties of natural religion, yet in the process of time the greatest part of the world made so
little use of their reason, that they are ignorant of God and the true
way of worshipping him. Sense and passion blinded some, and a careless indifference in others ensued.... Thus, whatever light there was in
the works of the creation and providence to lead men to the knowledge of the true God, yet very few found him.... Thus revelation
became very necessary to lead them into the knowledge of God's
unity and his other perfections, as well as to instruct them in their
duties towards him. It may be that you ask whether the revelation the
Jews received by Moses did not teach men all this and was sufficient
without that given by Jesus Christ. I answer, No! It was not sufficient.... For it was not long after the law was given on Mount Sinai
that men were entirely given up to idolatry and immersed in all manners of vice and wickedness; even the Jews, God's peculiar people,
forgot and forsook the laws of their fathers and worshipped the gods
of those very nations which were delivered into their own hands by
God himself for punishment of their unreasonable idolatry ... nor
would they hear the voice of God speaking through his prophets....

In this wretched state of darkness and error our Savior found
mankind and brought light and immortality to light by his coming. "For
this purpose the Son of God was manifested, that he might destroy the
works of the Devil" (John 3:8). And this could no way be done but by a
complete morality established in all its parts upon true foundations to

which mankind could have recourse upon all occasions. And upon its true foundations morality could never be fixed without a clear knowledge of the lawmaker and a just acknowledgement of him.... This required nothing less than an assurance of Jesus' being the Messiah, and a clear evidence of his mission was needed to prevail over men to repent and conform to his doctrine. For this reason our blessed Savior wrought so many miracles in the view of all the world. And as his love and pity to unhappy people was universal, so he broke down the wall of sanction between Jews and Gentiles. He did not confine his miracles and doctrine to worshippers at Jerusalem, but he preached at Samaria and wrought miracles in the borders of Tyre and Sidon, and people followed him from all quarters.

Scripture Meditation

Only be careful, and watch yourselves closely so that you do not forget the things your eyes have seen or let them slip from your heart as long as you live. Teach them to your children and to their children after them.
—DEUTERONOMY 4:9

Thought for the Day

Am I as educated and effective in reaching the younger generation with the Christian faith today as Susanna Wesley was in her day?

Prayer

Long ago I learned from your statutes that you established them to last forever.
—PSALM 119:152

JANUARY 17: DO NOT INDULGE IN WORLDLINESS NOW AND BE ASSURED OF HEAVEN LATER!

Susanna Wesley [see previous entry], now a widow, writes to her son John, March 30, 1734, about the vital role of meditation in Christian growth.

*D*ear Son,

Few insist upon the necessity of private prayer, but if they go to church sometimes, and abstain from the grossest acts of mortal sin, though they are ignorant of the spirit and power of godliness and have no sense of the love of God and universal benevolence, yet they rest well satisfied of their salvation and are pleased to think they may enjoy the world as much as they can while they live and have heaven in reserve when they die. I have met with the abundance of these people in my time. I think it is one of the most difficult things imaginable to bring them off from their carnal security and to convince them that heaven is a state, as well as a place; a state of holiness, begun in this life, though not perfected till we enter eternal life. Nor do they see that all sins are so many spiritual diseases which must be cured by the power of Christ before we can be capable of being happy....

You want no direction from me how to employ your time. I thank God for his inspiring you with a resolution of being faithful in improving that important talent committed to your trust.... You do not allocate enough time to meditation, which is incomparably the best means to spiritualize our affections, confirm our judgments, and add strength to our pious resolutions of any exercise whatever. Contrition ... as that sorrow for, and hatred of, sin, which proceeds from our love of God, surely comes when we meditate frequently on such subjects as will excite, cherish, and increase our love for that blest Being! And which is most proper for this end as deep and serious consideration of that pure, unaccountable love which is demonstrated in our redemption by God incarnate!

Verily the simplicity of divine love is wonderful. It transcends all thought, it surpasses our sublimest apprehensions! Perfect love indeed! No mixture of interest! No bye-ends, nor selfish regards! ... One word more and I am done.... Follow Mr Baxter's advice ... "Put your souls, with all their sins and dangers, and all their interests, into the hand of Jesus Christ your Savior, and trust them wholly with him, by a resolved faith.... It is he who is the owner of them by rights of redemption. And it is now become his own interest, even for the success and honor of his redemption, to save them." ... Dear Jacky, God Almighty bless thee!

Scripture Meditation

A wife of noble character who can find? ... Her children arise and call her blessed.
—PROVERBS 31:10, 28

Thought for the Day

Children live securely within boundaries created in love.

Prayer

May our Lord Jesus Christ himself and God our Father ... encourage your hearts and strengthen you in every good deed and word.
—2 THESSALONIANS 2:16–17

SPIRITUAL CONDITIONS TO CELEBRATE THE EPIPHANY

JANUARY 18: CELEBRATING THE EPIPHANY WITH OUR SPIRITUAL SENSES

Jean Guillaume de la Flechere (1729–1785), later known as John William Fletcher, was born to a noble family in Noyon, Switzerland [see January 7 entry]. After a brilliant academic education at the University of Geneva, he rejected the prospects offered him, immigrated to England in 1752, and ministered to Madeley Anglican parish church just north of London for the rest of his life. His pastoral letters are some of the finest examples of eighteenth-century Christian correspondence. In six pastoral letters, he describes how Christ is manifested to the believer in his Epiphany.

*S*ir,

When I had the pleasure of seeing you last, you seemed surprised to hear me say that the Son of God, for the purposes worthy of his wisdom manifests himself, sooner or later, to all his sincere followers in a spiritual manner that the world does not know about. The assertion appeared to you unscriptural, enthusiastic, and dangerous. So I want to show you that it is scriptural, rational, and of the greatest importance.… The manifestation I contend for, being of a spiritual nature, must be made to the spiritual senses.…

The Scriptures inform us that Adam lost the experiential knowledge of God by the fall. His foolish attempt was to hide himself from his Creator, whose eyes are in every place, the total blindness of his understanding. We are like Adam, not only devoid of the life of God, but alienated from it, through the ignorance that is in us.… Hence the things of the Spirit of God cannot be discovered, except by spiritual understanding.…

The exercise of these spiritual senses is peculiar to those who are born of God. They belong to what the Apostle calls "the new man, the inward man, the new creature, the hidden man of the heart." In believers, this hidden man is awakened and raised from the dead, by the power of Christ's resurrection. Christ is his life, the Spirit of God is his spirit, prayer or praise is his breath, holiness his health, and love is his element. On the other hand the Scriptures indicate that in unbelievers, the inward

105

man is deaf, blind, naked, asleep, past feeling, yea dead in trespasses and thus are incapable of perceiving spiritual things. So the apostle prays that the eyes of his converts may be enlightened, to know the hope of their calling.... Likewise our Lord repeatedly warns against those who have an ear but cannot hear. For "he who has heard and learned of the Father comes unto me." ... Likewise if believers have no spiritual faculty to taste for divine things, how can they talk about Christ's "fruit is sweet to their taste." ...

May Emmanuel, the light of the world, direct me to write with soberness and truth, and may you read with attention and candor; this is my sincere prayer.

Yours.

Scripture Meditation

For who among men knows the thoughts of a man except the man's spirit within him? In the same way no one knows the thoughts of God except the Spirit of God.
—I CORINTHIANS 2:11

Thought for the Day

Do we fear the world's condemnation as being "too religious" for believing in Christ's Epiphany?

Prayer

I pray also that the eyes of your heart may be enlightened in order that you may know the hope to which he has called you, the riches of his glorious inheritance in the saints.
—EPHESIANS 1:18

JANUARY 19: THE NATURE OF THE EPIPHANY

John Fletcher was so esteemed by John Wesley that Wesley once wrote of him,
"He writes as he lives. I do not know another clergyman in all England or
Ireland like him in this regard." Fletcher continues this second letter on our
encounter with the Epiphany.

$\mathcal{S}$ir,

Having proved in my first letter the existence of the spiritual senses to which the Lord manifests himself, I shall now enter upon that subject by letting you know, as far as my pen can do it, what is the nature of that manifestation which makes the believer more than conqueror over sin and death.

Don't gratify yourself by dismissing me as merely an "enthusiast"! For I am not insisting you need to hear voices, feel a body or see blood pertaining to our Lord. Pilate actually heard Christ's voice, while the Jews saw his body, the soldiers handled it, and some of them literally were sprinkled with his blood. But this served no spiritual purpose; they never knew God as manifest in the flesh.

Neither do I understand by the term "manifestation" merely a descriptive knowledge of the Redeemer's doctrine, offices, promises and performances that took place, which someone can recount from memory. All nominal believers ... can so acquire historical and doctrinal knowledge of Jesus Christ. Their understanding may be informed, but alas their hearts remain unchanged. Acquainted with the "letter" they continue of the Spirit ... and know nothing of Christ in them, as the hope of glory.

Much less do I mean by "manifestation" such a representation of our Lord's person and sufferings as "the natural man" can form by force of a vivid imagination. By seeing a striking picture of Jesus bleeding on the cross or hearing a sentimental sermon on his agony in the garden, many can be deeply affected and melted into tears....

Indeed, sir, I can tell you more easily what this divine revelation is not than what it is. For the revelation of Christ by which a nominal believer becomes a holy and happy possessor of the faith is a supernatural, spiritual and experimental manifestation of the Spirit, power and love—and sometimes of the person—of God manifest in the flesh, whereby he is known and enjoyed in a manner altogether new.... Sooner or later, every seeker of faith will, in a low or high degree, experience this personally....

If this experience of Christ is allowed to have its effect, the results will be admirable. The believer's heart is then set free from guilt and the dominion of sin. Drawn by the love of Jesus, it will desire more earnestly to do the will of God; it will rise up in prayer and praise. Now his or her life becomes one of cheerful "evangelical" obedience. Common actions are now interpreted as done for the glory of God. Outward things no longer entrap, and having found the great I Am, the eternal substance, one now looks upon all created things as shadows.... Yes, one now counts all things as worth little for the excellency of the knowledge of Christ Jesus our Lord.

Scripture Meditation

No eye has seen, no ear has heard, no mind has conceived what God has prepared for those who love him.

—1 CORINTHIANS 2:9

Thought for the Day

God is revealed by personal encounter, which is then our transformation.

Prayer

Surely you desire truth in the inner parts; you teach me wisdom in the inmost place.

—PSALM 51:6

JANUARY 20: WHY HAS CHRIST REVEALED HIMSELF?

When John Fletcher wrote against the American Revolution in 1776, George III offered him, as a political reward, to name his "preferment" in the Established Church of England. Fletcher declined by saying firmly, "I want nothing but more grace." With this spirit he continues with his third letter on the mystery of the Epiphany.

*S*ir,

Why has Christ manifested himself to us? This is an important question. It was certainly not to satisfy our curiosity. Rather it was for the purposes worthy of his wisdom. These we can reduce to those that were extraordinary, others commonplace, and yet others a mixture of the two.

Among the extraordinary occasions, some are calculated to arouse the thoughtless to have consideration. We may cite the occasion shortly before our Lord's passion. "As he prayed, there came a voice from heaven, saying, 'I have glorified my name, and will glorify it again.' The people who stood by and heard it, 'it thundered.'" They looked upon the extraordinary call as something commonplace and natural. "Others said, 'an angel spoke to him.' But Jesus said, 'This voice came not because of me, but for your sakes.'"

Others are intended as a last warning to the wicked. Such was the occasion when the king Nebuchadnezzar had in his second dream of a "watchman and Holy One coming down from heaven, and crying aloud, 'cut down the tree.'" And there was also the occasion when the mysterious hand wrote on the wall what would be Belshazzar's doom, while he profaned the sacred vessels in his night revelry.

Some are designed for the protection of God's people, and to destroy the pride of their enemies, as when "the Lord looked to the Egyptians, through the pillar of fire, and troubled their host." Or he manifested his presence in Nebuchadnezzar's furnace, to quench the violence of the flame and preserve the three young men, and to convince the raging tyrant that God's kingdom rules over all.

Again others are designed to encourage the children of God in dangerous enterprises, or to direct them in important steps. Such was the case with Joshua, before he began the conquest of Canaan.

Some are designed to appoint persons to undertake uncommon tasks or trials, as when Noah was commissioned to build the ark, or for Abraham to offer up Isaac, or Nathan to reprove David....

The ethical consequences of such manifestations is to make the Word life and spirit ... to ease an anguished conscience ... to reveal Christ to us and in us ... to open a blessed intercourse and keep a delightful communion with Christ ... to silence the self righteous ... even prepare us for great trials ... and finally to make us depart in peace, like Simeon ... or in great triumph of faith like Stephen....

Scripture Meditation

Now I know in part; then I shall know fully, even as I am fully known.

— I CORINTHIANS 13:12

Thought for the Day

The knowledge of God provides the greatest possible self-realism.

Prayer

Let me know thee, O my creator. Let me know thee, even as I am known.

— AUGUSTINE OF HIPPO

JANUARY 21: THE DIVERSITY OF CHRIST'S MANIFESTATIONS

In his fourth letter, Fletcher reflects on the diverse ways God manifests himself.

*S*ir,

That some persons are blessed with clearer, stronger or earlier manifestations of himself than others is undeniable. Why this is so, is one of the mysteries of God's Kingdom that shall not be disclosed until the day of Judgment. But meanwhile, the following reflection may cast some light on this obscure subject, and to help us to say that the Lord does all things well.

For first of all, the Lord suits his manifestations to the various states of the Church. Under the Mosaic covenant God dealt largely with externals, and so revealed himself externally also. But now that the Christian Church is founded upon a more spiritual plan, it is favored with a more spiritual and internal character.

Our Lord also has made us rational beings, in a state of probation. So he deals with us reasonably, not violently, in incessant and powerful ways, but gently would lead us to repentance and obedience. Every day is not a day of Pentecost. Soon after the Son of God had seen the heavens open, he was led into the wilderness to be tempted of the devil; and so too is the Church after him.

Also our wise Redeemer proportions the means to the end. If the effect of a manifestation of his love is to be exceeding great, the manifestation must be exceeding bright.... So the hotter the fight of afflictions that God's people have to go through, then the stronger and brighter is the celestial armor put upon them. Thus we cannot doubt that our good God arranges the nature and degree of his manifestations to us, in respect of our state and capacity, when he discloses himself to us.... Blessed then are the poor in spirit who are empty enough for God to appear to them. For he is like a good physician who knows how to treat each patient according to their condition.

Finally, let me remind you that the author or agent of every divine manifestation is the eternal; God, one in the three, and three in one. The Father reveals the Son freely, the Son freely discovers himself, and the Holy Spirit freely testifies of him. For the Scriptures attest, "No one can say 'Jesus is Lord' but by the Holy Spirit." Again Christ says, "He shall glorify me, for he shall take of the things of mine and show it unto you."

Outwardly too, there are what the Church calls "the means of grace," particularly hearing or reading the word, partaking of the sacraments, and praying together with one accord for the manifestation of the Spirit as the early Christians did in Acts 2:1. These are to be used with great diligence but not to be trusted blindly, for the only proper object of our confidence is God who works all in all.... Although the Lord works through many means, he does not tie himself to any of them ... so if Jesus visits us, it is not because of our prayers or other means, but for his own sake, because his truth and compassion fail not....

Scripture Meditation

Nothing in all creation is hidden from God's sight.
—HEBREWS 4:13

Thought for the Day

Help me to accept the challenge of God's self-revelation to me.

Prayer

Settle in my heart a serious and strong sense of the glory to which Jesus is advanced, by humbling himself even unto death.
—SIMON PATRICK

JANUARY 22: THE WORD OF GOD STILL PRESENTS HIMSELF TO US TODAY

Maximus the Confessor (580–662) was a Greek theologian and monk of the monastery of Chrysopolis. He had an amazing ability to synthesize the truth. This meditation comes from his Centuria.

*B*eloved,

Out of love for us the Word of God, born once for all in the flesh, wills continually to be born in a spiritual way in those who desire him. Becoming a little child, he fashions himself in them by their virtues and gives them as much knowledge of himself as he knows them capable of receiving. The revelation he gives them of his majesty is only partial, not because of any ill will on his part, but because he has regard for the capacity of those who long to see him. This is why the Word of God is always being manifested in the lives of those who share in him, yet remains forever invisible to all in the transcendence of the mystery.

Therefore, after profound reflection upon the meaning of the mystery, the holy apostle declares: "Jesus Christ is the same yesterday, today, and for ever." For the apostle knows that the mystery is always fresh and new, and that its freshness can never be diminished by our understanding of it.

Scripture Meditation

The Word became flesh and made his dwelling among us. We have seen his glory, the glory of the One and Only, who came from the Father, full of grace and truth.

—JOHN 1:14

Thought for the Day

The mystery of God's Word is that it finds its home in us while also being veiled in transcendence.

Prayer

Thou art my Way; I wander if thou fly:
Thou art my Light; if hid, how blind am I!
Thou art my Life; if thou withdraw, I die.

—FRANCIS QUARLES

JANUARY 23: CHRIST IS THE ONE WE SHOULD FOLLOW, NO ONE ELSE

John Wycliffe (1330–1384), one of the forerunners of the Reformation,
expressed the belief that the church should give up its worldly possessions
in order to truly reflect Christ. Wycliffe's writings were condemned in 1382,
and he was summoned to Rome. But in this, his last letter to Pope Urban
VI, he outlines his convictions and explains he is too old to leave England.

I suppose that if my faith be true, and given of God, the Pope will gladly keep it, but if my faith is in error, then he will wisely amend it. I believe the Gospel is expressive of God's law, for I believe Jesus Christ embodied the Gospel, as very God and very Man, and thus surpasses all other laws. I presume therefore that the Pope as the highest vicar on earth should be the most like Christ. For the greatness of Christ's vicars, is not measured by worldly greatness; but by virtuous living; for thus teaches the Gospel.

I take it to be expressive of the Gospel, that during the time Christ was on earth, he walked as the poorest of men, both in spirit and in possessions, for Christ states he had nowhere to lay his head. I also believe personally, that no one should imitate the pope, nor any saint now in heaven, for even the disciples who said they followed Christ, John and James erred, and Peter and Paul sinned. So I believe it is wholesome counsel that the pope should leave his worldly lordship to worldly lords, as Christ has set him a different example, and command his clerks speedily to do the same. For the devil has blinded the world from seeing these things.... Christ has taught me to obey God rather than men, concerning these things. So if the pope does not want to be the anti-Christ, then he will not want to reverse Christ and contradict his will.

Scripture Meditation

I glory in Christ Jesus in my service to God. I will not venture
to speak of anything except what Christ has accomplished
through me.
—ROMANS 15:17–18

Thought for the Day

To be Christlike is to be sacrificial, for Jesus Christ is the supreme sacrifice of God. So we owe him everything.

Prayer

When I stand before the throne
Dressed in beauty not my own,
When I see Thee as Thou art,
Love Thee with unsinning heart?
Then, Lord, shall I fully know
Not till then—how much I owe.
—Murray McCheyne

JANUARY 24: BE COURAGEOUS IN AFFLICTION

William Tyndale (1494–1536) writes this letter to John Frith while in the Tower of London sometime after May 9, 1535. He began printing the New Testament in English in 1525 in Cologne and also worked on the Old Testament from 1530 to 1535. Possibly 80 percent of the Authorised Version of 1611 is actually the genius of Tyndale's translation. Both Tyndale and Frith were martyred.

Dearly Beloved,

However the matter be [i.e. being persecuted for the dissemination of the English Bible], commit yourself wholly and only unto your most loving Father, and most kind Lord, and fear not men that threaten, nor trust men that speak fair; but trust him that is true of promise, and able to make his word good. Your cause is Christ's Gospel, a light that must be fed with the blood of faith. The lamp must be dressed and snuffed daily, and the oil poured in every evening and morning, [i.e. in daily prayers], that the light go not out. Though we are sinners, yet the cause is right.

If when we are buffeted for well-doing, we suffer patiently and endure, that is acceptable to God; for to that end we are called. For Christ also suffered for us, leaving us an example that we should follow his steps, who did no sin. Hereby have we perceived love, that he laid down his life for us: therefore we ought also to lay down our lives for the brethren. Rejoice and be glad, for great is your reward in heaven. For we suffer with him that we may also be glorified with him, who shall change our vile body that it may be fashioned like unto his glorious body....

Dearly beloved, be of good courage, and comfort your soul with the hope of this high reward, and bear the image of Christ in your mortal body, that it become like to his immortal. Follow the example of all your other dear brethren, which chose to suffer in hope of a better resurrection....

Scripture Meditation

When we are cursed, we bless; when we are persecuted, we endure it; when we are slandered we answer kindly.
—1 CORINTHIANS 4:12–13

Thought for the Day

William Tyndale shared, "To look for no human help, brings God's help to overcome."

Prayer

The Lord of peace, of hope, and of faith, be with you, Amen.
—WILLIAM TYNDALE

NARRATIVES OF CONVERSION

JANUARY 25: THE CONVERSION OF SAUL OF TARSUS

On this day, the church has celebrated the conversion of Saul of Tarsus as the archetype of what the eighteenth century began to take in a distinctive way. John Newton (1725–1807), best known for his hymn "Amazing Grace" and for his devotional collection of letters, Cardiphonia or Utterances of the Heart *(1781), was a leader of this conversion movement or Evangelical Revival as it became known. Since he was himself dramatically converted, he could identify with the conversion of the apostle Paul.*

*R*everend and Dear Sir …

The outward circumstance of many religious people has been uniform, knowing very little in life. Whatever changes took place inwardly, they were affected in secret, and unnoticed by others, and almost unperceived by themselves. The Lord has spoken to them, not in thunder and tempest, but with a still small voice he has drawn them gradually to himself.… Others he seems to select in order to show them the exceeding riches of his grace, and the greatness of his mighty power. He permits the natural rebellion and wickedness of their hearts to have full scope … then when others expect the full vengeance to then fall upon them, the Lord is pleased to pluck them as brands from the burning.… A case of this sort indicates a divine power no less than that at the creation of the world; it is evidently the Lord's doing, and it is marvelous in the eyes of those not blinded by prejudice and unbelief.

Such was the persecuting of Saul of Tarsus: his heart was full of enmity against Jesus of Nazareth, and therefore he persecuted and made havoc of his disciples. He had been a terror to the church of Jerusalem, and was going to Damascus with the same intent. He was yet breathing out threats and slaughter against all who loved the Lord Jesus. He thought little of the mischief he had hitherto done. He was engaged in the suppression of the whole.… Such was his spirit and temper, when the Lord Jesus, whom he hated and opposed, checked him in the height of his rage, and called this bitter persecutor to have the honor to become his apostle. Then the Lord inspired him with a new zeal and passion to preach that same faith, which he has so recently attempted to destroy....

Scripture Meditation

I thank Christ Jesus our Lord, who has given me strength, that he considered me faithful, appointing me to his service. Even though I was once a blasphemer and a persecutor and a violent man, I was shown mercy because I acted in ignorance and unbelief.
— I TIMOTHY 1:12–13

Thought for the Day

Who could most appropriately be chosen to communicate God's mercy than one who esteemed himself the least deserving of the apostles?

Prayer

Now to the King eternal, immortal, invisible, the only God, be honor and glory for ever and ever. Amen.
— I TIMOTHY 1:17

JANUARY 26: CONVERSION IN A STORM AT SEA

John Newton [see previous entry] is himself the archetype of eighteenth century narratives of conversion. He was first taken to sea at age eleven by his father, his mother having died when he was six. He then spent time in the West Indies, forced to join the navy at the outbreak of war with France. So his basic education was in "the school of hard knocks." Later he published several collections of letters, of which this is one written on January 19, 1763.

$\mathcal{D}$ear Sir,

Those and many other deliverances were all, at that time, entirely lost upon me. The admonitions of conscience, which, from successive repulses, had grown weaker and weaker, at length entirely ceased; and for a space of many months, if not for some years, I cannot recollect that I had a single check of that sort. At times I was visited with sickness, and believed myself near to death, but I had not the least concern about the consequences. In a word, I seemed to have every mark of final impenitence and rejection; neither judgments nor mercies made the least impression on me....

But now the Lord's time was come, and the conviction I was so unwilling to receive, was deeply impressed upon me by an awful dispensation. I went to bed that night in my usual security and indifference, but was awakened from a sound sleep by the force of a violent sea, which broke on board us; so much of it came down below as filled the cabin I lay in with water. This alarm was followed by a cry from the deck that the ship was going down or sinking. As soon as I could recover myself, I essayed to go upon deck: but was met upon the ladder by the captain, who desired me to bring a knife with me. While I returned for the knife, another person went up in my stead, and was instantly washed overboard. We had no leisure to lament him, nor did we expect to survive him long; for we soon found the ship was filling with water very fast. The sea had torn away the upper timbers on one side, and made a mere wreck in a few minutes.

I shall not affect to describe this disaster in marine dialect, which would be understood by few; and therefore I can give you but a very inadequate idea of it. Taking in all circumstances, it was astonishing, and almost miraculous, that any of us survived to relate the story. We had immediate recourse to the pumps; but the water increased against our efforts....

About nine o'clock, being almost spent with cold and labor, I went to speak with the captain, who was busied elsewhere, and just as I was returning from him, I said almost without any meaning, "If this will not do the Lord have mercy upon us." This (though spoken with little reflection) was the first desire I had breathed for mercy for the space of many years. I was instantly struck with my own words; and, as Jehu said once, "What hast thou to do with peace?" so it directly occurred, "What mercy

119

can there be for me?" … Yet still I was but half convinced, and remained for a space of time in a sullen frame, a mixture of despair and impatience. I thought, if the Christian religion was true, I could not be forgiven; and was, therefore, expecting, and almost, at times, wishing, to know the worst of it.

—I am yours.

Scripture Meditation

He lifted me out of the slimy pit, out of the mud and mire; he set
my feet on a rock.
—PSALM 40:2

Thought for the Day

The depths from which God delivers us become the assurance of the depths to which we can accompany others in their distresses.

Prayer

O Lord, open my lips, and my mouth will declare your praise.
—PSALM 51:15

JANUARY 27: THE GREAT QUESTION: HOW TO OBTAIN FAITH?

*John Newton [see previous entry] continues his narrative of how God entered
into his life in a letter written on January 19, 1763.*

*D*ear Sir,

The twenty-first of March 1748 is a day much to be remembered by me, and I have never suffered it to pass wholly unnoticed since then. On that day the Lord sent from on high, and delivered me out of the deep waters.... I began to pray; I could not utter the prayer of faith; I could not draw near to a reconciled God, and call him Father: my prayer was like the cry of the ravens, which yet the Lord does not disdain to hear. I now began to think of that Jesus whom I had so often derided: I recollected the particulars of his life and of his death; a death for sins not his own, but, as I remembered, for the sake of those who, in their distress, should put their trust in him.

And now I chiefly wanted evidence. The comfortless principles of infidelity were deeply riveted, and I rather wished than believed these things were real facts. You will please to observe, Sir, that I collect the strain of the reasonings and exercises of my mind in one view; but I do not say that all this passed at one time. The great question now was, how to obtain faith. I speak not of an appropriating faith, (of which I then knew neither the nature nor necessity), but how I should gain an assurance that the Scriptures were of divine inspiration, and a sufficient warrant for the exercise of trust and hope in God.

One of the first helps I received, (in consequence of a determination to examine the New Testament more carefully), was from Luke 11:13. I had been sensible that to profess faith in Jesus Christ, when in reality I did not believe his history, was no better than a mockery of the heart-searching God; but here I found a Spirit spoken of, which was to be communicated to those who ask it. Upon this I reasoned thus: If this book is true, the promise in this passage must be true likewise; I have need of that very Spirit, but which the whole was written, in order to understand it aright....

About this time I began to know that there is a God that hears and answers prayer. How many times has he appeared for me since this great deliverance!—yet alas! how distrustful and ungrateful is my heart unto this hour!

—I am, dear sir, your obliged humble servant.

Scripture Meditation

If you then, though you are evil, know how to give good gifts to

your children, how much more will your Father in heaven give the Holy Spirit to those who ask him!
—LUKE 11:13

Thought for the Day

Entering into Christian faith is believing God can and will give us his Spirit so we can believe in him.

Prayer

I will praise you, O LORD. Although you were angry with me, your anger has turned away and you have comforted me. Surely God is my salvation; I will trust and not be afraid.
—ISAIAH 12:1–2

JANUARY 28: CONVERSION REQUIRES HUMBLE SELF-KNOWLEDGE

Blaise Pascal [see entry for February 25] lost his mother as a child. His father's death in 1651 he felt keenly. His devout sister was then free to enter the reforming community of Port Royal. On a visit to his sister, Pascal heard a sermon that deeply affected him and resulted in his conversion in 1653. Here he reflects upon his coming to Christ.

Dearest Jacqueline,

If I had but seen a miracle, say some men, should I not be converted? They would not talk in this manner, if they knew what conversion really meant. They imagine there is nothing in it but merely to acknowledge there is a God; and that to worship him consists only in uttering certain verbal addresses, but little different from those which the heathens made to their idols. True conversion consists in deep abasement of ourselves before that sovereign Being whom we have so often provoked, and who every moment might justly destroy us; in acknowledging that we can do nothing without his aid, and that we have merited nothing of him but his displeasure. It consists in knowing that there is such an invincible opposition between God and ourselves, that without a Mediator there could not be any communion between us.

Think it not strange that illiterate persons should believe without reasoning. God gives them the love of his righteousness, and hatred of themselves. He inclines their hearts to believe. No man ever believes with a true and saving faith unless God inclines his heart; and no man when God does incline his heart, can refrain from believing. This David well knew when he prayed, "Incline my heart, O God, unto thy testimonies."

If some men believe without having examined the proofs of religion, it is because there is produced in them a disposition truly holy; and because what they hear affirmed of our religion is perfectly agreeable to that disposition. They are sensible that God is their Maker; they are resolved to love none but him, and to hate none but themselves; they feel that they are without strength, that they are incapable of going to God, and that, unless he is pleased to come to them, they can not have any communion with him; and they hear our religion declare that we are to love God alone, and hate only ourselves; and that, whereas we are altogether corrupt and incapable of coming to God, God became man that he might unite himself to us. There needs no more than this to convince men who possess such a disposition of heart, and such knowledge of their duty and of their own incapacity to perform it.

Scripture Meditation

Give me understanding, and I will keep your law and obey it with all my heart.

—PSALM 119:34

Thought for the Day

In his *Pensées,* Blaise Pascal wrote, "The heart has its reason that reason knows not of."

Prayer

Turn my eyes away from worthless things; preserve my life according to your word.

—PSALM 119:37

JANUARY 29: THE CONVERSION OF A MOTHERLESS CHILD

Francis Ridley Havergal (1836–1879), English hymn writer of such Revivalist hymns as "Just as I Am, without One Plea," recounts her conversion after her mother died when she was twelve years old. Three years later she was led gently to experience the eternal trust of Christ.

*D*ear Sister,

Up to the time I was six years old, I have no remembrance of any religious ideas whatever ... but I remember Mamma's words to me in 1848: "Dear child, you have your own little bedroom now, it ought to be a little Bethel." Having that small room to myself developed me much as a child; it was mine, and to me it was the coziest little nest in the world.

I know I did not love God at this time, the very thought frightened me; but sometimes a feeling not unlike love would make me go to sleep with a wet pillow. For going to bed I would determine to try to think about God, hard as it was, and whisper, "How good of God to send Jesus to die!" Nevertheless it usually ended in my crying most heartily, because I was so bad, and he was so good, and because I didn't and couldn't love him when he even died for sinners ...

[She recounts then how her sister Diana had become a Christian.] I could not help seeing—nobody could—a new and remarkable radiance about her countenance.... I looked at her almost with awe ... throwing her arm around me, she said, "O Fanny, dearest Fanny, the blessing has come to me at last. Jesus has forgiven me, I know. He is my Savior ... such a Savior, I never imagined, so loving, so kind!" ... Yes she had found peace, and more than peace—overflowing unspeakable joy!

Two months later ... I made a confidante of Miss Cook (shortly to become my step-mother).... I sat on the sofa alone with her, and told her I longed to know that I was forgiven. I assured her I desired it above everything on earth.... "Then Fanny, I am sure, it will not be very long before your desire is granted, your hope fulfilled.... Would his call, his promise, be enough for you? Could you not commit your soul to him, your Savior, Jesus?" Then came a flash of hope across me, which made me feel literally breathless. I remember my heart beat. "I could, surely" was my response. I flung myself on my knees, in my room, and strove to realize the new hope. I could commit my soul to Jesus.... I did trust the Lord Jesus.

Scripture Meditation

Out of the overflow of his heart his mouth speaks.
—LUKE 6:45

Thought for the Day

Let's say with Francis Havergal, "Only for Jesus! Lord keep it for ever, sealed on the heart and engraved on the life!"

Prayer

Take my life, and let it be, ever, only, all for thee.
—FRANCIS RIDLEY HAVERGAL

JANUARY 30: THE CONVERSION OF CHARLES DE FOUCAULD

Charles de Foucauld [see entries for February 14 and 15] became a monk
who lived alone with the Tuareg dwellers of the central Sahara. By his
example he rediscovered the lives of the Desert Fathers, in renewed "imitation
of Jesus." He lived in a life of apparent failure, his dream of others joining him
never being fulfilled. He writes this letter from Nazareth in November of 1897.

*D*ear Father,

As soon as I believed that there was a God, I understood that I could do nothing else than live for him exclusively: my religious vocation dates from the same hour as my faith....

In the beginning faith had many obstacles to overcome; I, who had doubted so much, I did not believe everything in a day. Sometimes the miracles of the Gospel seemed unbelievable to me, sometimes I wanted to mix passages from the Koran in my prayers. But God's grace and the counsel of my confessor dispersed the clouds.... I wished to be a monk, to live only for God, to do only what was most perfect, whatever that might be.... My confessor made me wait three years; I myself, although anxious to "breathe myself out in a total exhalation of self before God," as Bousset says, did not know which order to choose. The Gospel showed me that "the first commandment is to love God with one's whole heart" and that everything had to be contained in love.

Scripture Meditation

[God] chose the lowly things of this world ... —and the things
that are not—to nullify the things that are.
—I CORINTHIANS 1:28

Thought for the Day

Charles de Foucauld provided the insight "Love is always obedience when its object is God."

Prayer

> *O God, we should all hymn praises of your mercies—we who were all created for the everlasting glory and redeemed by the blood of Jesus.*

—CHARLES DE FOUCAULD

JANUARY 31: THE LONELY JOURNEY OF AN INTELLECTUAL

Simone Weil (1909–1943), French social philosopher and activist in the Resistance during World War II, was born of Jewish parents but converted to the personal and existential Christian faith, which she so much admired in Søren Kierkegaard. For that reason she never joined the Catholic Church, although she had Catholic mentors.

At fourteen I fell into one of those fits of bottomless despair that come with adolescence, and I seriously thought of dying because of the mediocrity of my natural faculties. The exceptional gifts of my brother, who had a childhood and youth comparable to those of Pascal, brought my own inferiority home to me. I did not mind having no visible successes, but what did grieve me was the idea of being excluded from that transcendent kingdom to which only the truly great have access and wherein truth abides. I preferred to die rather than live without that truth. After months of inward darkness, I suddenly had the everlasting conviction that any human being, even though practically devoid of natural faculties, can penetrate to the kingdom of truth reserved for genius, if only he longs for truth and perpetually concentrates all his attention upon its attainment. He thus becomes a genius too, even though for lack of talent his genius cannot be visible from outside....

There was a young English Catholic [at Solesmes] from whom I gained my first idea of the supernatural power of the sacraments because of the truly angelic radiance with which he seemed to be clothed after going to communion.... He told me of the existence of those English poets of the seventeenth century who are named metaphysical. In reading them later on, I discovered the poem of which I read you, what is unfortunately a very inadequate translation. It is called "Love." I learned it by heart. Often, at the culminating point of a violent headache, I made myself say it over, concentrating all my attention upon it and clinging with all my soul to the tenderness it enshrines. I used to think I was merely reciting it as a beautiful poem, but without my knowing it the recitation had the virtue of a prayer. It was during one of these recitations that, as I told you, Christ himself came down and took possession of me....

I never wondered whether Jesus was or was not the Incarnation of God; but in fact I was incapable of thinking of him without thinking of him as God.... During all this time of spiritual progress I had never prayed. I was afraid of the power of suggestion that is in prayer—the very power for which Pascal recommends it.... Last summer, doing Greek with T——, I went through the "Our Father" word for word in Greek. We promised each other to learn it by heart. I do not think he ever did so, but some weeks later, as I was turning over the pages of the Gospel, I said to myself that since I had promised to do this thing and it was good, I ought to do it. I did it.

The infinite sweetness of this Greek text so took hold of me that for several days I could not stop myself from saying it over all the time. A week afterward I began the vine harvest. I recited the Our Father in Greek every day before work, and I repeated it very often in the vineyard.... The effect of this practice is extraordinary and surprises me every time, for, although I experience it each day, it exceeds by expectation at each repetition.... Sometimes, also, during this recitation or at other moments, Christ is present with me in person, but his presence is infinitely more real, more moving, clearer than on that first occasion when he took possession of me.

Scripture Meditation

Our Father in heaven, hallowed be your name, your kingdom come, your will be done on earth as it is in heaven.
—MATTHEW 6:9–10

Thought for the Day

Grace alone uplifts against the downward gravity of the natural world.

Prayer

Lord, my first fruits present themselves to thee;
Yet not mine neither: for from thee they came.
—GEORGE HERBERT'S DEDICATION OF *THE TEMPLE*

FEBRUARY 1: EXPERIENCING AN EPIPHANY AT THE OLYMPIC GAMES

Kathy Kreiner-Phillips (b. 1957) joined the Canadian national ski team at age
thirteen and in 1976 became the youngest Olympic gold medalist in alpine
skiing in the giant slalom competition in Innsbruck, Austria. She writes to the
editor on February 13, 2004, the anniversary of her victory.

It is significant you should ask me my story, for it was on February 13, 1976 that a childhood dream came true. It all started in 1968, when I was ten years old and my father had come home from the 1968 Olympics as the team doctor, with stories of Nancy Greene winning her gold and silver medals. I remember thinking, wouldn't it be great to also stand on the podium to receive an Olympic gold medal around my neck and hear our National Anthem being played.

Eight years later, just a week before the opening ceremonies of the Innsbruck Olympic Games, our team was in a slump, and I was thinking I should retire with my sister Laurie and Betsy Clifford after the games. But my brother's friend, Tom Vukovich, began to ask me straight questions…. "How did I want to finish? Did I want to be first? What would I think about as I left the starting gate?" After that I needed to concentrate on just a few simple things, "outside ski," and "look ahead." Meanwhile, to relax I thought I would see a movie in the Olympic Village, and it so happened it was *Jesus Christ Superstar*. Well, I was deeply affected by what I saw, feeling the terrible injustice of what Jesus suffered, to the point that this seemed more important than the races ahead of me. I remember riding the chairlift to the start of my race, having a conversation with God, saying: "God, if you really are there, then you do what you want with me, and I will be happy with that." In other words I was recalling my childhood prayer "The Lord's Prayer," in the Sunday School of St. Matthew's Anglican Church, in Timmins, Ontario. But church practice had fallen away with our family life of skiing in winter, and summer at the cottage.

So now I skied the race of my life, not losing focus from top to bottom of the mountain. It was almost an out-of-body experience, where everything flowed effortless, as if I wasn't even trying. Was this really just a simple new beginning, of having a new spirit, of literally hurling oneself down the mountain in the arms of my heavenly Father? Had he really heard my little prayer? Was this really part of a larger plan for my life, or was it the only way that he might have got my attention? Does he think excellence is not to be despised?

How has this Olympic victory changed Kathy? Well to start with, it was more than an Olympic medal—it was about God getting my attention—showing me personally that he cares about me through his son Jesus. For he continually says to me now: *"You asked me for help so I gave it to you. You asked that my will be done—not what Kathy Kreiner wants. Though you had done everything you could do to prepare yourself physically and mentally you completed the picture by thinking about the spiritual also. You surrendered to me, your Creator. How else can I get through to you unless you let me? I have tried to get your attention over the years and you have come close to receiving it, especially when you were alone and quiet in the Northern Ontario woods. When you read those books of your brother's when he studied Theology at Knox College, that really delighted me. When you spoke to certain people about higher things I was excited. So here you are now trying to live in the center of my will, day to day, moment by moment. You are experiencing my peace, my love—isn't it so good?—and my joy."* Thank you, God!

Kathy

Scripture Meditation

[You shall] love the LORD your God with all your heart and with all your soul and with all your strength.

—DEUTERONOMY 6:5

Thought for the Day

"We live with superlatives when living in his presence: always joyful, praying continuously, giving thanks in all circumstances." (1 Thess. 5:16–18)

Prayer

O God of Peace,
You have taught us that in returning and rest we shall be saved:
In quietness and in confidence shall be our strength,
Lift us we pray to your Presence,
Where we may be still and know that you are God. Amen.

—KATHY KREINER-PHILLIPS

FEBRUARY 2: A DRUG ADDICT'S CRY: GOD WHERE ARE YOU?

Fred Milne (b. 1954) and his wife Janet are involved in a ministry to drug addicts in Kelowna, British Columbia. He writes this letter to the editor on December 22, 2003.

*A*ll I can remember in my childhood was constant change, moving 5 times before I was 10, never knowing what would happen tomorrow. I was always thinking, *where are my friends, and especially my teachers?* I had an alcoholic father, whose life was falling apart; and when he was home from a logging camp or a mine he wasn't there either but in bars. His violence progressed with his alcoholism, so I would hide under the bedcovers, praying to God "Where are you?" or seeking something or someone to stop it all and end his life. I was frightened, ashamed and powerless and very, very lonely. I swore I would never be like my father.

At 10, I acted out in violence to stop him and ran away to the streets of Vancouver. By now I was more frightened, more alone, now blaming God also. *For if you are real, God, what are all of us kids doing living on the streets?* Before I hit the streets I had always felt safe at school getting straight As. But at 12 I had started using drugs and missing school, selling drugs and rebelling. I had made a choice, unbeknown to me, to follow the road to hell.

I hated God, I hated society and again unknown to me I hated myself. My life became a grade B movie gangster, drug dealing, violent, and totally self-centered. People needed to fear me because I was scared. To prove my toughness I developed a heroin habit, which jumped from $12 a day to $300–400. One day I nodded out at the wheel of my car with my 15 year old, pregnant girlfriend beside me. I totaled the car and we dragged ourselves out and made our way home to wake up in a pool of blood. Our baby miscarried. I could go on sharing losses, pain and the suffering of others who crossed my path.

After years in jail, now 41, I just wanted it to end, putting enough heroin in a spoon to kill 5–10 men. Rescued, I fled from the hospital, to use more drugs. But twelve hours later, I miraculously made it into detox where for 17 days two of the workers laid their hands on me and prayed. One woman I had used drugs with over 25 years prior, and the other man I'd sold drugs to for many years. They had 23 and 7 years clean from addiction and both had become Christians. They offered help in the formula of a recovery program. I spent six months there to stay safe. Then another miracle happened, when Larry, a fellow gangster who I had met in the early 70's in prison was 18 months clean, stopped by to see if any of the men wanted a ride to church. Had it been anyone else asking me to Church the answer would have been "No Way!"

However, here was a man whose life paralleled mine. I went to church to see people smiling, happy and giving, so I knew that something was going on. Reading the Bible I was arrested by Psalm 40:1–5, all about the "god-stuff" I so long despised — "hearing my cry," (v. 1); "lifting me from a slimy pit," (v. 2); "putting a new song in my mouth," (v. 3); performing "many wonders," indeed (v. 4).

This has just been the beginning of a slow journey of helping others off the streets, where I had been, in the gutter.

Scripture Meditation

Therefore let us stop passing judgment on one another. Instead make up your mind not to put any stumbling block or obstacle in your brother's way.
—ROMANS 14:13

Thought for the Day

All individuals are persons of worth to whom God can extend his transforming grace.

Prayer

Here I am, I have come … I desire to do your will, O my God; your law is within my heart.
—PSALM 40:7–8

FEBRUARY 3: OUR SECOND BIRTH

It would be a mistake to think of Christian conversion as only a modern phenomenon. Fulbert of Chartres (960–1028) was a bishop who developed the Cathedral School of Chartres in Picardy, France, into one of Europe's chief centers of learning. He had the reputation of seeking the truth, beyond merely being skilled in erudition.

We know, and our knowledge is true, that we who were defiled by our first birth have been cleansed by our second birth; we who were enslaved by our first birth have been freed by our second birth; we who became children of earth at our first birth became children of heaven at our second birth; we who were fleshly because of the corruption inherent in our first birth have become spiritual by virtue of our second birth. The first made us children of wrath; the second, children of grace. Therefore let everyone know that any attack on the reverence due to holy baptism is an insult to God himself who told us: "No one who is not born again of water and spirit can enter the kingdom of heaven" [John 3:5].

Sound instruction therefore gives us the grace to understand the nature and purpose of saving baptism. As the apostle puts it: If we have died with Christ, we believe we shall also live with Christ; for the object of our dying and being buried with Christ is to enable us to rise again and live with him.

Scripture Meditation

God did not send his Son into the world to condemn the world,
but to save the world through him.

—JOHN 3:17

Thought for the Day

Has our religious culture emptied the radical meaning of being "born again"?

Prayer

Love is born of God, and cannot rest but in God, above all created things. Let me love thee more than myself, nor love myself
but for thee.

—THOMAS À KEMPIS

THE FAMILY TRANSFORMED BY THE EPIPHANY

FEBRUARY 4: A NEW ERA FOR WOMEN

St. Frances Xavier Cabrini (1850–1917), a missionary to the Alaskans, writes to some schoolchildren in New Orleans on May 31, 1904.

*D*ear Children,

The Indian woman has to work while the man quietly smokes opium. With this most powerful narcotic, the men make themselves drunk. The poor woman and mother of many little ones, who are too small to stand, is forced to tie her offspring round her waist in a sack, and in this unconventional way has to do her washing. If the baby cries, she moves it with a shrug of her shoulders and thus calms it. This is the way the Indian baby is fondled. How grateful we should be to Christianity, which has raised the dignity of a woman, reestablishing her rights, unknown to the pagan nations.

Until Mary Immaculate, the Woman *par excellence*, foretold by the prophets, Dawn of the Sun of Justice, had appeared on earth—what was woman? But Mary appeared, the new Eve, true Mother of the Living, and a new era arose for woman. She was no longer a slave but equal to man; no longer a servant, but mistress within her own walls; no longer the object of disdain and contempt, but raised to the dignity of mother and educator, on whose knee generations are built up. All this we owe to Mary.

Scripture Meditation

The virgin's name was Mary. The angel went to her and said, "Greetings, you are highly favored! The Lord is with you!"
—LUKE 1:27–28

Thought for the Day

Since antiquity, men have misused women, the source of all human beings. As the Lord's servant, Mary is indeed the exaltation of womanhood.

Prayer

My soul glorifies the Lord ... for the Mighty One has done great things for me.
—LUKE 1:46, 49

FEBRUARY 5: THE WISE SONSHIP OF JESUS

Aelred of Rievaulx (1110–1167) was Abbot of the Cistercian monastery of Rievaulx in Yorkshire, England. His special friendship with Yvo, a monk in Wardon, was brought out in the first part of Aelred's book on "spiritual friendship." In this letter, written between 1153–1157, Aelred wanted to help Yvo meditate upon the hidden years of Jesus' childhood, especially Jesus' presentation at the temple at the age of twelve.

My dearest Son Yvo,

You ask me to extract from the passage of the Gospel which tells what the boy Jesus did at the age of twelve some seeds of devout meditation and holy love, and, committing them to writing, as if putting them in baskets, to send them to you. While your messenger was still telling me this I became aware in the inmost depths of my heart how great, how ardent, how sweet and of what kind of affection I had for you! ... I am aware of the intimacy, devotion and tears you are accustomed to ask these very kinds of questions of Jesus himself in your own prayers. For you have in your heart's eyes the sweet likeness of that dear boy himself, reproducing imaginatively the features of that lovely face. With the gaze of his lovely eyes upon you, it is then that you burst out devoutly: "O dear boy, where were you? Where were you hiding? Who sheltered you? Whose company were you enjoying? Was it in heaven or upon earth, or in some house where you were staying?" [We ask such questions] because just as the Lord is born and conceived in us, so he grows and is nourished in us, until we all come to perfect manhood, that maturity which is proportioned to the complete growth in Christ [Ephesians 4:13].

"Then, as they could not find him, they returned to Jerusalem, and after three days they found him in the temple" (Luke 2:44). It is with good reason that at the end of three days he was found in the temple, in the midst of the doctors and elders. As he had revealed the loving design of God the Father for our redemption ... so he began gradually to manifest the same in the most sacred of all places in the world, the temple at Jerusalem, and to the guardians of this most precious treasure, the promise contained in Scripture. First listening and asking questions, then answering questions, he unfolded the most sacred mysteries. Then we read, "All were amazed at the wisdom of his answers" (Luke 2:47). This is an example of humility and modesty for all youths, teaching them to be silent in the midst of their elders, to listen and ask questions in order to learn.

Tell me, my dearest lady, Mother of my Lord, what were your feelings, your surprise, your joy, when you found your dearest son, the boy Jesus, not among boys but among teachers, and beheld the gaze of all eyes bent on him, everyone eagerly listening to him ... his wisdom and the answers he gave? "I found," she says, "him whom my soul loves" (Song of Songs 3:4). "So I held him fast and would not let him go" ... for in the sorrow of his absence, we asked: "Son, why have you behaved so, to us? Behold, your father and I have been looking for you in sorrow" (Luke 2:48).... "How is it," he replied, "that you have sought me? Did you not know that I must be concerned about my Father's business" (v. 49). Here already he begins to disclose the secret of the heavenly mysteries in which he had been occupied for the three days ... yet then "went down with them and was subject unto them" (v. 51).

Scripture Meditation

Jesus grew in wisdom and stature, and in favor with God and men.
—LUKE 2:52

Thought for the Day

Jesus had no high educational advantages, living simply with a father and mother who were poor working villagers in obscure Nazareth.

Prayer

My Jesus, you are so close to me: inspire in me the thoughts I should have about your hidden life.
—CHARLES DE FOUCAULD

FEBRUARY 6: GROWING SPIRITUALLY AS JESUS GREW PHYSICALLY

Aelred [see previous entry] continues his letter to Yvo, with further reflections upon the mystery of the Epiphany and of "the three days" of Jesus' absence from the parents who so loved him.

What you are looking for, my son, is not theological speculation but devotion. This is not something then to sharpen your tongue but something to arouse your affections. [As his master Bernard of Clairvaux was accustomed to say.] "My purpose is not so much to explain in words, as to move hearts."

The Lord our God is one God (Deuteronomy 4:6). He cannot vary, he cannot change, as David says: "You are always the same and your years will not come to an end" (Ps. 101:28). Now this God of ours, eternal, outside of time, unchangeable, in our nature became changeable, and entered time, in order to make the changeableness which he took upon himself for our sakes the way for changeable men and women, within time, to enter into his own eternity and stability; so that in our one unique Savior there should be the way by which we might mount on high, the life to which we might come, and the truth which we might enjoy. As he himself said: "I am the way, the truth and the life" (John 14:6).

So the Lord, without ceasing to be great in his own nature, was born as a little child in the flesh and through a certain interval of time he advanced and grew up according to the flesh, in order that we who in spirit are little children, or rather as almost nothing, might be born spiritually and, passing through the successive ages of the spiritual lie, grow up and advance. Thus his bodily progress is our spiritual progress, and what we are told he did at each stage of his life is reproduced in us spiritually according to the various degrees of progress.

Let then his bodily birth be the archetype of our spiritual birth, that is of conversion to holiness. Let the persecution which he suffered at the hands of Herod be a sign of our conversion. Let his upbringing in Nazareth become the image of our growth in godliness. Moreover, when Jesus was twelve years old he went up to Jerusalem.... This was fitting that he was twelve years old then, because he came not to abolish the Law but to fulfill it....

Scripture Meditation

He had to be made like his brothers in every way.
—Hebrews 2:17

Thought for the Day

Likewise, I must be like Jesus, poor in spirit, humble, loving, and serving others.

Prayer

> May Christ our Savior bring this desire of ours to fulfillment, for
> he took flesh for us.
>
> —RABANUS MAURUS

FEBRUARY 7: BECOMING A CHILD LIKE THE CHRIST CHILD

---

*Geert Groote (d. 1381) lived in Deventer in the eastern Netherlands. As a
well-educated layman of independent means, he resolved at age thirty-two to
repent and to devote himself wholeheartedly to live as a deacon of the
church, preaching repentance and conversion. Thus was inaugurated the
Devotio Moderna, a movement of spiritual renewal that included later
leaders such as Thomas à Kempis. His sermons, meditations, and letters are
one corpus of his teachings on conversion.*

Who is born an adult? It hardly seems necessary to say that someone
is born a child. But this was said for us, to make it understood that Jesus
was born and made a child for us, and thus to show that we must also be
born and become children with him. "Unless you become children like
unto this child, he said, you will not enter the kingdom of heaven"
(Matthew 18:3). "Like unto" is a comparative adverb, for just as we have
borne in our flesh the likeness of an earthly child, so we are to bear that
of a heavenly child. The birth of Christ teaches us in this way to become
like him in humility and stature. No one can be born with Christ unless,
as Christ, he becomes like unto a child.

Let us therefore be children with the Child, not thinking ourselves superior. Let us rather speak as children, think as children, and reason as
children. Milk and drink ought to suffice for us who cannot yet bear solid
food. For are we not still carnal, sold under sin? For there is still such strife

and contention among us, as we walk in the ways of human beings. So let us rather walk in the pathways of the Church, fortified by sharing in the holy sacraments and the Scriptures. Then who knows but that God will forgive and send mercy from on high, and by putting away childish milk and nourishing us with more solid food will bring us to a measure of maturity?

Scripture Meditation

Just as we have borne the likeness of the earthly man, so we shall bear the likeness of the man from heaven.

—1 CORINTHIANS 15:49

Thought for the Day

Lord, help me see that I cannot have human maturity without possessing the child Jesus.

Prayer

O compassionate, merciful Father ... I commend to you my children, whom you have put on my shoulders, for you commissioned me to keep them awake—me, who am always sleeping. Wake them up yourself, kind and compassionate Father, so that the eyes of their understanding may be always wide awake in you.

—CATHERINE OF SIENA

FEBRUARY 8: CHRIST'S CARE FOR THE CHILDREN OF BELIEVERS

Samuel Rutherford (1600–1661) was a leading pastor and professor of theology at St. Andrews University in Scotland. He resisted resolutely the prevalent spirit of natural self-improvement and suffered much injustice. But he is best known for his pastoral letters as being expressive of "the loveliness of Christ." He writes the following letter on November 26, 1631, seeking to bring comfort to a mother who had just lost a child.

*W*ell-Beloved Sister,

Know that I have been visiting my Lady Kenmure. Her child is with the Lord. I entreat you, visit her ... for her husband is absent, and I think she will be so grief-stricken.

Send me word about Grizel, your sick daughter, whom I remember in Christ. Urge her to cast herself into his arms, who was born of a woman, and being "the Ancient of Days," was yet made a young weeping child. It was not for nothing that our brother Jesus was an infant. It was that he might pity infants of believers, who were to come out of the womb into the world. I believe our Lord Jesus shall be waiting on, with mercy, mercy, mercy, to the end of that battle, and bring her through with life and peace, and a sign of God's favor. I shall expect to have news from you, and especially if you fear her possible loss....

I trust in God, that the Lord, who knit us together, shall continue to keep us together ... I know that you will, with love, cover infirmities; and our Lord give you wisdom in all things. I think love has broad shoulders, and will bear many things, so that love does not faint, nor sweat, nor fall beneath the burden.

Commend me to your husband and dear Grizel. I think of her. Lord Jesus, be in the furnace with her, and then she will smoke but not burn....

Yours in his sweet Lord Jesus,

S. R.

Scripture Meditation

*H*e gathers the lambs in his arms and carries them close to his heart.

—ISAIAH 40:11

Thought for the Day

It is not for nothing that our brother Jesus was an infant.

143

FEBRUARY 9: ARE YOU READY TO PERCEIVE CHRIST?

This is another of the six letters John Fletcher addressed to his congregation.
[See entries for January 7 and 18–21.]

Dear Friends,

The mere outward sight of our Savior's person and miracles rather confounded than converted the beholders. What glorious beams of his Godhead pierced through the veil of his mean appearances, when, with supreme authority, he turned the merchants and moneychangers out of the temple. When he entered Jerusalem in triumph, all the city was moved, saying "Who is this?" And when he said to those who apprehended him, "I am he," and they went backward and fell to the ground! ... Nevertheless, we do not find that one person was blessed with the saving knowledge of him, on any of these solemn occasions. The people of Galilee who saw most of him, believed the least in him. Instead, they questioned: "What wisdom is this which is given to this man, that such mighty works are wrought by his hands? Is this not the carpenter's son? ...

How inadequate then was the manifestation of Jesus, when it remained only external, and was not received within the heart! ...

Thus if our Lord had not called Zacchaeus, inwardly as well as outwardly, would he have come down from the pinnacle of his proud nature, as well as from a sycamore tree? ... The blind man restored to his bodily sight knew not his heavenly benefactor, until a second and greater miracle was wrought upon the eyes of his blind understanding....

As for the revelations of Christ to St. John in the book of revelation ... one of the things our Lord commanded John to write is a most glorious promise, that he stands at the door of the human heart, ready to manifest himself to poor lukewarm Laodiceans, and to confront their need of him, and to open their hearts by the prayer of faith, so that he will come in....

Some of you wonder why you cannot believe; why you cannot see Jesus with the eye of your mind, and delight in him with all the affections of your heart. I apprehend the reason to be one of the following, or perhaps, all of them.

First, you are not poor, lost, undone, helpless sinners in yourselves. You indulge spiritual and refined self-righteousness, you are not yet *dead* to the law, and quite slain by the commandment. Now the kingdom of heaven belongs to none but the poor in Spirit. Jesus comes to save none but the lost. What wonder, then, if Jesus is nothing to you, and if you do not live in his kingdom of peace, righteousness, and joy in the Holy Ghost?

Secondly, perhaps you spend your time in curious reasoning, instead of casting yourselves, as forlorn sinners, at Christ's feet; leaving it to him to bless you, when, and in the manner and degree, he pleases. Know, that he is the wise and sovereign God, and that it is your duty to lie before him as clay—as fools—as sinful nothings.

Scripture Meditation

Here I am! I stand at the door and knock. If anyone hears my voice and opens the door, I will come in and eat with him, and he with me.

—REVELATION 3:20

Thought for the Day

Conception predisposes perception, so who I believe Christ to be will condition what I experience of him.

Prayer

O God, whose only begotten Son has appeared in our flesh: grant we beseech you, that we may be conformed inwardly unto him, whom we confess to have been outwardly like unto us, even Jesus Christ your Son, our Lord.

—COLLECT ON THE OCTAVE OF THE EPIPHANY

FEBRUARY 10: BEING STEWARDS OF THE MYSTERIES OF GOD IN THE HOME

Richard Baxter (1615–1691), Puritan preacher and pastor, was known as one
of the great reconcilers in an age of religious dissension. He coined the phrase
"mere Christianity" to focus on the faith of the fathers of the church. He
organized a pastoral movement called the "Worcester Association" committed
to the catechism of families in each parish. For Baxter this involved traveling
exhaustively. Here he writes to a fellow pastor, the Reverend Thomas
Wadsworth, about the scheme in late January 1656.

ear Brother,

I am glad to hear of the success of your labour for the souls of those committed to your charge.... I recommend to you *The Agreement of Divers Ministers of Christ in the County of Worcester ... for Catechizing* (1656): I advise and entreat you to follow it presently with all your might. Use what Catechism you think meet, but see that you take all your parish personally person by person, in private as we do, and prudently and seriously set it upon their consciences.... I take our business of discipline itself to be far below this. And I never had more comfort in any work that I have set my hand to, except public preaching. I first briefly explained to them the reasons for our undertaking in the open congregation, and read over the Agreement, Exhortation, and Catechism. And then I preached 2 or 3 days (from Hebrews 5:11, 12), to show the necessity of it, even to the aged and ancient "professors" [i.e. of faith] who have been loiterers and remain ignorant of Principles.

Then, according to our Agreement, I caused my assistant himself with one of the deacons, to go from house to house through town and parish (nearly twenty miles) visiting each family. While 5 or 6 refused, over 800 accepted them. Then after giving them six weeks [to learn the Catechism] I cause one of the clerks to go every weekly, with a week's notice, of our visitation. We spend every Monday and Tuesday visiting each family from 1 pm. until night-time.... The seriousness of the discourse I find spends me much, even as much as two sermons daily might do. So I fear sometimes I will not hold out. But I see the hope of success, and this convinces me that we will pull down the Kingdom of the Devil. I fear nothing except that many Ministers will lazily, dully, and superficially slubber and do little more than hear the words [of the parishioners].

Scripture Meditation

Whoever gives heed to instruction prospers.
—PROVERBS 16:20

Thought for the Day

Give me a like passion to mentor others in the way of truth.

Prayer

Consecrate with thy presence the way my feet should go; and then the humblest work will shine, and the roughest places be made plain.
—JAMES MARTINEAU

THE JOURNEY WITH JESUS

FEBRUARY 11: PRAYING FOR "TRAVELING MERCIES" IN
THE PURSUIT OF THEOLOGICAL SCHOLARSHIP

*Julie Canlis (b. 1973) writes to the editor on February 4, 2004, as she is
completing her doctorate at the University of St. Andrews. She is married with
three young children.*

It is amazing how often we can just be in "survival mode" and stop praying and reflecting on what we are doing, and why we were called to it in the first place.... So, carried along by my studies, I have been completely unmindful of its dangers. Indeed, I am becoming convinced that getting a theological PhD is not a neutral experience. Rather it is a hardening of the arteries—a narrowing of heart and brain—of feeling myself to be out-of-balance, toning and strengthening my left brain while my right brain is rapidly deteriorating. I once felt this loss acutely in a dream. In some ways, it feels like a profound un-learning. For four years now, I have been in rigorous training to atomize everything, to turn things, people, and Scriptures into corpses, to write a complex defense of a concept of "participation in God" as I myself cease to participate.

Yet this reflection has come about ironically, because my studies are flowing so well: in publishing articles, being asked to conferences and weighty meetings on "The Importance of Spirituality for Theology." But in its midst there is a deeper dissonance. I sense that I am at a road that is forking, but I cannot see it cognitively. Only in prayer do I see that I am at a juncture, an opportunity to choose. One is the path God has chosen for me. The other is the path of my choice, to continue to do theology, to be "successful" at it, to publish, to receive acclaim. The more praise I receive, the more nervous I become, wondering, "am I just playing their game?"—and yet I do not even know what "the game" is! Somehow "the game" never forces me to face my essential loneliness; instead it fills it superficially. It allows me to "master" theology, and thus becomes an idol for self-assurance, for securing my place in this world. And that is its deception.

Slowly, I am understanding what it means to have a true vocation to theological scholarship; it is only in obedience and joy. I am called to the inefficiency of prayer, rather than to the efficiency of studies. Ironically, in our culture's mania for credentials, the very thing that is supposed to "certify" you usually kills you … especially if you are a professional theologian. You start relying on the fact that you at last have a PhD, rather than listening to your vocation. Credentials can so easily mask what was originally a call—tempting me to be "proficient" rather than faithful. It turns me into a "thing" and I begin to take pride in my being a "thing" (a person with credentials)! I also begin to look at my life through these credentials, subconsciously asking what is going to boost my C.V. [curriculum vita, a record of one's accomplishments] rather than what will lead me deeper into obedience to Jesus in this vocation, in this family I am in, with these children and husband I have been given.

I sometimes wonder if I have made a mistake to specialize in my topic, until I remember what I really seek is to live free and large before God. I sense that God has and is working powerfully in me (although to be honest, I mostly can't feel/see it but it is there), and I also sense that I have received a bedrock of good theology that I could not have just absorbed by osmosis. But also I sense I will be led *out* of this specialized focus into a broader vision of things that more naturally bring me alive. And for that I give God thanks, and attempt to work hard so I can be done with this PhD as quickly as possible!

So please pray with me for *traveling mercies*—that God would protect me through this time in my life. It is never a "crisis," but it is always the undertow that threatens to pull me under. I think it is the difference between ending up as a theologian or as someone-who-prays. Mostly, I want to follow God, not serve my credentials (or worse—mistake myself for them!).

This is a great mystery. The spirit of Jesus commands and, we must obey. I believe that is the fundamental idea in the teachings of the apostle Paul. Jesus is the master of our lives, our Lord. We do not teach theories about him—that is not the decisive test; rather, we teach what we are living now, the deed of obedience, with which we serve him.

Scripture Meditation

And to know this love that surpasses knowledge.
—Ephesians 3:19

Thought for the Day

Ireneaus said, "For the glory of God is a human being made fully alive, and the life of humanity consists of beholding God."

Prayer

Lord, lead me from an accurate theology of transformation to being transformed. Clear space in my life so that I am not always thinking about you, but I am thinking with you. Teach me to listen. Teach me to pray. Amen.

FEBRUARY 12: GOD'S GRACE IS BOTH SEEN IN PLACES
AND IN THE LIVES OF THE FAITHFUL

Gregory of Nyssa (330–395), younger brother of Basil the Great, was bishop of Nyssa in Cappadocia, or eastern Turkey. He was perhaps the greatest of the Cappadocian theologians. He writes in this letter to three ladies, Eustathia, Ambrosia, and Basilissa.

Greetings in the Lord!

Meeting with good and beloved Christians, as well as visiting the sacred sites of our Lord, have together given me intense joy and gladness. For as a double portion, the saving tokens of the God who gave us life, and in meeting with those in whose his grace is demonstrated, both are combined on the festive days. For by the Lord's grace, one can see very clearly that Bethlehem, Golgotha, and Mount Olivet, as well as the scene of the Resurrection are really seen in the heart indwelt by God.... For when by a good conscience, Christ has been formed within one, then godly fear also nails the prompting of the flesh, to become crucified with Christ. Then when the illusions of the world are rolled away, like the great stone at Christ's grave, one can walk in newness of life.

Further, in abandoning this low-lying valley of human life, a soaring desire transports one to the heavenly realm, where Christ now sits. Then lifted up by chastity, one no longer is burdened by the body of flesh. Thus visiting both the sacred places as well as seeing Christians like you, I am overflowing with such joy that I find no words to express the reality of it all.... Walk by the primitive Rule of Faith, and the God of peace shall be with you, and you shall be strong in mind and body....

Scripture Meditation

Praise be to the God and Father of our Lord Jesus Christ! In his great mercy he has given us new birth into a living hope through the resurrection of Jesus Christ from the dead.

—1 PETER 1:3

Thought for the Day

The sacred places of Christ's Epiphany dwell within us!

Prayer

May God keep you uncorrupted, is our prayer.

—GREGORY OF NYSSA

FEBRUARY 13: "PLACES" INTERPRETED AS SPIRITUAL CONDITIONS

Aelred of Rievaulx [see entry for February 5] reflects on how looking at
biblical truth through the lens of allegory can bring spiritual counsel. The
following are excerpts of his letter on "Jesus at the Age of Twelve."

My dear Son,

At Bethlehem the soul becomes poor, at Nazareth it grows rich, and at Jerusalem it abounds in delights. It becomes poor by complete renunciation of the world, it grows rich by developing the virtues, it abounds in delights through the sweetness of what it tastes spiritually.

Consider then the man from whom the spirit of fear has pruned away his former vices and innate covetousness as the one year old. Next, if the spirit of poverty makes him gentle and obedient, consider him to be two years old. If the spirit of knowledge brings him knowledge of his own weakness and a desire for God's help, then have no doubt that he has reached the age of three. If the spirit of determination makes him unyielding and resistant against all temptations and carnal pleasures that fight against the soul, then admire him as a boy of four. With the spirit of counsel and a virtue of discretion he will become five years old. If the spirit of understanding allows him to meditate upon the sacred Scripture, then a happy progress will bring him to the age of six. The spirit of wisdom brings him to seven years old, which proceeds from meditating upon God's Law and provides the developing soul with four virtues as if with the light of four years.

Sobriety is another name for temperance, which provides balance and prevents excess in making progress in virtue. Prudence then prevents one virtue being mistaken for another. Righteousness prevents a lack of due order in the use of the virtues. Strength is another name for fortitude that ensures that the will persists. Then follows a twelfth year which is the light of contemplation. This upraises the ardent soul to the heavenly Jerusalem itself, opens the gates of paradise, unlocks heaven, and reveals to the gaze of the pure mind the Bridegroom himself....

The first day on which the soul that thirsts for God dwells in the delights of contemplation as if in Jerusalem, is consideration of God's power. The second day is admiration of his wisdom. The third day is a sweet anticipation of his goodness and kindness. To the first belongs justice; to the second, knowledge; to the third, mercy. Justice creates fear, knowledge instructs, mercy nurtures. For those souls more purified, sublime and more profound in the discovery of these three things may find the following. In God's power they see the depths of his judgments; in his wisdom, his hidden purposes; in his goodness, the unutterable words of his grace. So "at the end of three days they found him in the temple."

Often when we lay aside all business to give ourselves to inner meditation or to private prayer, if we linger in the joy of this longer than is good for those who are under our care, the Spirit intervenes and love prompts us.... There are times then, when we need to put the needs of those in our care before the delights of contemplation. You must show the same preference for the unity and the harmony of the community. Above all never rely on your own unaided judgment to discern the times of these spiritual needs, that is to say, when you are to go down to Nazareth, in order to go up to Jerusalem, but you should always ask the advice of your elders.

And so you have my dearest son what you asked for.... Realize that we have not been concerned so much to give an exegesis of the passage from the gospel, as to draw from it as you asked, some seeds for meditation.

Scripture Meditation

"Why were you searching for me?" he asked. "Didn't you know I had to be in my Father's house?" But they did not understand what he was saying to them. Then he went down to Nazareth with them and was obedient to them.

—LUKE 2:49–51

Thought for the Day

Allegory transcends the literal sense to extend our horizons.

Prayer

Forth, pilgrim, forth! ... Know thy country, look up, thank God of all; hold the highway ... and Truth thee shall deliver.

—GEOFFREY CHAUCER

FEBRUARY 14: FOLLOWING IN THE STEPS OF THE MASTER

Charles de Foucauld (1858–1916) [see letter for January 4] lost both his
parents when he was six years old. As a college student he lost all faith,
experienced moral collapse, and was discharged from the military academy
for "ignominious conduct." Showing great courage, he explored the Sahara
desert at twenty-five, and three years later was dramatically converted at the
end of October 1886. He writes to the Abbe Huevelin, his mentor,
on February 1, 1887.

The state of my soul is unchanged: I am always full of joy, rejoicing at
the feet of Jesus.… I realize how good for me my stay here [in Palestine],
and how *necessary it is to me*.… For my interior life is one of union with
Jesus at different stages of his life in this world. Until tomorrow I shall
be at Bethlehem; tomorrow morning I am going to the Temple; tomorrow evening I shall leave during the night for Egypt. I shall be traveling
with the Holy Family until Ash Wednesday, then I shall go with our Lord
into the desert. A month before the end of Lent, I shall go to the raising
of Lazarus at Bethany and be with our Lord during the last part of his
life, and then with his apostles from the Ascension till Pentecost. From
Pentecost till Advent, I work and pray with the Holy Family at Nazareth.
That is my year.… It is as though I were with his holy parents, or St. Mary
Magdalene, sitting at his feet at Bethany.…

Our Lord is now on the way to Bethlehem—the journey on foot will
probably take five days, the last of them only two or three hours long:
from Nazareth to Engannim, then to Sichar, then Bethel, from Bethel
to Jerusalem, and finally from Jerusalem to Bethlehem. How full of
love and recollection the Blessed Virgin must have been when she
made that journey. How she must have burned with longing for the
salvation of mankind, for whose sake the Son of God had come down
into her womb.

At every moment of the journey, our Lord saw not only his Mother
and St. Joseph, and the angels worshiping him, but also this present
time and the future, every moment in the life of every human being.
What is more, at the prospect of the sins, ingratitude and damnation of
so many souls, his sacred heart was already experiencing the terrible

pain that was to be its lot throughout his life on earth. Yet he also tasted, as well as the great consolation afforded him by the holiness of his mother, a lesser, but still real, consolation at the prospect of all the souls of the saints, all the souls who had loved him and who would one day love him, all the hearts that would join with Mary's in beating for him alone. Shall we be among them, dear Father? Shall we be consolation or pain to our blessed Savior?

If Christmas marks the beginning of our joys, it is also the beginning of Jesus' agonies. There are only eight days between Christmas and the Circumcision. Bethlehem is only five miles from Jerusalem. In Palestine one is made painfully aware of this fact: having spent the Christmas of 1888 in Bethlehem, hearing midnight Mass and receiving Holy Communion in the cave, I returned to Jerusalem at the end of two or three days. The delight I had experienced at praying in the very cave which had echoed to the voices of Jesus, Mary and Joseph—the cave where I had been so close to them—was indescribable. But, alas, after an hour's traveling there rose up before me the dome of the Church of the Holy Sepulchre, Calvary and the Mount of Olives, and whether I wanted to or not, I was compelled to begin a new line of thought and go back to the foot of the cross.

Scripture Meditation

Even if I am being poured out like a drink offering on the sacrifice and service coming from your faith, I am glad and rejoice with all of you. So you too should be glad and rejoice with me.
—PHILIPPIANS 2:17–18

Thought for the Day

Ours is a historic faith, lived out in geographical realities of space and time. We need then to live within its living symbols as Jesus did.

Prayer

May our Lord draw you closer to him in this world, until it pleases him to do so in the next.
—CHARLES DE FOUCAULD

FEBRUARY 15: BRINGING JESUS TO OTHERS

On April 26, 1901, Charles de Foucauld [see previous entry] wrote to Abbe
Huevelin, his spiritual director in Paris, that "my vocation is to imitate as
perfectly as possible our Lord's hidden life at Nazareth." Ordained on
June 9, 1901, Foucauld here writes his friend, Fr. Jerome,
on July 17, 1901, about his call.

Dearest Father:

If I depended on myself my plans would be mad, but I depend on God who said, "If anyone wants to serve me, let him follow me." He said "Follow me" so often and told us "to love your neighbor as yourself, do for others what you would wish them to do for you." It's impossible for me to practice this precept of brotherly love unless I devote my life to doing all the good I can do to those brothers of Jesus who lack everything because they lack him. If I were a Muslim knowing neither Jesus nor his sacred heart, nor Mary our mother, nor the holy Eucharist, nor the bosom of our holy Church, nor the gospels, nor any of the things that constitute our happiness down here and our hope up there, and if I were aware of my tragic condition, oh how I would long for someone to come and get me out of it!

And what I would wish for myself, I *must* do for others: "Do for others what you would wish them to do for you," and I must do it for the poorest, the most abandoned, the most lost sheep, I must share my feast, my divine banquet, not with my rich brothers and neighbors (rich in the knowledge of things unknown to these unhappy people) but with the blind, the crippled, the beggars, a thousand times more to be pitied than those who suffer only in their body. And I don't think I can do them a greater good than by bringing Jesus to them as Mary brought him to John's house at the Visitation; Jesus, the good of goods, the supreme sanctifier; Jesus present among them in the tabernacle.... I would try to show our ignorant brothers what our religion is, what the Christian spirit is, what the heart of Jesus is.

Scripture Meditation

[Jesus said,] "Whoever serves me must follow me."
—JOHN 12:26

Thought for the Day

As Foucauld said, "I shall always look for the lowest place, because God made himself the least of men."

Prayer

Give us in our hearts pure love, born of your love to us, that we may love others as you have loved us.
—ANSELM

FEBRUARY 16: CHRIST IN THE REAL PLACES OF THIS WORLD

Father Rene Voillaume was trained in the Saint-Sulpice seminary in Paris, and with four other colleagues founded the Small Brothers to follow in the steps of Charles de Foucault. They commenced in 1933 in the Saharan community of Abiodh Sidi-Sheikh, and then scattered into many of the "urban deserts" of the world's largest cities. He writes this pastoral letter after visiting the real places Jesus had been.

My Son,

The [holy places in Palestine] sharply confront us with the earthly reality of the mystery of our Lord's life and death, and through them we come to realize the feebleness of our faith. We find it easy enough to say:

"Lord, Lord," and yet still do not believe. If our Lord does not seem to us to belong to the real world, is it surprising that his words no longer affect our lives? If they are to take us out of the rut of custom and deliver us from its bondage, those words must come alive. Otherwise, they are far from being the sword that penetrates to the very muscles of our daily behavior.

If our Lord is not in fact a real individual for us, a living person, then dare we say that we belong to him, that we will give him our lives? Well, here we are faced with the places where he lived, died his agonizing death, and came out of the grave alive. That since these events took place, days, or years, or centuries, have passed, is immaterial. These places make one feel infinitely empty and squalid, appallingly egotistic and hidebound in routine and conformity. I am reminded of Peter who in this very place declared that he did not know Jesus, and of the other apostles who the moment he was arrested and brought to judgment, made themselves scarce. I should have been among them, and God knows whether! ...

Jerusalem has not altered since my last visit. What was dilapidated remains so. The Holy Sepulchre is perhaps the only Christian sanctuary in the world propped up by a mass of wood and iron scaffolding, and looking as though the intention of maintaining it had been given up. It is always almost empty, and few people come to this place where their Friend, their greatest Friend and the Lord their God, once died ... and from whose rock their life came forth!

I found this desolation all the more striking after I had traveled round the world. Everywhere else there is life; but not here.

Scripture Meditation

For in Christ all the fullness of the Deity lives in bodily form, and you have been given fullness in him.
—COLOSSIANS 2:9–10

Thought for the Day

Do Christians need to fight over the Promised Land, if Christ dwells in our hearts by faith?

Prayer
My Jesus, be always with you!
—Charles de Foucault

FEBRUARY 17: LIVING IN SEVERAL WORLDS AT THE SAME TIME

Fr. Rene Voillaume [see previous entry] continues in a further letter to the Small Brothers.

y Daughter,

The reality of existence on this earth is made up for each of us of several worlds. First, we have ourselves, with our defects and limitations, with the pull of the flesh, but also with the goodness of our will. This is our own, our personal world. Secondly, there is the external world, stable and tangible, with its painful or happy events—what is called *life*. It is a world that contains other people, other men in their objective reality. Why should we resist the necessity of honestly accepting this world as it is, and especially other men, our brothers, as they are, in flesh and blood, and not as they ought to be, or as we imagine they ought to be, but with both their defects and their qualities, and be ready to love them as such? Jesus knew the whole truth about every one; he had no need to be told about it; he had no illusions—and yet he loved them....

And lastly, and above all, there is the great reality that is God. This is the world of the risen, living Lord, and of all the invisible realities that bind us to him. This invisible world is supernatural; but it is not a dream; it is reality in its absolutely concrete form.

To live *now, this instance*, is to welcome these three realities: ourselves, the external world, the universe of other men, and that over which our

Lord reigns.... [It means] that we refuse to escape into dreams either of the past, the future, or the unreal.... One gains spiritual health when one is in possession of the present moment and no longer indulges in dreams of escaping from it, but steps out into the daylight of him who made all things and all life's passing moments and said that *they were good*. The cross of Calvary, which was a harsh but real moment, has transformed everything that harms us in this world into a source of perennial good. Do not be afraid then, to become a living being, to grasp the present moment with both hands, and to make it completely your own.

Scripture Meditation

Our light and momentary troubles are achieving for us an eternal glory that far outweighs them all. So we fix our eyes not on what is seen, but on what is unseen. For what is seen is temporary, but what is unseen is eternal.

—2 CORINTHIANS 4:17–18

Thought for the Day

He who guards his way, guards his life. (Prov. 16:17)

Prayer

O for a closer walk with God,
A calm and heavenly frame;
a light to shine upon the road
That leads me to the Lamb!

—WILLIAM COWPER

FEBRUARY 18: RECOLLECTIONS OF WRONGS

Francis de Paola (1416–1507) followed the Franciscan ideal, seeing in the life of poverty the ideals of the Desert Fathers, as needed for the reform of the church. He writes this letter to an undesignated friend.

𝒮et your minds on the passion of our Lord Jesus Christ. For inflamed with love for us he came down from heaven to redeem us. For our sake he endured every torment of body and soul and shrank not from any bodily pain. He gave himself to us as an example of perfect patience and love. We are then to be patient also in our adversities.

Put aside your hatred and bitter, combative spirit. Make the effort to refrain from saying sharp words. If they escape from your lips, do not be ashamed to let your lips also provide for the needy, since they are what have caused the wounds. Forgive one another, so that later on you will have forgotten the injury ever occurred. For the recollection of an injury is wrong in itself. It only adds to our anger, nurtures our sin, and hates what is good. It is like a rusty arrow which poisons the soul, putting all virtue to flight. Or it is like a worm within the mind that confuses our speech and tears to shreds our petitions to God. Indeed, it is quite foreign to charity, and remains embedded within the soul like a nail. It is wickedness that never sleeps, sin that never stops acting negatively. It is indeed a daily death of the soul.

Scripture Meditation

Forgive us our debts, as we also have forgiven our debtors.
—MATTHEW 6:12

Thought for the Day

The unforgiving spirit cannot receive the forgiveness of God.

Prayer

O Lord, make us to love thee, and each other in thee, and to meet
before thee, to dwell in thine everlasting love, Amen.
—E. B. PUSEY

FEBRUARY 19: THE FIRE OF GODLY DESIRE

---

*Walter of Hilton (d. 1396) was an Augustinian canon living in the English
Midlands near the Priory of Thurgarton, in the county of Nottingham. His
ministry was personal to lay Christians, and he was described by Evelyn
Underhill as "one of those hidden figures, those quiet and secret friends of
God who have never failed the Church."*

Our Lord has put into your heart a little spark of this blessed fire—that
is, himself. Scripture says, "Our God is a consuming fire." For as a physical fire consumes physical fuel that may be burned, just so spiritual fire
that is of God, consumes all manner of sin wherever it reaches, and
therefore our Lord is likened to a consuming fire.

I pray that you will nourish this fire in you, that is, love and charity.
This is the kind of fire that God himself sent into the world, even as
our Lord says in the Gospel: "I am come to send fire on the earth, and
what will I, if it be already kindled?" (Luke 12:49). That is, God has
sent a fire of love, a good desire and a great will to please him into the
human soul. And this is his purpose, that this fire should be recognized, preserved, nourished, and strengthened, for it is sent for our
salvation.

The more desire then you have towards him, the more is this fire of
love within you. The less this desire is present, the less then is the fire.
The measure of this desire, in yourself or anyone else, is not recognized

by the person himself, nor can you discern it, but only God that gives it. And therefore do not set out to analyze and measure how much of this desire you possess. Instead, be busy to desire as keenly as is possible to you the love of God, but not to take the measure of your own ardor.

St. Augustine says that the life of each Christian is a continual expression of desire towards God. And that is a great virtue, for it is the voice of the heart crying out in the ears of God. The more you yearn for him, the more audible will be your heart's cry; the same will be true as you pray more effectively and think more wisely.

Scripture Meditation

Since we are receiving a kingdom that cannot be shaken, let us be thankful, and so worship God acceptably with reverence and awe, for our "God is a consuming fire."
—HEBREWS 12:28–29

Thought for the Day

God, who fulfills the desires of heart, cleanses our hearts for such desires of love divine.

Prayer

O fire ever blazing! The soul who comes to know herself in you, finds greatness of desire wherever she turns.
—CATHERINE OF SIENA

ISSUES OF LAW AND GRACE

FEBRUARY 20: TRYING TO BE GOOD WITHOUT CHRIST

*The letter excerpted here and in the following entry was found in a
collection of letters by Augustine of Hippo (354–430). It was addressed to
Pope Innocent (ca. 416) and cosigned with Aurelius, Alypius, Euodius, and
Possidius. It discusses the heresy of Pelagianism, the belief that our own
self-effort can overcome our sinful condition.*

We have sent your holiness letters from the two councils of the
province of Carthage and of Numidia, signed by a large number of bishops. These letters condemn the enemies of the grace of Christ, who trust
in their own virtue and say, in effect, to their Creator: "You have made
us men, but we have made ourselves good." They say that human nature
is free, so that they look for no liberator; and safe, so that they consider
a savior superfluous; they claim that this nature is so strong of its own
strength, acquired once and for all at the moment of creation, without
any helping grace from him who created it, that it can subdue and extinguish all passions and overcome all temptations....

But the family of Christ, which says: "When I am weak, then I am
strong," and to which the Lord says: "I am thy salvation," its heart quiv-
ering with fear and trembling, awaits the help of the Lord....

But when a man says in prayer: "Lead us not into temptation," he certainly does not pray to be a man, which he is by nature; he does not pray
to possess free will, which he received when his nature itself was created;
he does not pray for the forgiveness of sin, because in a previous phrase
the prayer says: "Forgive us our debts," nor does he pray to receive the
commandment; he manifestly does pray to fulfill the commandment.

If he is led into temptation, that is, fails under temptation, it is plain
that he commits sin, which is against the commandment. He prays,
therefore, not to commit sin, that is, not to do any evil; that is what the
Apostle asks in prayer for the Corinthians when he says: "Now we pray
the Lord that you may do no evil." From this it is quite clear that,
although the freedom of the will is called into play in refraining from
sin, that is, in doing no evil, its power is not efficacious unless there is

help for its weakness. Therefore, the Lord's prayer itself is the clearest testimony of grace. Let him admit this and we will rejoice over him as being either in the right or set right.

Scripture Meditation

It is God who works in you to will and to act according to his good purpose.
—PHILIPPIANS 2:13

Thought for the Day

Do we ever live sufficiently aware of the grace of God in our lives?

Prayer

O Almighty God, without whom we can do nothing, grant what you command us and command what you will.
—AUGUSTINE OF HIPPO

FEBRUARY 21: ON THE DISTINCTION BETWEEN LAW AND GRACE

Augustine of Hippo continues to write with his colleagues in the same letter to Pope Innocent.

There has to be a distinction between the Law and grace. The Law knows how to command; grace, how to help. The Law would not command if there were no free will, nor would grace help if the will were sufficient. We are commanded to have understanding when the

167

Scripture says: "Do not become like the horse and the mule that have no understanding," yet we pray to have understanding when it says: "Give me understanding that I may learn thy commandments." We are commanded to have wisdom when it says: "You fools, be wise at last," but we pray to have wisdom when it says: "If any of you lack wisdom, let him ask of God who gives to all men abundantly and upbraids not." We are commanded to have continence when it says: "Let your loins be girt," but we pray to have continence when it says: "As I knew that no one could be continent except God gave it, and thus also was a point of wisdom to know whose gift it was, I went to the Lord and besought him."

Finally, not to be too lengthy in listing all the rest, we are commanded not to do evil when it says: "Decline from evil," but we pray not to do evil when it says: "We pray the Lord that you do no evil." We are commanded to do good when it says: "Decline from evil and do good," but we pray to do good when it says: "We cease not to pray for you, asking," and among other things that he asks he mentions: "That you may walk worthy of God in all things pleasing, in every good work and good word." As then we acknowledge the part played by the will when these commands are given, so let him acknowledge the part played by grace when these petitions are made....

This is the grace that was being called into question when those whom Pelagius had offended and disturbed told him that he was making war on grace by the arguments in which he asserted that human nature, through its own free will, was sufficiently strong, not only to carry out the divine commandments but even to fulfill them perfectly. But the teaching of the Apostles gives the name of grace to that gift by which we are saved and justified through our faith in Christ, and of this it is written: "I cast not away the grace of God, for if justice be by the law, then Christ died in vain." Of this grace it is written: "You are made void of Christ you who are justified in the law; you are fallen from grace." Of this grace it is written: "And if by grace it is not now by works; otherwise grace is no more grace." This is the grace of which it is written: "Now to him that works, the reward is not reckoned according to grace but according to debt. But to him that works not yet believes in him that justifies the ungodly, his faith is reputed to justice."

There are many other passages which you can recall for yourself, with your prudent understanding and your well-known gift of expression. As to that other grace by which we are created as human beings, even though we understand that it may reasonably be called grace, it would be surprising if we found it so used in any of the authentic writings of the Prophets, of the Gospel, or of the Apostles.

Scripture Meditation

It is by grace you have been saved.
—EPHESIANS 2:5

Thought for the Day

In an age of techniques, we may be more tempted than ever to ignore the grace of God.

Prayer

Lord, I fling myself with all weakness and misery into your ever open arms, for I know that I am ignorant and much mistaken about myself.
—FATHER BESSON

FEBRUARY 22: ON THE RIGHT USE OF THE LAW

John Newton [see entry for January 25] had many remarkable experiences during his life. His father was a sea captain who took his son to sea early in his boyhood. As a wild youth, John Newton was engaged for a time on slave ships between West Africa and the Caribbean. He confessed his own lawlessness, saying: "I lost all sense of religion and became deaf to the remonstrance of conscience and prudence." From such experience he writes to an inquirer later in his mature years of pastoral ministry.

*D*ear Sir,

You desire my thoughts on I Timothy 1: 8, "We know that the law is good if a man use it lawfully," and I willingly comply. I do not intend to give you a sermon on this text, but a little attention to method may not be improper upon this subject, although given as a letter to a friend. Ignorance of the nature and design of the law is at the bottom of most religious mistakes. For this is the root of self-righteousness, the great reason why the gospel of Christ is no longer regarded, and the cause of so much uncertainty and inconsistency in many people, who though they profess themselves to be teachers, do not really understand what they are saying, nor what they are affirming....

The Law, in many passages of the Old Testament, signifies the whole revelation of God, as in Psalms 1:2 and 19:7. But the law in the strict sense of the term is contra-distinguished from the Gospel ... as the apostle does in his epistles to the Romans and the Galatians....

The Law of God then, in the largest sense is that rule or prescribed course, which God has appointed for all his creatures, according to their several natures and capacities that they may answer the end for which he has created them.... The Law of God in this sense, or what some may choose to call "the law of nature," is no other than the impression of God's power, whereby all things continue and act according to his will from the beginning. For "he spoke, and it was done; he commanded, and it stood fast."

But ..., when God created mankind, he taught him more than the beasts of the earth, and wiser than the birds of the air. For he formed himself for himself, breathing into him an immortal spirit, incapable of dissolution, giving him a capacity not to be satisfied with any creature-good. He endowed him with an understanding, will, and affections, which qualified him for the knowledge and service of his Maker, and of a life of communion with him. The Law of God, therefore, concerning mankind, is that rule of disposition and conduct of which a human being is constituted and ought to conform....

But as man and woman was capable of understanding it, so they were capable of forsaking it. They did so and sinned, by eating of the forbidden fruit.... Yet still the Law remained in force ... the depravity they had brought upon human nature remained. Their children and all their posterity were born in their sinful likeness, without the ability or inclination to keep the Law. So the whole earth was soon filled with violence. But a few in every successive age were preserved by grace and faith in God's promise ... Abraham—Moses—godly Israelites....

But how can we know the law is good, if by our fallen nature we do not, nor can we think so.... For we cannot be at enmity with God, and at the same time approve of his law.

Scripture Meditation

The ordinances of the Lord are sure and altogether righteous.
—PSALM 19:9

Thought for the Day

The law of God expresses both his sovereign will and his mercy.

Prayer

Oh, that my ways were steadfast in obeying your decrees.
—PSALM 119:5

FEBRUARY 23: CHRIST AND THE LAW

John Newton, continuing his letter on the right use of the law [see previous entry], writes from deep experience of God's grace just as his famous hymn expresses: "Amazing Grace."

The Decalogue or Ten Commandments uttered by the voice of God is an abstract of the original Law under which mankind was created. But it was published in a prohibitory form, since the Israelites, like the rest of mankind, being depraved by sin, was strongly inclined to the commission of everything evil. This law could not be designed as a covenant, by obedience to which man could be justified. For long before its publication the Gospel had already been preached to Abraham (Gal. 3:8). But the law entered to expose sin, showing its extent and evil consequences, for it reaches to the most hidden thoughts of the heart, yet requires absolute and perpetual obedience, and denounces a curse upon all who continue in sin. To this was further added the ceremonial or Levitical law. This prescribed a variety of institutions, ceremonials, purifications, and sacrifices, the observance of which were absolutely necessary to the acceptable worship of God. By obedience to these prescriptions, the people of Israel preserved their legal right to the blessings promised to them as a nation....

But Christ as the Lamb of God, who in the fullness of time came to take away the sin of the world by the sacrifice of himself, has done away with all need to keep the ceremonial law and its sacrifices. Now all other sacrifices, other than his own, became unnecessary and vain. The Gospel supplies the place of the ceremonial law.

Moreover, Christ has removed the enmity we naturally had against God and his Law, by the power of the Holy Spirit. For it is the Spirit's office to enlighten and convince the conscience; to communicate an impression of the majesty, holiness, justice, and authority of the God with whom we have to do, and thus to understand the nature and seriousness of sin. The sinner is then stripped of all his vain pretences, and compelled to plead guilty.... But the office of the Holy Spirit is also to discover the grace and glory of the Savior, as having fulfilled the Law for us, as well as to enable us to honor the Law with a due personal obedience. Then a change of judgment takes place in us helping us to begin to see the Law is holy, just, and good. As holy, it manifests the holiness of God. Conformity to it is the fulfillment of our perfection as God originally purposed. Thus we begin to recognize that there can be no excellence in mankind, except as we are influenced by God's law.

Scripture Meditation

We know the law is good if one uses it properly.
— I TIMOTHY 1:8

Thought for the Day

We need to discern the legitimacy of the law and the illegitimacy of legalism.

Prayer

You have laid down precepts that are to be fully obeyed. Oh that my ways were steadfast in obeying your decrees.
—PSALM 119: 4–5

FEBRUARY 24: ABUSE OF THE DOCTRINE OF HOLINESS

Pierre de Berulle (1575–1629), cardinal, reforming statesmen, and founder of the Oratory of Preachers in France, was convinced that being enflamed with the love of Christ was for the church "a Copernican revolution." He writes this letter to a priest.

I feel obliged to speak to you a bit at length about the subject of which you wrote me so that, when appropriate, you can instruct those people of note who might wish to understand it. You should know that the church is divided into two parts and both of them are holy, if we consider its institution and origin. One is the people, and the other is the clergy. One receives holiness, and the other brings it about. In the period closer to its birth these two parts brought forth many virgins, confessors and martyrs who blessed the church, filled the earth, populated heaven and diffused everywhere the odor of the sanctity of Jesus.

This holy body, animated by a Holy Spirit and governed by holy laws, has lost its fervor and diminished in holiness through the corruption of the ages. This slackening began in its weakest part, the people. Then, from among the people, some withdrew to preserve in themselves the holiness proper to the whole body. These were the monks who, according to Saint Denis, constitute the highest and most perfect part of the people. They were governed by priests in the early church, receiving from them direction and perfect holiness, to which they aspired in an extraordinary way....

However, time, which corrupts all things, brought about laxity in most of the clergy. These three qualities: authority, holiness and doctrine, which the Spirit had joined together, were separated by the human spirit and the spirit of the world. Authority has remained in prelates, holiness in religious, and doctrine in the schools. In this separation God preserved in different segments of his church what he had joined in the clerical state. Such is the plan of God and the institution of his Son, Jesus. Such is the excellence of our state. Such is the power, light and holiness of the priestly condition.

However, alas! We have fallen from it. The evil of the world in which we live has demoted us from this dignity. It has passed into foreign hands, and we can rightly utter these words of lamentation: *Our inheritance has been handed over to strangers* (Lam. 5:2). For no matter how much they are at home in grace and in the unity of the body of Jesus, they are foreign to the ministry; and God, in his original, primary plan did not choose them for it.

Scripture Meditation

[Jesus said,] "My house will be a house of prayer; but you have made it a den of robbers."
—LUKE 19:46

Thought for the Day

Does organized religion need another Reformation today?

Prayer

*Lord, destroy everything that is not of you, and help us to form
no ideas of which you are not the center, so that we are compelled
to a more living love.*

—ANDRIENNE VON SPEYR

FEBRUARY 25: PLAYING POLITICS WITH GRACE

---

*Blaise Pascal (1623–1662), French mathematician and inventor of the first
calculating machine, was converted to Christianity after reading the
seventeenth chapter of John's gospel. He was encouraged in his growing
faith by the reforming community of Port-Royal. When its Jansenist leader,
Antoine Arnauld, was defamed by the theological faculty of the Sorbonne
in Paris University in one of the most famous examples of "casuistry"
theologians have ever exhibited, Pascal defended him in a series of
anonymous "Provincial Letters." These are excerpts of the
first letter, dated January 23, 1656.*

*S*ir,

We have been greatly mistaken. It was only yesterday that I was unde-
ceived. For, until then, I had imagined that the disputes of the [faculty of
Theology] of the Sorbonne were truly of greatest importance to the
interests of the Christian faith.... Two subjects are under consideration.
One is a question of *fact*. The other is a question of *right*.

The question of fact is whether Mr. Arnauld is guilty of rashness of
saying in his second letter that he has carefully read the book of
Cornelius Jansen and has not been able to find those propositions there
condemned by the late Pope [Innocent X]. Yet, as he condemns these
propositions wherever they occur, he also condemns them in Jansen *if*

they should be there.... This is where the question of fact finishes.... But instead, I found a strange refusal on the part of everyone to show me where they were. I haven't met a single person who could say he had actually seen them for himself....

The question of *right* seems at first much more important. So I have therefore taken the utmost trouble to inform myself upon the subject.... The investigation questioned Mr. Arnauld's words in the same letter, "that the grace without which we can do nothing was deficient in the apostle Peter when he fell." We might have expected that the great principles of grace would have been examined, as to whether grace is bestowed on all men, and whether it is certainly efficacious. But alas! How we were deceived! For myself, I soon became a great divine, of which you will have some evidence [as Pascal searched Jesuit casuistry about their interpretation of "grace," when it was "efficacious" or not].

To find out the truth, I went to my near neighbor Mr. N., a doctor of the College of Navarre, who is, as you know, one of the bitterest opponents of the Jansenists.... I asked if, to remove all further doubts, they could come to a formal decision "that grace is given to all men." ... [H]e confirmed by a famous passage of Augustine: "We know that grace is not given to all men." I ... asked to know whether they would at least condemn that other opinion of the Jansenists, which had created such heated debate, namely, "that grace is efficacious and determines the will in the choice of good." Again I was unfortunate: "You know nothing about it," he retorted. "That is no heresy; it is perfectly orthodox. All Thomists maintain it and I have done the same myself in my debates in the Sorbonne."

I dared not proceed; still, I could not discover where the difficulty lay. So in order to gain some insight, I begged him to state exactly in what consisted the heresy of Mr. Arnauld's proposition. "It is this," he said, "that he does not admit that the righteous possess the power of fulfilling the commands of God, in the manner in which *we understand it.*" ... For the Jansenists were agreed upon the just possessing power to perform the commandments.... "Hold," he said, "a man must be an excellent theologian to discriminate these niceties; so fine and subtle is the difference between us that we can scarcely discern it ourselves. So you cannot be supposed to understand it, but simply we are satisfied the Jansenists will tell you that the just always possess the power of fulfilling the divine commandments. This we do not dispute, but they will not inform you that this is *near power.* This is the point."

This term was to me quite new and nonsensical. I thought I had grasped the whole situation but now it was all, once more, obscure. When I asked for some explanation he made a great mystery of it and dismissed me without any further satisfaction to inquire of the Jansenists whether they admitted this *near power....* They are determined mutually to use the term *near*, although they understand it themselves in many different ways, in order to seek to undermine and ruin Mr. Arnauld.

This answer amazed me....

Scripture Meditation

The Pharisees and Sadducees came to Jesus and tested him by asking him to show them a sign from heaven.
—MATTHEW 16:1

Thought for the Day

Theological casuistry—like that of the Jesuit contestants with Pascal—can be more a conflict of issues of power than a genuine pursuit of truth.

Prayer

O Lord, we beseech thee to keep your church and household continually in your true religion ... defended by your almighty power; through Jesus Christ our Lord.
—COLLECT FOR THE FIFTH SUNDAY AFTER THE EPIPHANY.

FEBRUARY 26: WHEN LAW IS NOT OBLIGATORY

Alphonsus de Liguori (1696–1787), born to a noble family in Naples, was trained in law and ministered among the poor, prisoners, and criminals as a

*priest, bishop, and ecclesial reformer. Pope John Paul II said of him: "He did
for modern Catholicism that which Augustine of Hippo accomplished in
ancient times." He writes to Father Pietro Paolo Blasucci in November 1768.*

ear Father,

I think I have clearly proved, with the grace of God, the principle
that a doubtful law is not obligatory. The reason is that the law is not
obligatory if it is not promulgated, as St. Thomas and all the theologians say. When you have two probable opinions, it is not the law that
is promulgated but only a doubt whether there is a law or not. So when
there are equally probable opinions the law, because it is doubtful, is
not obligatory....

But you object, that the rule to be followed is, "In doubt, take the safer
view, and so forth." This rule refers to cases where we are in doubt. But
whoever works with the reflex principle explained above is not acting in
doubt but with a moral certainty. So we are not dealing with the point
that is at issue.

Let us come now to your feeling that one has to follow a rigid opinion
which has one or two degrees of greater weight. This rule seems to me to
be very confused and likely to cause scruples, since it is difficult to find
the measuring scale which identifies these one or two degrees of greater
weight.

My rule seems very clear and certain to me. When the view in favor
of the law is definitely more probable, I say that you cannot follow the
less probable view. When I know that the rigid view is more probable, I
say that it has to be followed—here I am against the system of the
Jesuits. But when the rigid opinion is only equally probable or very
doubtfully more probable, then it is safe to follow the more benign
opinion. And why? Because when a view is equally probable or there is
a doubt about it being a little bit more probable, the law is doubtful in
the real sense of the word. So then the principle that a doubtful law does
not oblige comes into play, since what has been sufficiently promulgated
is the doubt about the law, but not the law itself.... I hope that I have
made myself sufficiently clear.

Scripture Meditation

Woe to you, teachers of the law and Pharisees, you hypocrites!
You shut the kingdom of heaven in men's faces.
—MATTHEW 23:13

Thought for the Day

When we become technicians of the law rather than its exemplars of justice, then unrighteousness prevails.

Prayer

Though rulers sit together and slander me, your servant will meditate on your decrees. Your statutes are my delight; they are my counselors.
—PSALM 119:23–24

FEBRUARY 27: TRUE RELIGION IS SO LITTLE UNDERSTOOD

Henry Scougal (1650–1678) was ordained into the ministry at twenty-two
years old and elected professor of divinity a year later at King's College,
Aberdeen. He wrote the classic The Life of God in the Soul of Man. *His*
great concern was the state of nominal religion, which he writes about to a
friendly patron of his book here and in the following two entries.

Dear Friend,

I cannot speak of religion but I must lament that, among so many pretenders to it, so few understand what it means. Some place it in the understanding, in orthodox notions and opinions. All the account they can give of their religion is that it is this or that persuasion. So that is why they have chosen to join this one of many other sects into which Christendom is unhappily divided. Others place their religion into externals for the outward man, expressed by public duties and claim to have a model of performances. Provided they live peaceably with their neighbors, keep a temperate diet, observe public worship, frequent the church, or their own room for private prayer, and sometimes show charity to the poor, then they think they have acquitted themselves well. Others again, put all their investment in religion into their emotions, with rapturous and ecstatic devotion. So they aim to pray with passion, thinking pleasurably of heaven and constantly being melted into sentimentalism about their Savior. They think they are mightily in love with him, and assume great confidence about salvation, which they esteem as the chief of Christian graces ... such are frequently assumed to be the whole content of Christianity.

But true religion is quite another thing, and those who have experienced it will entertain very different thoughts about it. For they know by personal experience that true religion is a union of the soul with God, a real participation of the divine nature, in the apostle's phrase, it is Christ formed within us. Briefly, I do not know how one can put it more succinctly that to simply call it divine life given to us....

Scriptural Meditation

My dear children, for whom I am again in the pains of childbirth until Christ is formed in you.
— GALATIANS 4:19

Thought for the Day

Nominal Christendom can never catch the depth of true religion.

Prayer

O most gracious God ... let us neither presume on our own strength, nor distrust your divine assistance. But while we are

doing our utmost endeavors, teach us still to depend upon you for
success.
—HENRY SCOUGAL

FEBRUARY 28: FEATURES OF TRUE RELIGION

Henry Scougal continues in the same letter to explore further upon the nature
of the Christian life.

Frue religion is life indeed. Firstly, it is marked by stability and per-
manence. Enthusiasms will rise and fall, passions will have starts and
fits, hot moods will turn to coldness.... But the motions of holy souls
are constant and regular, proceeding from a permanent and lively principle.... True religion is also inward, free ... not driven merely by
threats, nor bribed by promises, nor constrained by laws. But it is powerfully inclined towards the good, and delights in its performance. The
love which a devout saint will have toward God is not so much by a
command given, but as a new nature prompting and instructing him to
do it.... "Who shall prescribe a law to those who love? Love's a more
powerful law which doth them move." For such it is their meat and
drink to do their Father's will....

It is of course true that external motives can often be of great help
to stimulate and stir up this inward principle of living the Christian
faith, especially at the infancy of a new Christian, when in its weakness, it is so languid that there is still little Christian consciousness, of
even taking one step forward. Then to be propelled by his hopes, his
fears, the pressure of affliction, the deep sense of mercy, the authority
of the law, or indeed by the persuasion of others. If then, such a person is conscientious and consistent in his obedience to the truth, and

groans earnestly under the sense of his depression, and is desirous to perform his duties with more spirit and vigor, these may well be the first motions of divine life within him. But if one is entirely destitute of this inward principle of divine life, and does not aspire for it, but is content with mere performances that are prompted by education, habit, by fear of hell, or by carnal notions of heaven, then he can no more be accounted as a religious person, than a puppet can be a man. For it remains artificial and enforced … law compels such, as peevish and narrow minded. Whereas the spirit of true religion is frank and liberal. Indeed, the one who gives himself entirely to God will never think he can ever do too much for him.

Scripture Meditation

Indeed, the water I give him will become in him a spring of water welling up to eternal life.
—JOHN 4:14

Thought for the Day

Never can our life be richer, fuller, deeper, and more life-giving than when Christ dwells within us.

Prayer

Infinite and eternal Majesty! Author and Fountain of being and blessedness! How little do we poor sinful creatures know of you, or the way to serve and please you! We talk of religion, and pretend to be so; but alas, how few there are, who know and consider what it really means!
—HENRY SCOUGAL

FEBRUARY 29: THE BASIC NEED OF SELF-ABANDONMENT

Jean-Pierre de Caussade (1675–1751) was born and brought up in the region of Toulouse in southern France and was the most distinguished Jesuit spiritual director of his time. His emphasis was the central need to "self-abandonment" (including "self-surrender") in order to take the Christian life seriously. He still speaks directly to all suffering desolation in one form or another. Here he writes to a nun, Sister Marie-Antoniette de Mahuet, in 1731.

My dear Sister,

Our Lord has given me something better than what you desired ... a summary of general principles to guide the conduct of your life, explaining the easiest way of putting them into practice.

Firstly, the mainspring of the spiritual life is the will, so a sincere desire for God entirely and unreservedly is basic.... Secondly, a firm resolve to belong only to God helps you to think only of him. So let idle thoughts just drop like a stone into the sea, rather than worrying about having them. Gradually the habit will become easier ... but in concentrating only about God may take you into a great emptiness of spirit and of understanding, which in turn may make you numb of all will and of feelings also.... Value however this twofold void, for they make pride and self-love difficult to survive. Thirdly, we must confine our whole attention to fulfilling as completely as possible the holy will of God, abandoning everything else to him ... acknowledging that every care, fear, projects of self-interest, we say to God, "Lord, I sacrifice all this; I give up all my miserable interests to You." ...

The consequences will be that I begin to develop the gifts of prayer, humility, sweetness and the love of God.... Then I discover I am still very imperfect, and I cry out, "when shall I be free of these miseries?" But I begin to have no affection for them, and though still self-blind I begin to long to have more self-understanding.... Then I begin to long also to be more in tune with God's will, prepared to walk in darkness if that is his will for me. It is his business to know my state, mine to occupy myself with Him alone, to serve him, and to love him as much and as well as I can.... He is the Master, may his will be accomplished in all things....

Scripture Meditation

We have this treasure in jars of clay to show that this all-surpassing power is from God and not from us.

—2 CORINTHIANS 4:7

Thought for the Day

In the words of Jean-Pierre de Caussade, "Abandonment implies the gift of our whole self to God to be used as he thinks fit."

Prayer

Oh my God, I renounce my own will which is very blind, perverse and corrupt, in consequence of its wretched self-love, the mortal enemy of your grace, of your pure love, of your glory, and of my own sanctification.

—JEAN-PIERRE DE CAUSSADE

MARCH 1: BEING ROMANTIC ABOUT FAITH IS NOT ENOUGH

John Newton [see entries for January 25 and February 22],
now a seasoned pastor of over thirty years in the ministry, replies to
Hannah More wisely and with some humor.

*M*y dear Madam …

Reflecting on your hermitage—my imagination went to work at that, and presently built one. I will not say positively as pretty as yours, but very pretty. It stood (indeed without a foundation) upon a southern declivity, fronting a woodland prospect, with an infant river, that is a brook, running between. Little thought was spent upon the house, but if I could describe the garden, the sequestered walks, and the beautiful colors with which the soil, the shrubs, and the thickets were painted, I think you would like the spot. But I awoke, and behold it was a dream! ... The noises which surround me in my present situation, of carriages and carts, and London cries, form a strong contrast to the sound of falling waters and the notes of thrushes and nightingales. But London, noisy and dirty as it is, is my post, and if not directly my choice, has a much more powerful recommendation; it was chosen for me by the wisdom and goodness of him whose trust I am, and whom it is my desire to serve. And therefore I am well satisfied with it. And if this busy imagination (always upon the wing) would go to sleep, I would not awaken her to build me hermitages; I want none....

What you are pleased to say, my dear Madam, of the state of your mind, I understand perfectly well; ... I have stood upon that ground myself.... I trust that he who has already taught you what to desire will, in his own best time, do everything for you, and in you, which is necessary to make you as happy as is compatible with the present state of infirmity and warfare. But he must be waited on, and waited for, to do this; and for our encouragement it is written as in golden letters over the gate of his mercy, "Ask, and ye shall receive; knock, and it shall be opened unto you."

We are apt to wonder that when what we accounted hindrances are removed, and the things which we conceived would be great advantages are put within our power, still there is a secret something in the way which proves itself to be independent of all external changes, because it is not affected by them. The disorder we complain of is internal.... We are defiled and impeded by that which is within.... But till we are so far apprised of the nature of our disease as to put ourselves into the hands of the great and only Physician, we shall find, like the woman in Luke 8:43, that every other effort for relief will leave us as it found us.

Scripture Meditation

Create in me a pure heart, O God, and renew a steadfast spirit within me.

—Psalm 51:10

Thought for the Day

Self-honesty helps to give good counsel to others.

Prayer

God, strengthen me to bear myself,
That heaviest weight of all to bear,
Inalienable weight of care.
—CHRISTINA ROSSETTI

MARCH 2: FURTHER STEPS INTO THE CHRISTIAN LIFE

John Newton continues to guide Hannah More [see previous entry] into the
realities of the Christian life. He reminds her of the first steps for each
Christian and offers hope for her future maturity in Christ.

My dear Madame,

As sinners, the first things we need are pardon, reconciliation, and a principle of life and conduct entirely new. Till then we can have no more success or comfort from our endeavors than a man who should attempt to walk while his ankle was dislocated; the bone must be set before he can take a single step with safety, or attempt it without increasing his pain. For these purposes we are directed to Jesus Christ, as the wounded Israelites were to look at the brazen serpent (John 3:14–15). When we understand what the Scripture teaches of the person, love and offices of Christ, the necessity and final causes of his humiliation unto death, and feel our own need of a Savior, we then know him to be the light, the sun of the world, and of the soul, the source of all spiritual light, life, comfort, and influence, having access to God by him, and receiving out of his fullness grace for grace.

Our perceptions of these things are for a time faint and indistinct, like the peep of dawn, but the dawning light, though faint, is the sure harbinger of approaching day (Prov. 4:18). The full-grown oak that overtops the wood, spreads its branches wide, and has struck its roots to a proportionate depth and extent into the soil, arises from a little acorn; its daily growth, had it been daily watched from its appearance above-ground, would have been imperceptible, yet it was always upon the increase. It has known a variety of seasons, it has sustained many a storm, but in time it attained to maturity, and now is likely to stand for ages. The beginnings of spiritual life are small likewise in the true Christian; he likewise passes through a succession of various dispensations, but he advances, though silently and slowly, yet surely—and will stand forever.

Scripture Meditation

The path of the righteous is like the first gleam of dawn, shining ever brighter till the full light of day.
—PROVERBS 4:18

Thought for the Day

Allowing God to settle the issue of sin in our life is the greatest step we can take.

Prayer

O God within my breast, almighty, ever-present deity! Life—that in me has rest, as I—undying life—have power in thee!
—EMILY BRONTË

MARCH 3: LEARNING MORE DEEPLY IN THE SCHOOL OF CHRIST

Rev. William Romaine [see entry for December 14] writes the following letter,
undated in his collection, to an unnamed friend.

*Y*ou may depend upon this, as one of the sweetest axioms in divinity: whatever it makes you pleased with yourself, is not true grace; and whatever
makes you displeased with yourself, is not true grace either, unless it brings
you humbly to Christ, and makes you put more trust and confidence in him.
The good Lord teaches you these things practically. I have learned them by
long experience. Although I know but little of them, yet I am getting on in the
school of Christ, and hope soon to be in the lowest form, for there we learn
most and fastest. We there depend entirely upon the teachings of our divine
Master, who reveals the secrets of his kingdom to none but babes. As a newborn babe depends entirely upon the care of its parents, so must we on God,
our prophet and teacher. I would wish you to be the humblest person on
earth, not only that you might know most, but also you might love most. He
that feels his sins most … is in the fittest way to love Christ most….

When you are going to measure Christ's high grace, do not get upon
a mountain, but go down into a valley; lower still, to the depth from
which David cried, or lower still, to the belly of hell from which Jonah
prayed. From thence, take the heights of Jesus' grace, and from thence
see how lovely he is. When the Spirit of Jesus is humbling you, showing
you your deceitful heart, laying open your ruined nature … did it not
weaken your faith, and so lessen your love? … May he teach you better,
that every future sense of sin may greatly endear you to the Lamb of
God, whose blood cleanses from all sin. Depend upon it, that it is only
true [self-]humbling for sin, that makes his blood more precious.

—William Romaine

Scripture Meditation

Unless you change and become like little children, you will never
enter the kingdom of heaven.

—MATTHEW 18:3

Thought for the Day

We learn the ways of grace fastest in the school of humility.

Prayer

I conceal nothing: I make no excuses. I give thee glory, O Lord.

—LANCELOT ANDREWES

SEASON OF LENT

*I*f the seasons of Advent and Epiphany challenge us by God's gracious intervention in human affairs, the season of Lent prepares us for the death and resurrection of Christ. The transition between the seasons of Epiphany and Lent is marked by a deepening realism about the cost of discipleship. It involves facing our temptations, knowing ourselves, having new attitudes, changing dispositions, living prayerfully—all to become more Christlike. As a penitential season of the church, it provides for a forty-day period of fasting, in imitation of Jesus' fast in the wilderness.

Since Easter is a moveable feast it can occur as early as March 22 and as late as April 25. There are six Sundays of Lent prior to Holy Week, and Ash Wednesday is the first day of Lent. In the Eastern Church it begins eight weeks before Easter. During World War II, Roman Catholics were dispensed of this Lenten period of fasting, now reduced to two days, Ash Wednesday and Good Friday.

LEARNING THE MEANING OF LENT

MARCH 4: THE LENTEN FAST

Archbishop Hovnan Derderian of the Armenian Church of Canada writes a pastoral letter to explain the significance of the Lenten fast to his church members.

The term "to fast" designates certain acts, such as "to control," "to restrain," "to abstain," etc., which are to be practiced by individuals during specific religious ceremonies. However, we must apply these concepts to our own lives. While fasting, we abstain from animal products, but we must not neglect to see the other side of the coin; for the tradition of fasting does not only consist of abstinence from nourishment. In fasting, we also abstain from all kinds of evil thoughts and words. Therefore, fasting should be maintained inseparably in both its meanings.

The tradition of fasting is not a custom practiced among Christians only, for we find it in many religions. It was a commonly accepted practice in the times of the Old Testament. Isaiah, the prophet of the people of Israel, explains the manner one should adopt while fasting, and not abuse it unrighteously. "'Why have we fasted,' they say, 'and you have not seen it? Why have we humbled ourselves, and you have not noticed?' Yet on the day of your fasting you do as you please and exploit your workers. Your fasting ends in quarreling and strife.... You cannot fast as you do today and expect your voice to be heard on high.... Is that what you call a fast, a day acceptable to the Lord?" [Isa. 58:3–5].

In the Christian Church, the canon of fasting was established in the year 325, in Nicea at the First Ecumenical Council. The Armenian church has dedicated 160 days of the year to fasting. The days designated for that purpose are on Wednesdays and Fridays. The weeks that precede the five major feast days of the Armenian church, known as "Daghavars," are also fasting days. The Lenten period, called the Great Lent, is the longest and comprises seven weeks, beginning from Monday following the eve of the Great Lent, up to the Eve of Easter — forty days in all. The duration of the forty days is a special period for prayers and fasting, a time to examine oneself. During the Lenten season, every one has to pass in review his deeds, his behavior, and correct himself, his errors, just as an auditor would do looking through the accounts of an institution. We should fast and pray, thus cleansing our own selves, our minds and our souls ... and as a means of teaching Christian behavior. The forty days of fasting and praying are a period of preparation for every Christian. Christ himself was in favor of fasting, for he proved its necessity by his own example....

Prayer and fasting—these are the means that will approach us to the feast of Easter, to our Lord's Resurrection, with purified feelings and renewed faith, ... to welcome him who "by his death defeated death, and granted life to us by his resurrection."

Scripture Meditation

When you fast, put oil on your head and wash your face, so that it will not be obvious to men that you are fasting, but only to your Father, who is unseen; and your Father, who sees what is done in secret, will reward you.
—MATTHEW 6:17–18

Thought for the Day

Fasting is any spiritual discipline of restraint we may exercise before God to live righteously.

Prayer

Grant, O Lord, to your faithful people, that they enter upon the holy solemnities of the fast with true reverence and continue the same with steadfast devotion.
—A COLLECT OF THE ANGLICAN PRAYER BOOK FOR LENT

MARCH 5: THE SUNDAYS OF THE LENTEN SEASON

*Archbishop Hovnan Derderian [see previous entry] explains the meaning
of each Sunday feast of the Lenten period in the practice of the
Armenian Church as the period of the need for spiritual
renewal in the lives of Christians.*

The first Sunday (after Ash Wednesday) is "Poun Paregentan" the doorway to the Spiritual Journey of the Lenten period. "The Expulsion from Paradise" falls on the second Sunday of Lent. This day reminds us of the loss of man's happiness caused by his disobedience.... The third Sunday of Lent is known as "the Sunday of the Prodigal Son," for it mirrors the life of each one of us ... lost and then found ... with the figure of the Father helping us to grasp the love of God for the salvation of mankind.

The fourth Sunday of Lent is dedicated to the parable Jesus told his disciples about a rich man who ... is aware of his steward's dishonest actions, yet he gave him a second chance ... just as God's power of forgiving love helps the fallen person to renew his life and thus find salvation. The fifth Sunday of the Lenten period is known as the Sunday of the Unrighteous Judge ... told to the effect that Jesus' disciples "ought to pray and not lose heart." ... This is a parable which closely relates to our everyday life.... Consistency is vital to overcome our difficulties.... The sixth Sunday is called the Sunday of the Advent (or Second Coming) ... to commemorate our Savior as the Second Adam, who sacrificed his life for mankind.... In the admonition of the Apostle we are to examine ourselves, to see whether we are holding to the Christian faith.

Scripture Meditation

Examine yourselves to see whether you are in faith; test yourselves.
—2 CORINTHIANS 13:5

Thought for the Day

The specificity of faith is such that to be personal it must also be historical.

Prayer

> *O God, we have heard with our ears, and our fathers have declared unto us, the noble works that you did in their day, and in the old time before them. O Lord, arise, help us, and deliver us for your honor.*
> —THE LITANY

MARCH 6: PRACTICING THE FAST

St. Theophan the Recluse (1815–1894), a pious Russian seminary student in Jerusalem, was inspired to follow the life of a staretz *or spiritual director like Bishop Tikhon of Zadonsk. Throughout his life, he was in contact with countless disciples, whom he never saw but with whom he communicated by letters. His name at birth was George Govorov, but at baptism he adopted the name derived from "Theophanes," meaning "manifestation of God." Here he writes about* govenie *or fasting, interpreted in the Orthodox church as a preparation for communion, as well as for the Lenten season. It takes seriously our eucharistic life in God.*

Glory be to Thee, O God! The fast [i.e. Lent] has drawn near. You bring me joy to know that you intend to begin fasting and to attend Divine Services immediately. Do not change your intention. People usually fast and attend services during Holy Week, but do not postpone it yourself until then. Those who fast and attend services during Holy

Week include people who have already fasted, attended services and taken Communion during the preceding weeks who desire to take Communion a second time....

Lord, give me the blessing for you to perform *govenie* [i.e. Lenten disciplines] in a fitting manner. Each faster must do everything that you intend to do. Fast, go to church, seclude yourself, read, think and study yourself; all of this is necessary. But all of these actions must be directed toward one goal: to seek worthy Communion of the holy Mysteries of Christ. In order to commune worthily, the soul must be cleansed with repentance. All the various actions of *govenie*—going to church, prayer at home, fasting, and everything else, are undertaken in order to accomplish repentance as it should be, with sincere contrition and a firm resolution not to offend the Lord anymore.

The first thing to do in making repentance is to go inside yourself. Earthly matters and cares and unrestrained, wandering thoughts, do not allow us to go inside ourselves and to study ourselves. Therefore the faster, to the extent possible during the time of the fast, shuts off his cares, and instead of going about his usual business, stays "at home." Cutting off our cares is a matter of extreme importance in *govenie*. Whoever does not do so, will certainly spend the fast haphazardly. You, too, must cut off your cares. No matter how few these cares are, they do exist and distract us. So set about *govenie* having laid aside all cares.

Scripture Meditation

Jesus' disciples asked him, "Where do you want us to go and make preparations for you to eat the Passover?"
—MARK 14:12

Thought for the Day

In a culture of "techniques," help me O God, to cast all my cares upon you, not trusting in fixing everything by myself.

Prayer

O God, draw tight thy noose about my life that in my haste and my ardent comings and goings in this world's affairs, I may be

*brought low and come into the realization of my utter depend-
ence upon thee, Amen.*
—BERNARD OF CLAIRVAUX

MARCH 7: ENTERING THE SCHOOL OF HOLY POVERTY

---

*Catherine de Hueck Doherty (1896–1985) was a married Russian Catholic
woman living in North America. She founded a community called the
Madonna House. She was a true* staretza, *a spiritual mother who fed her
spiritual children with gospel wisdom. Here in a letter of March 30, 1962, she
explores the depths of holy poverty as an essential part of the gospel.*

*D*early Beloved,

It is only since the coming of Christ that poverty truly found her place
in the hearts of men. She came from the heart of God, the God who was
born in a stable and died naked on a cross.

The first impact that poverty makes on souls who fall in love with God
is a tremendous desire for physical poverty. One wants to be truly dispossessed of all the created goods that people crave with such a passionate
hunger and greed. They have made these goods the yardsticks or symbols of their status before others, and one almost shivers to think before
God. The soul falling in love with God, I repeat, first desires to dispos-
sess herself of all these worldly symbols—these possessions that possess.

However, as time goes on, and one grows in the depths of love—as
dedicated souls will   the words of the Gospel about poverty withdraw
their veils, or sometimes just simply explode in your face, revealing new
depths and understanding of the mystery. This is what has been happening to me and what I want to share with you. Slowly, as the years
went by and the graces of God filled my soul, I began to realize that

physical poverty, being dispossessed as we truly were in the early days of Harlem and Toronto, was but the kindergarten of God's novitiate of love. I began to understand that poverty would not grow unless obedience walked with her. For a soul must surrender not only its goods, but itself. Obedience surrenders the will of a human being, truly his most precious possession, becoming the crown of poverty and the footstool of charity.

Time went on and more graces came, more words of God exploded in my face. As God led me to the high school or maybe college of his love, I understood that both poverty and obedience lived in the house of True Humility, that the poor had nothing to hide and, therefore, if their poverty was offered to God, they lived in humility and truth.

Detachment and holy indifference had to be embraced also if one wanted to be poor: detachment from family and friends, indifference to heat, cold, kinds of food, and living conditions. A deep detachment and true holy indifference would lead into the heart of poverty, the Sacred Heart of God. There it would be stripped naked of all attachments to created things and return to the world with a flaming love of all things now as a reflection of God himself—a love that sings his glory alone.

The implementation of this mystery of poverty into the reality of everyday life beggars the imagination.

Scriptural Meditation

He who gives to the poor will lack nothing.
—PROVERBS 28:27

Thought for the Day

Both poverty and obedience live in the house of true humility.

Prayer

O Lady, holy poverty, may the Lord save thee, with thy sister holy humility!
—FRANCIS OF ASSISI

MARCH 8: THE QUEST OF DEEPER SELF-UNDERSTANDING

Macarius of Optino (1788–1860) was a Russian staretz, or spiritual director,
who wrote more than 447 letters between 1834 and 1860. To preserve
anonymity, regrettably, all names, places, and dates of correspondence were
eliminated by later editors. But this letter appears to have been written to a
princess of the Czar's court.

Do not limit yourself to striving for the right outward order: fasting and prayer. Strive also for greater inward order, only to be attained through intensified love and deep humility.

You say that the longing for obedience has pierced your heart, and you ask, "How can I attain to it?" Shall I tell you?

In the world you live in, Princess, you must have seen how long it takes an artist to train for his art, and how much effort he must devote to it. Is it not natural that the art of arts should exact even more time and even greater effort?

Pray that you may be granted the grace to read the Fathers with the right understanding, and the grace to live clearly to see your own frailty. You will not long be left wanting and waiting. God will give you help.

In the meanwhile carefully examine the movements of your heart, the patterns of your thoughts, the intention of all your words and actions. In your case, it may even be good to do this in writing. It may help to make clearer to you your utter poverty; it may humble your pride of mind.

Scripture Meditation

He humbles those who dwell on high ... the path of the righteous
is level.

—ISAIAH 26:5, 7

Thought for the Day

God directs us appropriately in the circumstances of our life.

Prayer

My soul rejoices in the Lord ... The Lord sends poverty and
wealth; he humbles and he exalts.

—1 SAMUEL 2:1, 7

MARCH 9: THE GIFT OF TEARS

---

*John Ilyitch Sergieff (1829–1908), known as John of Kronstadt, was bishop of
Kronstadt for six years before relinquishing his position to have a ministry of
letter writing as a* staretz *to thousands of correspondents across Russia. The
practice of* penthos, *or the gift of tears, was exercised by the Eastern Fathers,
and mourning of sins indeed is appropriate as a Lenten exercise, as this letter
encourages.*

he Lord turned and looked upon Peter ... and Peter went out, and
wept bitterly." And even now, when the Lord looks upon us we weep bitterly over our sins. Yes, our tears during prayer mean the Lord has
looked upon us with his gaze that gives life to everything and tries our
hearts. Ah! The soul is sometimes entangled and ensnared by sins, like a
bird in the net. We do not sometimes see any outlet from our sins and
they torment us; the heart sometimes feels terribly anxious and sorrow-
ful on account of them; but Jesus looks on us and streams of tears flow
from our eyes, and with tears all the tissue of evil in our souls vanishes.
We weep and rejoice that such mercy has been suddenly and unexpec-
tantly granted to us. What warmth then do we feel in our heart, and what
lightness as though we could fly up to the Lord God himself! I thank the
Lord with all my heart for freely forgiving all my sin!

Scripture Meditation

Blessed are those who mourn, for they will be comforted.
—MATTHEW 5:4

Thought for the Day

Without the presence and gaze of God in my life, I will never know sin.

Prayer

Forgive what seemed my sin in me;
What seemed my worth since I began:
For merit lives from man to man,
And not from man, O Lord, to thee.
—ALFRED, LORD TENNYSON

EXPERIENCING THE SERMON ON THE MOUNT

*We continue Lenten meditations as expressive of the Sermon on the Mount.
So Catherine Doherty [see entry for March 7] writes this letter to a family
relative on February 22, 1961, about the importance of meekness.*

Dearly Beloved,

During this most holy season of Lent when we prepare for the death and resurrection of Our Lord, I would like to share with you two little words which came to me during Mass. I have been meditating upon them, for they are very profound. Did you know that words dealing with God in any way have great depths, which often do not reveal themselves immediately? Like all the things of God, they open the doors of their beauty slowly and gently, revealing their full meaning only to those who persevere.

These two words which came to me are meekness and rejection. At first glance, they seemed to have little in common. As the days went by, a pattern emerged. Those words grew, intertwined, separated, and came together again. I want to prayerfully and lovingly share with you my thoughts. I hope they may help you as I have been helped, for I love you so very deeply, and one of the proofs of love is serving those whom we love by sharing what has been meaningful to us.

Meekness: I have often meditated upon meekness. It is a virtue that has always attracted me. I love the Beatitudes where meekness is truly extolled. "The meek shall inherit the earth," said the Lord. He also said: "Learn of me for I am meek and humble of heart."

Ours is a century of neuroses and psychoses. Slowly, the Christians of the world have been drifting away from God, until finally they have cut themselves off from God completely by becoming atheists. People without God easily become neurotic and psychotic. From such mental conditions stem the fruits of the devil—fears, confusion and insecurity. So, as the atheists grow, the devil obtains more of a foothold. The stench of all that is evil spreads in ever widening circles until everyone, even the believing people, are affected in one way or another. Because of this

201

tragic situation of the world's soul, all of us are somewhat confused; all of us are frightened of threats and attacks from everything to the "A" bomb, to our next-door neighbor.

I too am on the defensive, emotionally speaking. It is not too noticeable to the untrained eye and, until now perhaps, I did not pay too much attention to it myself, but many of you sense it.

Remember the times when you and I had our private counseling conversations? I would not take time to listen to what you had to say. Because you were emotionally blocked, you took a long time to say what you had to say. Seemingly impatient, I would rush in and tell you that I knew what you thought or felt or hoped, and proceeded to solve (or think I solved) your problems. This didn't always happen, but sometimes it did. Naturally, you reacted violently. You became more hostile to me. Well, today I know why I did that. I was defending myself against your hostility.

At such times, you were a threat to me. It didn't matter that I was a nurse, that I understood that I was only a symbol, and that your hostility was directed against one or both of your parents. Those were the days when I was exhausted, humanly speaking, from the huge waves of hostility that constantly beat against the shores of my person.

I certainly was not defenseless before you. I defended myself on such occasions from you, my dearly beloved, unconsciously or semiconsciously. Each one of us has experienced many of these situations. However, today with new insights into meekness and its gentle attribute, defenselessness, I understand better.

Scripture Meditation

Blessed are the meek, for they will inherit the earth.
—MATTHEW 5:5

Thought for the Day

Meekness helps us to respond compassionately to the negative emotions of others.

Prayer

See, O LORD, how distressed I am! I am in torment within, and in

my heart I am disturbed, for I have been most rebellious.
—LAMENTATIONS 1:20

MARCH 11: TRAINING IN THE SCHOOL OF DAILY ACCEPTANCE

Amy Carmichael (1867–1951) went to India as a missionary and never
left, building a home for needy children. For the last twenty years of her
life, she was confined to her room as an invalid. She died in
her mission at Dohnavur on January 18, 1951.

*D*ear Daughter,

The best training is to learn to accept everything as it comes, as from Him whom our soul loves. The tests are always unexpected things, not great things that can be written up, but the common little rubs of life, silly little nothings, things you are ashamed of minding one scrap. Yet they can knock a strong man over and lay him very low.

It is a very good thing to learn to take things by the right handle. An inward grouse is a devastating thing. I expect you know this, we all do; but it is extraordinary how the devil tries to "get" us on the ordinary road of life. But all is well if only we are in him, deep in him and he in us, our daily strength and joy and song.

I have read and reread the bit in your letter about the love that constrains. Nothing less will hold on to the end. Feelings can be shaken and the fight can be fearfully discouraging, for sometimes we seem to be losing ground and all seems to be going wrong. Then the devil comes and paints glorious pictures of what might have been. He did to me—I can see those pictures still. But as we go on steadfastly obeying the word that compelled, we do become aware that it is all worth while. We know it, we know him with us, and that is life.

I am going to ask that the consciousness of his presence with you may be constant and very sweet. I know the difference this makes. But you are not a child in him; you have passed the point where that is needful. You know him near, with you and in you. It is indeed joy, to be conscious of that blessed One, yet the great thing is not about my feelings, but his reality. So if there are fogs on the sea on any day or any night—still all's well.

Scripture Meditation

I have learned to be content whatever the circumstances.
—PHILIPPIANS 4:11

Thought for the Day

The God of little things will help us see his sovereignty over everything.

Prayer

What? Shall I ever sigh and pine?.. But as I raved and grew more fierce and wild at every word, me thoughts I heard one calling, "Child!" And I replied, "My Lord."
—GEORGE HERBERT

MARCH 12: FOCUS UPON THE PRESENT MOMENT IN GOD'S PRESENCE

Jean-Pierre de Caussade [see entry for February 29] recognized that discouragement was a deadly affliction of those seeking a devout life, as he writes here to a nun, Sister Marie-Therese de Viomenil.

*M*y dear Sister,

At this moment you are suffering from one of the most dangerous temptations that could assail any soul of devout will; the temptation of discouragement. I urge you to resist it with all your might. Have confidence in God, and be convinced that He will finish the work He has begun in you. Your foolish fears about the future come from the devil. Think only of the present, abandon the future to divine providence. It is the good use of the present that assures the future. Apply yourself to obtaining attachment and conformity to the will of God in all things and everywhere, even to the smallest things, for in this consist all virtue and perfection. For the rest, God only allows our daily faults to keep us humble. If you know how to gain this fruit, and to remain in peace and confidence, then you will be in a better state than if you had not committed any apparent fault, which would have flattered greatly your self-love, and have exposed you to the extreme danger of being satisfied with yourself.

On the contrary, nothing can be easier than to make use of your faults, to acquire a fresh degree of humility, and so build deeper foundations for the life of holiness. So ought we not to admire and bless the infinite goodness of our God, who knows how to make even use of our very faults, to serve our greater good? For this it suffices to dislike them, to rise humbly above them, working peaceably and with untiring perseverance to correct them.... If you are faithful in this practice, you will be able to live in peace even in the midst of disturbances ... conforming your will to the will of God.

Scripture Meditation

Do not be anxious about anything, but in everything, by prayer and petition, with thanksgiving, present your requests to God.
—PHILIPPIANS 4:6

Thought for the Day

When God is accepted as Lord of little things, he can be God of everything.

Prayer

*May God be blessed by all vicissitudes and in all circumstances,
now and forever Amen.*

—JEAN PIERRE-DE CAUSSADE

MARCH 13: ACCEPTING REJECTION AS FOLLOWERS OF THE LAMB

---

*Catherine Doherty [see entry for March 7] continues her letter of February
22, 1961, on meekness and rejection, the first part of which
we recorded for March 10.*

Dearly Beloved,

A few days later, the Lord sent me another word to think about: rejection. This puzzled me again. Now what had the word rejection (which belongs to the textbooks of psychiatry) to do with God and me? What did it have to do with Lenten meditation? I confess that it puzzled me for quite a while. But one Friday in the great silence of the Lord in St. Kate's, (for you remember that Friday, these days, is a prayer day for me in the desert, or *poustinia*, as the Russians called the desert), I began to see light. Rejection belongs to the passion of Christ too. In fact, it belongs to his whole life. Let's briefly consider it.

St. Joseph, when he found out that Mary was pregnant, and he had not known her as a husband, would have rejected her had it not been for the angel's message. But rejection of Our Lady would have also meant the rejection of Christ—the fruit of her womb.

The innkeepers of Bethlehem rejected the Holy Family's need for shelter and hospitality. Because Christ was still in Mary's womb, this was a rejection of him also. We know for a fact that the Pharisees and the Sadducees, with the exception of a few, rejected him completely. That must have been a terrible pain for Christ.

One day when he was proclaiming that he would give his own flesh for the life of the world, many of his followers rejected him publicly, saying: "Your sayings are too hard. We will not walk with you anymore!"

There was Philip who was constantly rejecting the words of Christ by asking silly questions. (So many of us still do!) I think that Christ was touched to the quick by this rejection on the part of his beloved disciple, for he scolded him. The momentary rejection of Peter made him terribly sad. But what the rejection of Judas did to him—a rejection sealed with a lying kiss—only his Father knew!

When he went to his home town, Nazareth, the people there rejected him violently and were going to stone him. After all, he was "just the son of Joseph, the carpenter!"

In Gethsemane all the disciples slept, instead of watching with him during his tremendous hour of great agony. Love shares. Sleep is a rejection—a non-sharing. It must have added to his agony for he said: "Couldn't you watch one hour with me?"

From the time that he was arrested in the Garden of Olives to the time that he was nailed to the cross, rejection accompanied him. He was rejected by the very people he had taught and healed. Yes, rejection, like pain and loneliness, were the shadowy companions of his whole passion and indeed of his whole life....

Finally, the supreme (seeming) rejection that tore out of his parched, pain-filled mouth and lips those terrible words, "Father, Father, why has Thou forsaken me?"

I began to see that rejection was a word that I had to meditate upon, if I wanted to enter the passion of my Beloved. I also saw more. I saw the tremendous love of Christ in a new light. It is said that he was like us in everything but sin, and that he knew and experienced all that we in our humanity have to know and experience of pain and of sorrow. It stands to reason that he would experience the feelings of rejection also so as to help us in our neurotic, psychotic century. He wanted to help us understand, and to overcome that terrible feeling of rejection which is so neurotic, so deadly and life-shattering.

To put it another way: we seek approval from people who matter. We crave it and hunger for it because we equate it with love. Rejection almost means death to us—a sort of living death, filled with loneliness. Rejection means aloneness, pain, sadness. It means being unloved. It is, in fact, a hell on earth—a living death.

Scripture Meditation

Blessed are those who hunger and thirst for righteousness, for they will be filled.
   —Matthew 5:6

Thought for the Day

Experiencing rejection by others often gives us a stronger appetite for the things of God.

Prayer

Though earth and man were gone,
and suns and universes ceased to be,
and Thou wert left alone,
every existence would exist in Thee.
   —Emily Brontë

MARCH 14: A CHILD'S EXPERIENCES OF REJECTION

A Chinese friend writes anonymously to the editor on July 20, 2002, about her narrative of rejection.

*D*ear Dr. Houston,

Mother Teresa when she was interviewed by a journalist for *Time* magazine observed: "It is sad to see people who suffer, especially from a broken family, unloved, uncared for. It is a big sadness … and is the greatest poverty. If you pick up a person dying of hunger, you can give him food and it is finished. However, the hunger for love is much more difficult to remove than the hunger for bread."

Certainly this has been my experience. My insatiable hunger for love had its roots in a broken family, trying to survive. In 1972, I was born into a Chinese immigrant family that just arrived to New York City. It was difficult for them to provide full time care for a newborn, so they sent me to live with my aunt and her family in Taiwan. At age four, I returned to a family that did not know me nor know the implications of being separated at a young age. In addition to the challenge of receiving a "new" member into the family, we had other dysfunctional family patterns such as parenting responsibilities passed on to older siblings, physically absent father, and emotionally absent mother. This environment was the seedling to feelings of deep insecurity, alienation, rejection and abandonment. As a child, these feelings manifested themselves in several ways. Out of my insecurities and need to be reassured of an unlimited love, I would constantly ask my sister how much she loved me…. Out of my need to belong and have meaning for my existence, I would also question why I lived on Earth, in my family context, and for what purpose. Never receiving satisfaction left me feeling more alienated and confused. Out of my feelings of being forsaken or forgotten, my childhood was plagued with nightmares about people kidnapping me from my family, without my family noticing. Often times I needed someone to hold my hand before I could fall asleep.

As I grew older, many other events occurred that only watered these weeds of deep insecurity, alienation, rejection and abandonment. When my sister went away for college, I was devastated, feeling she had abandoned me; from then on, emotional distance crept into our relationship. At aged 12, my father died of stomach cancer. Having struggled to relate with him, his death brought a "death" into my own spirit. Following this, my mother went into a depression and so becoming even more emotionally absent—yet another form of abandonment. Needing space to recover, she then sent me to spend the summer with my sister. In many ways, this decision paralleled the decision to send me in Taiwan, and so I felt rejected once again. All of these events and more, only served to deepen my wounds, and left me entering young adulthood quite broken.

As I entered young adulthood, I looked for many sources to give me that love, acceptance and belonging I desperately yearned for. Before I fully committed myself to Jesus, this search led me astray for several years. In his grace, He allowed me to fall into the abyss and to experience his saving presence there. As I put my trust in Jesus, He began to fill my insatiable need for love, acceptance and belonging. He first did this by placing me in a community of faith where it was safe for Him to expose my wounds and bring healing. As I grow towards maturity in Jesus, I am continually challenged to find my main source of sustenance in himself. Through divine relationships, I began to experience God's love and presence. God would also use these key relationships to prune me. These relationships that brought so much healing in my life, also brought new awareness of pain and old feelings of abandonment and rejection—as one by one, these relationships would change as a result of geographic relocation on their part.

My daily prayer is that Jesus would deeply reassured me of his infinite love which no one else can give me, and that I will never be abandoned or forsaken by him. I continually seek comfort in his word which tells me: "See, I have engraved you on the palms of my hands" (Isa. 49:16).

Scripture Meditation

Can a mother forget the baby at her breast and have no compassion on the child she has borne? Though she may forget, I will not forget you!

—ISAIAH 49:15

Thought for the Day

Hungering for love needs more fulfillment than ever having physical needs met.

Prayer

O Heavenly Father, grant that I may preserve within my soul the grace that makes me Thy child! Keep me from all evil that might separate me from Thee!

—DOM COLUMBA MARMION

MARCH 15: TRANSCENDING REJECTION WITH MEEKNESS

Catherine Doherty [see March 7, 10, 13] concludes her Lenten meditations on living with the spirit of the Beatitudes.

Dearly Beloved,

The feeling and fear of rejection, and the putting up of defenses, constantly places us in a straitjacket—a prisoner of fear and a thousand other emotions. The result of this is that we are half alive in the reality of living, unable to love, yet desiring to be loved and accepted.

Gently, Christ comes to our rescue. He comes with two words: *meekness* and *rejection*, showing us, I think, that if we are truly meek, we will be defenseless and exposed. A defenseless person is a trusting and meek person, a person full of faith, with the heart of a child to whom belongs the kingdom of heaven. People who are defenseless are open to all the pain and thrusts of the knives of other people's words, glances, and deeds, because they are strong in faith and strong in love; because they don't retaliate, nor defend themselves; in a word, they are meek. They are not hurt, for the sharp arrows of words and deeds bounce off the shield of meekness and fall at the feet of the attacker and the attacked.

From their hearts and souls streams an almost unbearable light, for they are truly Christ-like. The light of Christ shines forth from them unimpeded and envelops the attacker with its gentle love, and illuminates his soul and heals him.

From this, it follows that meek and defenseless people who practice this virtue for Christ's sake will never feel rejected, because they are anchored in Christ. What is more, they realize this and feel secure. They have walked with Christ through every step of his rejection, and have seen how meekly, forgivingly, and lovingly Love Itself dealt with rejection. If they ever were neurotics, dearly beloved, by following in the footsteps of Christ they become healed, and they heal others.

Such was my meditation for the Lent of 1961. Lovingly, I share it with you, praying that the humble and rejected Christ may make you meek, defenseless, and hence secure in his Sacred Heart against any rejection.

Scripture Meditation

Learn from me, for I am gentle and humble in heart.
—Matthew 11:29

Thought for the Day

Only in being without self-defense can we "put on the whole armor of God."

Prayer

Spirit of God, descend upon my heart … stoop to my weakness, mighty as thou art.
—George Croly

MARCH 16: THE IMPLICATIONS OF "SEEING GOD"

Augustine of Hippo [see entry for December 19] writes to a noble lady, Pauline,
in 413 about the conditions of "seeing God." The letter, numbered 147, is really a
long treatise, although addressed personally, from which the following short
excerpts are paraphrased.

Devoted servant of God, Pauline,

I have postponed replying to your request to have a full treatise about the invisible God, and whether we can actually "see" him. Alas, I have been very busy, and needed time to reflect on the matter. For what you ask for is so profound a subject, that the more one "thinks" about it, the deeper it gets. You see, it is not so much a matter to "think" about, but a way of life "to be" before God, so that the manner of life is what counts, not the matter of speech. Those who have learned from our Lord Jesus Christ to be meek and humble of heart make greater progress by meditation and prayer, than by reading and hearing a lot of information. So when speech has played its role, just as planting and watering have had their part, then the rest is up to Him who gives the increase (1 Cor. 3:7).

To "see God" is not an external anything like reading this letter, or looking at the sun, anymore than you use your physical eyes to look at yourself, and examine your thought processes of seeing how you live, wish, seek, and know inwardly your own inner consciousness. Yet Scripture does promise us: "Blessed are the pure in heart for they will see God." We ought, and can, really believe this.

But first let us note that we both see and believe. We see what is present, and we believe what is absent. We are our own witness of the former, while we believe by trusting the testimony of others. So the apostle summarizes these issues by saying: "though you have not seen him you love him; and even though you do not see him now, you believe in him now" (1 Peter 1:8). So too, Jesus says: "Blessed are those who have not seen but believed" (John 20:29). For actually we can believe far more than we can see, since we cannot witness so much that has already happened. The Resurrection of Christ is a past event, but those living at that time, did not see it either. But they believed it very firmly, because they witnessed the living Christ, before and after the event. So while the actual fact is not visible and tangible to us, that Christ dies no more, and "death shall no more have dominion over him" (1 Cor. 2:1). But we believe it absolutely.

But the apostle takes us further when he observes, "for who among men knows the thought of a man except the man's spirit within him." In the same way no one knows the thoughts of God except the Spirit of God (1 Cor. 4:11). So we come now to the main point. We know we can see God, since we read: "Blessed are the pure in heart for they shall see God." Perhaps I should rather have said—not "know" but—we "believe" we shall see God.... So a distinction has to be made between the meaning "no one has seen God any time," the way those saints of God saw God kataphatically, by responding to his acts of love, in love. Neither of these is the false claim to know him only mentally so.

But we need to continue in another letter....

Scripture Meditation

Blessed are the pure in heart, for they will see God.
—MATTHEW 5:8

Thought for the Day

Can we no longer today "see God" as the biblical characters seemed to have "seen" him so frequently?

Prayer

My God, when I walk in those groves
and leaves thy spirit doth still fan,
I see in each shade that there grows
an angel talking with a man.
... Is the truce broke? Or 'cause we have
a Mediator now with thee? ...
Look down, great Master of the Feast; O shine,
and turn more our water into wine!
—HENRY VAUGHAN

MARCH 17: "SEEING GOD" IN PURITY OF HEART

Augustine of Hippo continues his letter to Pauline [see previous entry],
sharing with her how Ambrose, bishop of Milan, had mentored him about this
mystery of "seeing God" as a young Christian convert.

*D*evoted Servant of God Pauline,

My own initial struggles as a young Christian arose from issues of Neo-Platonism. For it was asserted by followers of Plotinus that if God in his deity is invisible, but Christ by his humanity is visible, then we can't believe in the divinity of Christ. The Arian heretics are saying the same thing [just as Unitarian sects still argue]. Ambrose's rebuttal was that the triune God of Father, Son, and Holy Spirit, being self-revelatory, are "seen" as they will to be "seen," but not by our desires or fancies. One God, Indivisible, Unchangeable, he appears to whomsoever he wills, and however he wills. There are devout souls who truly long to see God within their lives, burning with love for God. God did appear to Moses, just as he does appear to his ardent saints, but not as he is in his *essence*, only as he *wills* to appear to them. Just as the apostle declares: "No one has ever seen God, but God the One and Only, who is at the Father's side, has made him known" (John 1:18).

So when Philip burned with longing to be satisfied asked: "Show us the Father and it is enough for us," Ambrose observed: "God is not seen in any place," as at the oak of Mamre, or on Mount Sinai, "but in the clean heart." He continues: "God is not sought by physical eyes ... nor held by physical touch ... nor heard by the ear...." No, it is only by increase of "the Spirit," indeed by those who keep his commandments. As Jesus promised to Philip: "Whoever hears my commands and obeys them, he is the one who loves him. He who loves me will be loved by my Father, and I too will love him and show myself to him" (John 14:21) [i.e. God shows us himself in the way he wills to reveal himself, only in Jesus Christ].

For that reason, however hard we try to pursue the beatific life, this gives us no warrant for "seeing God." They will see him as he wills to be seen, not even because in this life they were poor in spirit, or they were meek, mourned and hungered after righteousness, were merciful or peacemakers, but because they were pure of heart. That is to say, it is a moral vision, not physical, in no way determined by our own faculties or abilities ... Rather "seeing God" is the process of being transformed by God. When "we, who with unveiled faces all reflect the Lord's glory, are being transformed into his likeness with ever-increasing glory, which comes from the Lord, who is the Spirit" (2 Cor. 3:18).... So that just as the Father "sees" the Son, and the Son "sees" the Father, so we shall "see" the Father, through the Son, by his Spirit. So let it suffice, as you probably read and reread this letter, all is summed up in this certainty, that only with a clean heart can you "see" God.

Scripture Meditation

No one has ever seen God, but God the One and Only, who is at the Father's side, has made him known.
—JOHN 1:18

Thought for the Day

Since the sinful life is "seeing idolatrously in self-absorption," I need transformation to "see iconically, as always relating towards God."

Prayer

Open my eyes, that I may see glimpses of truth thou hast for me ... open my eyes—illumine me, Spirit divine!
—CLARA H. SCOTT

MARCH 18: LEARNING IN THE SCHOOL OF SILENCE

Bernard of Clairvaux (1096–1153), great Cistercian reformer and one of the
most influential leaders of the church, writes to Oger, Canon Regular of Mont-
Saint-Eloi, near Arras, France, a learned scholar who had resigned from a
position of leadership. Note that silence has always had a central importance
in Cistercian spirituality [see entries for December 21].

I feel you may be annoyed or at least surprised that I answered your long letter with only a short note. But I beg you to remember those words of the Wise Man [i.e. in the book of Ecclesiastes], "All things have their season: there is a time for speaking and a time for keeping silence." And what time would there be for silence if conversation claimed even these holy days of Lent, and a sort of conversation all the more laborious for being so engrossing? When we are together it is possible quickly to say what we want, but being absent from each other we must laboriously compose what we want to ask or reply. And where, I ask you, is the leisure, where is the quiet of silence even when one is thinking, composing, and writing? You say that all this can be done in silence. I am surprised that you can seriously mean this. For how can the mind be quiet even in the composition of a letter, when the turmoil of expressions are clamoring and every sort of phrase and diversity of senses are jostling with one another? When words spring into the mind, but just the word one wants escapes one; when literary effect, sense, and how to convey a meaning clearly, and what should be said, and in what order it should be said, has to be carefully considered; all the things which those who understand these matters scrutinize carefully? And do you tell me there is any quiet in all this? Can you call this silence, even if the lips are not moving?

It is not only that I have not the time, it is also that the sort of work you want me to do is not suited either to my profession or ability. To lament, not to teach, is the duty of the monk I am supposed to be, and of the sinner that I am. There could not be anything more foolish than for an untaught man, such as I confess I am, to presume to teach what he knows nothing about.... To avoid this, I have flown far away and dwelt in solitude. Like the Prophet I have determined to "take heed to my ways that I sin not with my tongue," for "a glib tongue shall not have its way upon earth"; and again, "the tongue holds the keys of life and death." Isaiah calls silence "the work of justice" and Jeremiah says "it is good to await the salvation of the Lord in silence." Therefore so that I shall not seem entirely to ignore your request I invite and incite you, who by speaking press me to teach what I do not know, and, if not by my teaching, at any rate by the example of my silence … foster (silence) as the guardian of all virtues.

(Even as I write) what am I doing? I wonder you do not laugh. For, while appearing to condemn strongly much speaking, I still continue to pour out words, and in recommending silence I am actually thwarting silence by my verbosity! …

Scripture Meditation

There is a time for everything … a time to be silent, and a time to speak.
—ECCLESIASTES 3:1, 7

Thought for the Day

To be silent before the Lord clarifies the mind and stills the false desires.

Prayer

Silent in the house: all are laid to sleep … Strange Power! I trust thy might; trust thou my constancy.
—EMILY BRONTË

FOLLOWING THE WAY OF THE LORD

*John of Avila (1500–1569) was a great preacher and missioner as well as
friend and spiritual director of Spanish leaders such as Ignatius of Loyola
and Teresa of Avila. He wrote many letters to inquirers,
such as this one written about 1563.*

*D*ear Friend,

You ask me to tell you how to become a good Christian, and I am most
glad to hear your question, for to wish to be a good Christian is to have
already started well on the road. But take care not to resemble the many,
whose knowledge of God's Will, as it does not make them follow it, only
condemns them to more severe punishment; for, as Christ tells us: "That
servant who knows his Master's will and does not get ready or does not
do what his Master wants will be beaten with many blows" (Luke 12:47).
Therefore, to ask to be shown the way of God is to lay oneself under no
small obligation, but as I believe you wish to learn it with the full intention of practicing all that it involves, it is my duty to direct you in it....

What we need, above all things, is a new heart, but this is the last
thing we should think ourselves capable of obtaining by our own
power. No man has faith who does not believe that he has received his
being from God; neither has he faith, who thinks that any other than
the Almighty can give him strength to become good, for holiness is a
higher gift than mere existence. Those who imagine they can attain to
holiness by any wisdom or strength of their own will find themselves
after many labors, and struggles, and weary efforts, only the farther
from possessing it, and this in proportion to their certainty that they of
themselves have gained it.

Humility and self-contempt will obtain our wish far sooner than will
stubborn pride. Though God is so exalted, his eyes regard the lowly, both
in heaven and on earth, and we shall strive in vain to please him in any
other way than by abasing ourselves.

The Son of God came down from heaven and taught us by his life and
words the way to heaven, and that way is humility, as he said: "He who

humbles himself will be exalted" (Luke 18:14). Therefore, if you wish God to give you a new heart, you must first of all amend your deeds, and then lament your faults and accurse yourself of your sins. Do not extenuate your defects, but judge yourself justly; let not your self-love blind you, but when conscience accuses you of wrong, do not forget it, but keep it before your eyes and manifest it to Jesus Christ, your savior and physician. Weep for it before him, and he will comfort you without fail. No force can prevail with a Father like the tears of his child, nor is there anything which so moves God to grant us, not justice, but mercy, as our sorrow and self-accusation. Call upon the Almighty, for he will not be deaf to your cries; show him your wounded soul, for you have not to deal with one who is blind; speak to him of all your miseries, for he is merciful and will heal them.

Scripture Meditation

How great is your goodness, which you have stored up for those who fear you, which you bestow … on those who take refuge in you.
—PSALM 31:19

Thought for the Day

Receiving a "new heart" is never within human capacities; it is solely God's gift to us.

Prayer

Have your own way, Lord! Have your own way! … till all shall see Christ only, always, living in me!
—ADELAIDE A. POLLARD

MARCH 20: A PILGRIM, NOT A VAGRANT

*Sir Robert Southwell (1561–1595) hid in England as a Jesuit priest
and a preacher until he was discovered, arrested, imprisoned for three years,
and martyred but not before gaining a reputation as
a wise and gentle spiritual director.*

I am much grieved to hear of your unsettled way of life, visiting many people, at home with none. We are all, I acknowledge, pilgrims, but not vagrants; our life is uncertain, but not our road. The curse made Cain a vagabond and wandered upon the earth. Conscience wounded by sin renders life also uneasy. Inconstancy is a disease of the mind, always changing to new places, never able to find a holy thought wherein it can rest. Variety of company is the mother of idleness and instability, and is more apt to corrupt than to perfect the disposition, however good. Who is more sunburned than he who is always traveling? A change of objects maybe feeds the eyes, but they suffer heavier damage from the wind and dust. Virtue is seldom found in the highway, and rare is the company from which you come forth more innocent. Experience is dear, if bought with danger to a good life. It is better to be ignorant of other men's manners, than to be a stranger at home. It is difficult to adapt one canvas to so many different models.

Diversity begets confusion, but perfects not art. It is difficult to imitate even one thing correctly. Graft your thoughts into some good stock, suck the sap from a fruitful root. Change of juices does not ripen, but rots the fruit. He who is familiar with all is friend to none. You will never be your own, if always with everybody. Among many strangers you will have but few friends. Transplant not your mind into such varieties; suffer it to take root in some one soil. Plants frequently transplanted sooner wither than blossom. It is an unwholesome appetite that tastes of everything and relishes nothing. He who sips of all and sticks to none is unsteady of heart. Recall then your senses. Restrain your wandering mind. Think upon a new course. Count yourself worthy of something to which you may in future adhere. Be at home somewhere, and there live by rule; then go forth to other places, like a guest looking towards home. Imitate the bees which suck the honey from the flowers, and immediately return to the hive, and there go about domestic duties, which begin with prudence and end with profit....

Learn while at home how to behave in company, and instruct your mind how to nourish in secret holy thoughts, which in the exercise of every virtue will prove to you sweeter than all possible delights; wherewith may you live both a long and a holy life (which from my heart I wish you). Farewell.

Scripture Meditation

Therefore, my dear brothers, stand firm. Let nothing move you. Always give yourselves fully to the work of the Lord, because you know that your labor in the Lord is not in vain.
—1 CORINTHIANS 15:58

Thought for the Day

Today the moral danger of many Christians is not so much to be "vagrants" but "tourists of the faith."

Prayer

Keep me safe, O God, for in you I take refuge.
—PSALM 16:1

MARCH 21: THE JOURNEY OF FAITH IS PURIFYING

In 1861 Frances Ridley Havergal [see entry for January 29] was asked by her married sister to act as governess for her two young nieces and live with the family. During this time because of delicate health, Frances

oscillated between the sunshine and the shadows of depression. She writes
the following letter in 1865.

*D*earest,

I had hoped that a kind of table-land had been reached in my journey, where I might walk awhile in the light, without the weary
succession of rock and hollow, crag and morass, stumbling and striving;
but I seem borne back into all the old difficulties of the way, with many
sin-made aggravations. I think the great root of all my trouble and
alienation is that I do not now make an unreserved surrender of myself
to God; and until this is done I shall know no peace. I am sure of it. I
have so much to regret: a greater dread of the opinion of worldly
friends, a loving of the world, and proportionate cooling in heavenly
desire and love. A power utterly new and unexpected was given me
[singing and composition of music], and rejoicing in this I forgot the
Giver, and found such delight in this that other things paled before it.
It need not have been so; and, in better moments, I prayed that if it
were indeed hindering me, the gift of song might be withdrawn. And
now that through my ill health it is so, and that the pleasure of public
applause when singing in the Philharmonic concerts is not again to
exercise its delicious delusion, I do thank him who heard my prayer.
But I often pray in the dark, as it were, and feel no response from
above. Is this to test me? Oh that I may be preserved from giving up in
despair, and yielding, as I so often do, to the floodtide enemy.

I want to make the most of my life and to do the best with it, but here
I feel my desires and motives need much purifying; for, even where all
would sound fair enough in words, an element of self, of lurking pride,
may be detected. Oh, that he would indeed purify me and make me
white at any cost! No one professing to be a Christian at all could possibly have had a more cloudy, fearing, doubting, sinning, and wandering
heart history than mine has been through many years

Scripture Meditation
O that I had the wings of a dove! I would fly away and be at rest.
—PSALM 55:6

Thought for the Day

While we waver in our desire and faithfulness, Christ is our rock.

Prayer

Listen to my prayer, O God, do not ignore my plea; ... my thoughts trouble me.

—PSALMS 55:1–2

MARCH 22: THE LAMB, OUR WAY

Catherine of Siena (1347–1380) became the voice of conscience for the church in crisis during the Great Schism. She wrote courageous letters of rebuke, encouragement, and peacemaking to many of its leaders. In this bold letter to the King of France, Charles V, Catherine of Siena writes from Avignon, the scene of the schism of the church, which she had visited.

Dearest lord and father in Christ, sweet Jesus: I Catherine, servant and slave of the servants of Christ write to you in his precious Blood:

This sweet Lamb, our Way, has despised the world, with all its luxuries and dignity, and has hated vice and loved virtue. Do you, as son and faithful servant of Christ crucified, follow his footsteps and the way which he teaches you: bear in true patience all pain, torment, and tribulation which God permits the world to inflict on you. For patience is not overcome, but overcomes the world. Be a lover of virtue, founded in true and holy justice, and despise vice. I beg you, by love of Christ crucified, to do in your state three especial things. The first is, to despise the world and yourself and all its joys, possessing your kingdom as a thing lent to you, and not your own. For well you know that neither life nor health nor riches nor honor nor dignity nor lordship is your own. Were they yours, you could possess them in your own way. But in such an hour a man wishes to be well, he is ill; or living, and he is dead; or rich, and he is poor; or a lord, and he is made a servant and vassal. All this is because these things are not his own, and he can only hold them in so far as may please him who has lent them to him. Very simple-minded, then, is the man who holds the things of another as his own. He is really a thief, and worthy of death. Therefore I beg you that, as The Wise, you should act like a good steward, made his steward by God; possessing all things as merely lent to you.

Scripture Meditation

Blessed are the peacemakers, for they will be called sons of God.
—MATTHEW 5:9

Thought for the Day

Being a peacemaker may mean being morally courageous for God's sake.

Prayer

Extol the LORD, O Jerusalem; praise your God, O Zion.
—PSALM 147:12

MARCH 23: THE DESERT AS THE PATHWAY TO GOD'S WILL

*Fr. Rene Voillaume [see entries for February 16 and 17] continues his letters
to the Little Brothers. They had chosen to live in "the deserts" not of the
Sahara, but of the great cities of the world.*

Our Lord's visits to the desert were intimately connected with his mission as Savior. It was in the desert that he confronted the total cost of that mission: the proclamation of the gospel and his death for his people and for mankind. The nights he spent in prayer, amidst his crowded life, also formed part of his mission as Savior. This prayer, together with the adoration of his Father, is the complete expression of his function as Redeemer, incorporating the totality of his mission and his responsibility for the salvation of mankind. The temptations to which he was subjected by Satan prove this, and also those nights of prayer before he chose his apostles and in the Garden of Gethsemane. This was prayer in its absolute reality; our Lord was alone, neither eating nor working, alone before God. The apostles and the saints chosen by God for some great work of evangelization experienced some similar states of prayer: St. Paul in the Arabian desert, Francis of Assisi in his various hermitages, especially at Alverno.

If then, the desert is to be a pathway to God, it must be welcomed by a mind that has really abdicated worldly desires. That inner stripping of desire by which our poverty should lead us is now a necessity if the desert is not to crush us but becomes an emancipation in our journey towards God. It is also in the desert that we can make a periodic clearance of those illusions which prevent us from obtaining a clear view of all the things that clutter our heart. Traveling in the desert soon becomes impossible if one's heart is not open and unattached, and if one continues to expect from life something that only God can give. That is why temptations are used to make ourselves useful to others ... through the example of our lives. So the temptation, for instance, to establish God's reign by any other means than those employed by our Lord himself, can ultimately only be overcome, as our Lord overcame them, in the desert.

Scripture Meditation

*Can God spread a table in the desert? ... Can he also give us
food? Can he supply meat for his people?*
—PSALMS 78:19–20

Thought for the Day

Our desolations, or "deserts," can be the sphere God uses to free us from
our fantasies.

Prayer

*Who is this coming up from the desert leaning on her lover? ...
Come away, my lover, and be like a gazelle or like a young stag
on the spice-laden mountains.*
—SONG OF SONGS 8:5, 14

MARCH 24: CLOTHED WITH THE SYMBOLS OF LIFE IN THE DESERT

*Evagrius Ponticus (d. 399) dwelt as a monastic leader in the Egyptian desert
and was the first to organize the sayings of the Desert Fathers into a coherent
system. In this letter to Anatolius, he explains the clothing worn by the desert
monks, as expressive of their conflicts with the Devil.*

Anatolius my dearest brother,

Recently you wrote to me here in Scete, from the Holy Mountain, to
request an explanation of the symbolism of the habit of the monks who
live in Egypt. You have well understood that not without purpose is this

227

habit made in a form so very different from what other men employ for the style of their clothes. So let me go on to tell you what I have learned about these matters from the holy Fathers.

The cowl [a child's dress in late antiquity] is a symbol of the charity of God our Savior. It protects the most important part of the body and keeps us, who are children in Christ, warm. Thus it can be said to afford protection against those who attempt to strike and wound us. Consequently, all who wear this cowl on their heads sing these words aloud: "If the Lord does not build the house and keep the city, unavailingly does the builder labor and the watchman stand his guard." Such words as these instill humility and root out that long-standing evil which is pride and which caused Lucifer, who rose like the day-star in the morning, to be cast down to the earth.

That the monks go with their hands bare is a symbol of a life lived free of all hypocrisy. For vainglory has a frightful power to cover over and cast virtues into the shade. Ever searching out praise from men, it banishes faith. Our Lord has put it very well: "How can you believe when you get your praise from other men and are not interested in the praise that God alone gives?" The good must be pursued for its own sake, not for some other cause....

The scapular, which has the form of a cross, and covers the shoulders of the monks is a symbol of faith in Christ. This raises up the meek, removes obstacles and provides for free, untrammeled activity.

The belt they wear about their loins signifies their rejection of all impurity ... fleeing from avarice, the mother of idolatry.

They carry a staff that is the tree of life, affording secure footing to those who hold on to it. It allows them to support themselves upon it as upon the Lord.

Scripture Meditation

We groan, longing to be clothed with our heavenly dwelling, because when we are clothed, we will not be found naked.
—2 CORINTHIANS 5:2–3

Thought for the Day

Being clothed of God is our greatest need, for since the Fall, humanity has been naked in unrighteousness.

Prayer

> O LORD my God, you are very great; you are clothed with splendor and majesty.
>
> —PSALM 104:1

RESISTING THE REALM OF TEMPTATION

MARCH 25: UNDERSTANDING OUR DOMINANT TEMPTATIONS

Evagrius Ponticus [see previous entry] further categorizes the evil thoughts that a solitary is prone to encounter when left alone with one's inner life. He teaches that all our affective life is indirectly affected by the sin of self-love.

ntolius my dearest Brother,

There are eight general and basic categories of thoughts in which are included every thought. First there is gluttony, then avarice, sadness, anger, *accedia* [i.e. boredom], sadness, vainglory and last of all, pride. It is not in our power to determine whether we are disturbed by these thoughts, but it is up to us to decide if they are to linger within us or not, and whether or not they are to stir up our passions.

The thought of gluttony suggests to the monk that he give up his ascetic efforts in short order.... The demon of impurity impels one to lust after bodies. It attacks more strenuously those who practice continence, in the hope that they will give up their practice of this virtue, feeling that they gain nothing by it.... Avarice suggests to mind a lengthy old age ... the pinch of poverty, the great shame that comes from accepting the necessities of life from others. Sadness tends to come up at times because of the deprivation of one's desires.... On other occasions it accompanies anger ... the most fierce passion ... defined as a boiling and stirring up of wrath against one who has given injury—or is thought to have done.... Then there comes a time when it persists longer, and is transformed into indignation. But the demon of *accedia*—also called the noonday demon—is the one that causes the most serious trouble of all. He presses his attack upon the monk ... first making it seem that the sun barely moves, if at all, and that the day is fifty hours long.... Then he instills in the heart of the monk a hatred for the place, a hatred for his very life itself ... leaving no leaf unturned to induce the monk to forsake his cell and drop out of the fight.

The spirit of vainglory is most subtle and it readily grows up on souls who practice virtue. It leads them to desire to make their struggles known publicly, to hunt after the praise of men.... The demon of pride is the cause for the most damaging fall for the soul. For it induces the monk to deny that God is his helper and to consider himself the cause of virtuous actions....

Reading, vigils, and prayer—these are the things that lend stability to the wandering mind. Hunger, toil, and solitude are the means of extinguishing the flames of desire. Hot anger is calmed by singing the Psalms, by patience and almsgiving. But all these practices are to be engaged in according to due measure and at the appropriate times.

Scripture Meditation

The acts of the sinful nature are obvious ... those who live like this will not inherit the kingdom of God.
—GALATIANS 5:19, 21

Thought for the Day

It is in the "desert places" of our lives when we can come to most intimate self-knowledge.

Prayer

O LORD, you have searched me and you know me.
—PSALM 139:1

MARCH 26: ADDICTIONS EXPOSED IN THE DESERTS OF LIFE

The author of this letter to the editor wishes to remain anonymous because of her husband's distinguished medical career. She writes on January 11, 2003.

ear Jim,

One morning in 1986 my husband, who is a neurologist, woke early and realized that I was not breathing properly. He took me to the sleep laboratory at the university hospital and I spent the night hooked up to machines. There I was told that I was not receiving 85% of the necessary oxygen to my heart and brain, and that I would be dead in a year if I did not lose the weight I had gained (up to 265 lbs). I was also addicted to prescription drugs and chain-smoked 5–6 packs of cigarettes per day.

They wanted to do an emergency tracheotomy, but I refused because I wanted to die. I had been suicidal for years, but had been too cowardly to do anything about it. I knew that I couldn't lose the weight. I was relieved that the decision was out of my hands, and I went home to die, I even ate more. I was 38 years old.

I also had agoraphobia, and rarely left the house—my social life at this point consisted of twice-weekly visits to my current therapist. I had seen approximately 75 counselors or therapists along the way, and I had to have someone drive me. I slept most of the time, which is how I coped with my clinical depression of 23 years. I came across the term "anestheticae," (despair beyond despair), and that perfectly described me. I had had a sad childhood full of insoluble problems for which I could find no answers. I knew that the Jesus of the Bible had to be the solution, but I had no ability to believe in him. All the doctors told me that there was nothing they could do, and wrote me new prescriptions. I had given up.

But God had other plans for my life. Sometime after I came home from the hospital, I woke early one morning, and walked downstairs to my living room. I took a Bible off the shelf, and opened it to John 1:1. It was if a light appeared under that verse, and suddenly immense joy filled my heart. I had no idea why—I could not in any way understand why the connection of Jesus' Name with the Word and God was so wonderful, I just knew that it was. I woke my husband, and told him that it was going to be all right, and it has been! My life changed dramatically in every way. I lost 153 lbs. in 16 months, and quit the pills and cigarettes in one afternoon. I had no withdrawal symptoms, no seizures or heart problems, just more energy. I went back to school, have traveled the world, and speak publicly. When I go for check-ups, the doctors think they have the wrong chart, and people think my husband has remarried (also part of my miracle is my dear, faithful husband of 34 years).

I was in a dark world without hope, and then I met the One for Whom nothing is impossible, the Lord, Jesus Christ, Who died that I might live. There is not human reason for me to be sitting here writing this letter.

Scripture Meditation

In the beginning was the Word, and the Word was with God, and the Word was God.
—JOHN 1:1

Thought for the Day

The rescue of those "in the despair beyond despair" encourages all of us to reach out in hope.

Prayer

To God be the glory great things he has done!
—FRANCIS CROSBY

MARCH 27: WARFARE WITH THE PASSIONS

St. Theophan the Recluse [see entry for March 6], who had spent time in the deserts of the Near East, experienced there the need of spiritual warfare against our passions. He writes this to a directee.

My Son,

Your inner remaking will begin properly from the time your heart becomes warmed with divine warmth.... But passions are like dampness in firewood. Damp firewood does not burn. Our "firewood" consists of all the faculties of our souls and all the functions of our bodies, but all of these are saturated with dampness—with negative passions.... All of these passions come from the desire to please one's self, selfishness and pride; and they are sustained by these. As soon as a person has denied himself, he is inspired with resolve to please God alone; in this very spiritual act all the passions lose their foothold, and are outside the consciousness and will that they formerly controlled. Once they have lost their foothold, they are deprived of their former distinctive power by which the person was dragged along like a young ass on a cord behind its owner. Formerly, as soon as some passionate enticement appeared, the person immediately tried with all his strength to satisfy it, but this is no longer the case. Now when such enticements appear, instead of hurrying to gratify them as soon as possible, the person immediately rejects them and banishes them from his sight....

For example, there was your righteous indignation or your self-righteous pride, although as far as righteousness goes, they are as unrighteous as anything else. They used to be there, and they controlled you at times almost without your knowing; they appear now and again, but you must not be controlled by them. I would like to say that they will not, because now, through you resoluteness, every power of theirs has been cut off. This happened the moment you decided not to spare yourself for God ... without making concessions. Self-pity is so deceitful; the passions sometimes adopt an attractive form. It would not be unusual if you were to work again for your passions as you used to, although without being fully aware of or observing this....

Be very careful then, how you live—not as unwise but as wise, making the most of every opportunity, because the days are evil (Ephesians 5:15–16). These days are an evil situation, in which we find ourselves, because of the crafty passions that are within us. Be self controlled and alert (1 Peter 5:8).

Scripture Meditation

Be on guard! Be alert!
—MARK 13:33

Thought for the Day

Be wary of how our own materialism and consumerism have almost eliminated living with ascetic disciplines.

Prayer

Almighty God, who sees we have no power of ourselves to help ourselves; keep us both outwardly in our bodies and inwardly in our souls; that we may be defended from all adversities … and all evil thoughts which may hurt the soul; through Jesus Christ our Lord. Amen.

—COLLECT FOR THE SECOND SUNDAY OF LENT

MARCH 28: INTERPRETING THE TEMPTATIONS OF JESUS IN THE WILDERNESS

In his seminal novel, The Brothers Karamazov, *Russian writer Fyodor Dostoevsky (1821–1881) had the Grand Inquisitor represent the rise of "European Socialism," with his condemnation of Jesus' responses to the Devil's temptations in the wilderness. In a letter to V. A. Alekseyev, a soloist with the Marinsky theatre orchestra, Dostoevsky prophetically echoes the scene of the trial of Jesus. The letter, which is continued in the next entry, was written on June 7, 1876, well before the completion of his novel (1880), as his prophetic indictment of Russian socialism.*

*D*ear Sir …

There are three colossal, universal ideas blended together in the devil's Temptation of Christ; and now 18 centuries have gone by and there is nothing more difficult, i.e., more complex, than these ideas, and they have not been worked out even yet.

"Stones and bread" means the social question of the day, a question of *environment*. There is no prophecy here; it has always been this way. [This is Satan speaking.] "Rather than going to the downtrodden beggars, who, suffering from starvation and oppression, look more like wild beasts than human beings, rather than going to the hungry and preaching abstention from sins and humility and chastity—would it not be better to *feed* them first? That would be more humane. Others before you have come to preach, but you are the Son of God, the whole world has been waiting for you with impatience; act then, as One superior to all in intelligence and justice, give them all food, *sustain* them, give them a social organization that will ensure them bread and order forevermore—and only then, ask them to account for their sins. Then, if they will sin, they will be ungrateful, but now, if they sin they do so out of hunger. It is a sin to call them to account....

"You are the Son of God and are therefore omnipotent. Here, you see these stones, they are legion. You have only to will it and the stones shall be turned into loaves of bread.

"Order things, then, so that henceforth the earth will produce without toil, give people the wisdom or show them the order that will guarantee their welfare. Surely you do not doubt that the vices and miseries that afflict man have come from cold, hunger, and poverty and from the impossible struggle for existence."

This is the first idea that the spirit of evil held up to Christ. You must agree that it is one that is quite difficult to deal with. Contemporary *socialism*, both in Europe and here at home, eliminates Christ from everything and is concerned, above all, with *bread*; it calls in science and asserts that the sole cause of all human miseries is *poverty*, the struggle for existence, the "Corrupting environment."

Scripture Meditation

Jesus, full of the Holy Spirit, returned from the Jordan and was led by the Spirit in the desert, where for forty days he was tempted by the devil. He ate nothing during those days, and at the end of them he was hungry. The devil said to him, "If you are the Son of God, tell this stone to become bread."

—LUKE 4:1–3

Thought for the Day

Being tempted is not evil, but falling into temptation is evil.

Prayer

Our Father in heaven ... lead us not into temptation, but deliver us from the evil one.
—MATTHEW 6: 9, 13

MARCH 29: JESUS REVEALS HIS SONSHIP BY HIS REBUTTAL OF TEMPTATION

Dostoevsky continues his discussion of Jesus' temptations in the desert.

[W]hen] Christ answered, "Man does not live by bead alone"—i.e., he gave expression to the axiom that man is spiritual in origin. The idea of the devil could apply only to man as a beast. But Christ knew that bread alone does not bring life to man. And if, besides bread, man is not possessed of a spiritual life, an ideal of beauty, he will languish and die, go insane, kill himself, or abandon himself to pagan fantasies. And since Christ carried the ideal of beauty in himself and in his Word, he decided that it was better to inculcate in the soul of man the ideal of beauty; bearing it in their souls, all men would become brothers and then, of course, they would work for one another and would all be rich. Whereas, if they are given bread, they will become enemies to one another out of sheer boredom.

But what if they are given both beauty and bread at the same time? Then man would be deprived of *labor*, of *individuality*, of the opportunity to *sacrifice his goods for the sake of his neighbor* — in a word, he would be deprived of life as such, the ideal of life. And therefore, it is best to do only one thing: to proclaim the spiritual ideal.

The proof that this is precisely the meaning of that short passage in the Gospels, and not merely that Christ was hungry and the Devil advised him to pick up a stone and will that to become bread — the proof lies precisely in Christ's answer, revealing the mystery of human nature: "Man does not live by bread alone" [i.e., merely as an animal].

If the question had been simply one of satisfying Christ's hunger, would there have been any reason to broach the subject of man's spiritual nature in general? Besides, Christ did not have to wait for the Devil's advice on how to obtain bread. He could have obtained it before if He had chosen to. By the way, remember Darwin's and other contemporary theories about man's descent from the ape. Without going into any theories, Christ declares directly that, besides belonging to the animal world, man also belongs to the spiritual world. Well then, it does not really matter what man's origins are (the Bible does not explain how God molded him out of clay or carved him out of a stone), but it does say that God *breathed life into him.* (But what is bad is that by sinning man can once again turn into a beast.)

Your obedient servant, F. Dostoevsky

PS: According to my observations, these very socialists, awaiting a socialist order in which there will be no individual responsibility, meanwhile love money tremendously and attach even excessive value to it, precisely because of the idea they have of it.

Scripture Meditation

Man does not live on bread alone, but on every word that comes from the mouth of God.
— MATTHEW 4:4

Thought for the Day

Help me realize every day that I am a child of God.

Prayer

And lead us not into temptation, but deliver us from the evil one.
—MATTHEW 6:13

MARCH 30: TEMPTATIONS EARLY RESISTED
IN CHRIST'S NAME ARE EASIER TO OVERCOME

---

*Thomas à Kempis (1380–1471), in this letter from around 1467, echoes the
counsel he has also expressed in his classic devotional text,* The Imitation
of Christ. *There he said, "We must be especially watchful against temptation
at the beginning of it, for the enemy is more easily overcome if he is not
allowed to enter into the door of our hearts, but resisted at
the very gate of his first knocking."*

My Brother, beloved in Christ,

You see how cautiously you ought to walk, since the days are evil.
Great caution should be observed by a servant of God in all his words
and works. For whoever does not exercise some forethought in his
affairs, will very soon either receive or do some hurt. And whoever in
the beginning has been either negligent or rash, will feel great loss in
the end....

Wherefore let your eye go before all your actions, and do everything
with foresight. Do not busy yourself with other people's matters and
neglect yourself; because no one is wiser than the one whose soul is
always in his own hands.... For the more prone one is to consider others, the more indisposed that one will be to look after one's self. Would
you have peace, then dwell in Zion. For it is profitable for those who
cannot find rest in this world to flee unto God, and to desire to be with
Christ, since there is no one to fight for us except he who made us....

Sometimes anger, pride, or at other times lust, will vehemently inflame our heart. But when this is so, with the shield of prayer, contrition of heart, and by calling upon the holy name of Jesus, you can look steadfastly to heaven, whence your help comes.

Scripture Meditation

See, I lay a stone in Zion, a tested stone, a precious cornerstone for a sure foundation; the one who trusts will never be dismayed.
—ISAIAH 28:16

Thought for the Day

Preoccupation with Christ, our Messiah, will protect us always.

Prayer

O gracious Jesus, help me at this present time ... what can I do without you!
—THOMAS À KEMPIS

MARCH 31: MANNA IN THE WILDERNESS

Thomas à Kempis [see previous entry] elaborates to another correspondent on the promise given by the Apostle John in his letter to the church of Pergamum concerning the promise of the "Hidden Manna" to those, who tempted, remain faithful in the journey of life.

*D*earest Brother,

Today the Lord came to meet his beggar, with the sweet bread of heaven. A discourse exceedingly savory and gracious was poured into mine ears. A long lesson out of the Book of the Revelation of St. John was read aloud, but … only one short verse was retained by me.… "He who has an ear, let him hear what the Spirit says to the churches. To him who overcomes, I will give some of the hidden manna. I will also give him a white stone with a new name written on it, known only to him who receives it" [Rev. 2:17].

The outward, carnal, natural man, he also who is lifted up in himself, is not able, therefore, to understand the secrets of Divine Revelation, as St. Paul attests.… But for those who have received the first fruits of the Spirit, cannot be ignorant of what this Hidden Manna is. For by tasting, rather than by reading or hearing, they have learnt what it is.

This Manna is given to the beloved Children, who serving the Father out of filial love, study to be always doing his will, and advancing his glory. And if you are not averse to receive what I offer, know that the Manna here promised describes the interior sweetness of the mind, or the consolation of the Saints in this life.…

The Israelites were nourished with this food as long as they were in the wilderness, even till they arrived at the land of promise; and as long as the Elect are sojourners in the world, so long are they nourished with the Bread of Life and spiritual understanding.…

Scripture Meditation

To him who overcomes, I will give some of the hidden manna. I will also give him a white stone with a new name written on it, known only to him who receives it.

—REVELATION 2:17

Thought for the Day

Thomas à Kempis shared this insight: "To walk inwardly with God, and not be kept abroad by any outward affection, is the state of a spiritual person."

Prayer

Lord, … I would rather choose to be a pilgrim on earth with you, than to possess heaven without you. Where you are is heaven; and where you are not, is death and hell.

—THOMAS À KEMPIS

MOVEABLE SEASON
OF EASTER

*A*ll the feasts of the Christian church are celebrated on Sundays, so we count the duration of Advent, Epiphany, Lent, Easter, and Pentecost by their number of Sundays.

Indeed, Maundy Thursday or "Mandate Day" commemorates the command of our Lord to partake of the sacrament of the Lord's Supper after the celebration of the Passover. Easter has been fixed in the church's calendar as the first Sunday after the full moon. This moveable date was determined by the astronomers of Alexandria. It became the practice for the bishop of Alexandria to announce to all the churches in Christendom the date of Easter for the coming year. It is probable that Athanasius, bishop of Alexandria, wrote forty-two Easter pastoral letters from AD 329 onwards, although some are now only fragments of the originals. But he is emphatic that the spiritual significance of Easter is the focus of each letter, not the astronomical date, which he merely mentions on each annual occasion.

ENTERING INTO THE
SIGNIFICANCE OF EASTER

WHY IS EASTER A SACRAMENTAL CELEBRATION?

Augustine of Hippo [see letter for December 19] writes two letters to
Januarius, otherwise unknown, collated in this response on why Easter is a
sacramental celebration and Christmas day is not.

It is vital to realize that our Lord Jesus Christ, as he states in the gospel, put us under an easy yoke and a light burden. So he put his new people together, under only a few sacraments, easy to celebrate, and yet so rich in meaning. Such is baptism, celebrated in the name of the Trinity, and the Eucharist, celebrating his blood and body given for us; and there are a few others prescribed in the Scriptures. But God's ancient people were in servitude to many more, needed perhaps because of the state of their hearts, described in the five books of Moses, and whose abused practices the prophets later denounced.

Also, there are events we celebrate universally by tradition, unwritten, yet preserved by the apostles, and promoted by the plenary councils of the Church. Such are: the Lord's passion, his resurrection, his ascension into heaven, and the coming of the Holy Spirit from heaven, celebrated every year with special solemnity.... Other practices have evolved in diverse times, places, and ethnically, such as some fasting on Saturday, receiving communion every day, or offering daily Mass, or doing both only on Saturday and Sunday, or only on Sunday, etc.... My advice then, would be that you follow the practice of the local church wherever you happen to be ... as I was advised by my own wise mentor, Ambrose, of blessed memory....

But you also ask me why the annual remembrance of the Lord's passion doesn't fall on the same day every year (like Christmas) ... this is because the day of our Lord's birth is not celebrated as a sacrament, but as a festal day. Whereas a sacrament is present in a celebration when the commemoration of the event is personally significant and applied to oneself. When we celebrate *Pasch*, or what we now call Easter, we are not just recalling the event itself, that Christ died then rose again, but that this event has become eventful and actualizing for us. As the apostle puts it: Christ "died for our trespasses and rose for our justification." Easter we may say is when we experience our own passing from death into life, in the light of our Lord's passion and resurrection.

The meaning of *Pasch* further brings this out. It is not a Greek word, nor does it mean "passion" or "to suffer" as popularly assumed. It is a Hebrew word *Pesach,* or Aramaic *Pascha*, meaning to "pass over" or Passover. The apostle emphasizes this, by saying: "When Jesus saw that his hour was come, that he should depart (lit. "Pass over") from this world to the Father ..." then Jesus gave them the sacramental meal. For as Jesus was "passing over" from this life into the next, so too his disciples are to pass from death into life eternal. By faith then, this "passing over" continues in the faith experience of every believer, for now "the just shall live by faith," and "faith works by love," and "our old self has been crucified with him." ... God too, has "raised us up with Christ, and made us sit with him in the heavenly places." ... So we are "to seek the things which are above, where Christ is seated at the right hand of God ... and to set our minds on things that are above, not on the things which are on earth." ... For now we are body of our Lord Jesus Christ, "the first-born from the dead," since the body of which he is the head is nothing else than the Church.

Scripture Meditation

Christ, our Passover lamb, has been sacrificed for us. Therefore let us keep the festival.
— I CORINTHIANS 5:7

Thought for the Day

This world in its present form is passing away (1 Cor. 7:31). How then does Easter help us to not be engrossed in this passing world?

Prayer

Father, the time has come. Glorify your Son, that your Son may glorify you.
—JOHN 17:1

ASH WEDNESDAY: BEGINNING THE SEASON OF EASTER

---

*Baron von FriedrichHugel (1852–1925), son of an Austrian diplomat and
Scottish mother, was a Catholic philosopher, who, like Charles de Foucauld,
had been given spiritual direction by Abbe Huevelin. He writes this letter on
Shrove Tuesday, February 17, 1920, to his niece Gwendolen.*

My darling Child,

I want this letter to reach you on Ash Wednesday, when we all start
Lent, because there is one little practice I should like to dwell upon for
a minute, in case you have not yet waken up to it, or that you require,
perhaps, a little encouragement in it. I mean the practice of some little voluntary renunciation. I know well, of course, my Gwen, how
much vague and airy wisdom oozes out of the comfortable and shal-
low modern mind about this. But then you see, we have the *little* (!)
examples of the Baptist in the wilderness, with his wild honey and
locusts meal; Our Lord's Fast of forty days; St. Paul's mastery of his
body; and really, without a break, the asceticism of all the great saints.
I say this not to suggest anything special in your food, sleep or dress;
and as to the amount of church, half an hour a day will be enough, and
it would be unwise to add to it, even in Lent. But I am thinking of
something without thinking *what*—that would correspond, say, to my
not buying any books for myself during Lent. Depend upon it, such little self-checks—checks on good propensities, and checks
self-imposed—where they spring from love, really feed love. They are
good things and still useful to your spiritual growth.

Loving old, Father-Uncle.

Scripture Meditation

*When you fast, put oil on your head and wash your face, so that
it will not be obvious to men that you are fasting, but only to your
Father, who is unseen; and your Father, who sees what is done in
secret, will reward you.*

—MATTHEW 6:17–18

Thought for the Day

Fasting is not undertaken to despise the body, but to suppress greed and creatively to make our lives more spiritual and less carnal.

Prayer

O Lord, who for our sake didst fast forty days and forty nights: Give us grace to use such abstinence, that, our flesh being subdued to the Spirit, we may ever obey thy godly motions in righteousness and true holiness, to thy honor and glory.... Amen.
—COLLECT FOR THE FIRST SUNDAY IN LENT

PALM SUNDAY:
ANTICIPATING AN ETERNAL PALM SUNDAY

Aelred of Rievaulx [see letter of February 5], Cistercian Abbot of Rievaulx in Yorkshire in the twelfth century, writes to his sister late i n his life, date unknown.

Let the glorious procession go into the high Jerusalem, the everlasting city of heaven. Christ himself will be at its head, and all the members of his Body that are gathered together in him shall follow in his train. There the glorious King shall reign in them, and they in him. And they shall receive the kingdom of eternal bliss as their inheritance that was prepared for them even before the world was created. We cannot know what that kingdom will be like, and so how can we write about it? But this I know for sure, and I make so bold as to say—that you will lack nothing that you desire, and you will not have anything that you would rather be without. There shall be no weeping nor wailing, no sorrow nor dread, no discord nor envy, no tribulation nor temptation. There will be no such thing as corruption, suspicion or ambition; no such things as the sickness of old age, death or poverty; no trace of need or weariness or faintness. And where none of these things is to be found, what else may there be but perfect joy and mirth and peace; perfect security, and unmarred love and charity; perfect riches, beauty and rest; health and strength and the perfect sight of God? And in that everlasting and perpetual life what more could you want?

There shall we see the Father in the Son, the Son in the Father, and the Holy Ghost in them both. There God our creator will be seen, not as in a mirror or in darkness, but face to face, as the Gospel says. For God will be seen as he is, when the promise that he made in the Gospel is fulfilled: "Who loves Me shall be loved by My Father, and I shall love him and show him My own self." It is from this clear sight of him that the blissful knowledge comes, of which Christ speaks in the Gospel: "This is eternal life, that they may know Thee, the one true God, and Jesus Christ whom Thou didst send." From this knowledge there springs so great a fervor of blissful desire, so much fullness of love, so much sweetness of charity, that the completeness of bliss may not take away the joyful desire, nor may the desire stand in the way of completeness. And how can we say all this in a few words? Surely, sister, it is in this way: "Eye hath not seen, nor ear heard, what God has made ready for those who love Him."

Scripture Meditation

As [Jesus] approached Jerusalem and saw the city, he wept over it.
—LUKE 19:41

Thought for the Day

In the momentary triumphs of ephemeral acclaim, do we weep over the true situations of life that are estranged from God?

Prayer

It was but now their sounding clamors sung,
"Blessed is he that comes from the Most High"

And all the mountains with "Hosanna" rung,
And now, "Away with him, away," they cry,
And nothing can be heard but "Crucify!"
—GILES FLETCHER

MONDAY BEFORE EASTER: KEEPING THE FAST RIGHTEOUSLY

In this first Easter letter of Athanasius (296–373), written in the spring of AD
329, he began a tradition of announcing the date of Easter to all the
churches, as well as writing an extensive pastoral letter in which
he shared his own reflections.

*D*ear brothers and sisters,

It is our obligation to remember and be aware of the significance of the event of Easter every year. As Paul admonishes Timothy: "Be prepared, in season and out of season" (2 Tim. 4:2). I interpret that to mean Timothy was to be ready to do the things he was supposed to do, and not be in default of doing things at the wrong time. For God has set the times and seasons for everything (Eccl. 3:1), so that in due time salvation would be brought to people everywhere. Thus at the right time "the Wisdom of God, our Savior Jesus Christ appeared (1 Cor. 1: 24). Many had been praying for his coming, saying with the Psalmist, "O that salvation would come out of Zion" (Ps. 14:7) … for the same reason the blessed apostle Paul urged us to keep Easter, the season of our salvation, when he said: "Behold, now is the accepted time, now is the day of salvation" (2 Cor. 6:2).

In Old Testament times, the Lord called Israel with the call of the trumpet, sometimes to celebrate, or to fast, or on occasion for war. The trumpet call was reserved for serious occasions, so that the people would respond accordingly ... sometimes for war ... against the spiritual forces of the wickedness in the heavenly places" (Eph. 6:12).... Sometimes the call is to fasting, and sometimes to a feast. Prophetically, Paul "blows the trumpet" when he declares: "Christ our Passover has been sacrificed for us; therefore let us keep the feast, not with the old leaven, nor with the leaven of malice and wickedness" (1 Cor. 5:7, 8). And there was an even greater trumpet call than all of these, when our Savior "on the last day, the great day of the feast, Jesus stood up and cried saying, 'If any man thirst, let him come to me and drink'" (John 7:37).

Since then, as I have pointed out, there are many kinds of proclamation. Let us obey the trumpet of the prophet: "Blow a trumpet in Zion, consecrate a fast" (Joel 2:15). This is a warning trumpet, which commands us solemnly that we should fast in a holy manner, for God is holy and has his pleasure only in a holy people.... So the apostle tells us how some dishonor God ... going through the motions of a fast, but their hearts are still polluted by doing evil against others, or daring to cheat God, or act in many other unrighteous ways.

Remember the parable of the Pharisee who fasted twice a week. But his fasting did him no good, simply because he considered himself better than the Publican. He had quite forgotten the admonition of the prophet Isaiah: "Your fasting ends in quarreling and strife, and in striking each other ... you cannot fast as you do today and expect your voice to be heard on high. Is this the kind of fast I have chosen, only a mere day for one to humble himself? ... is this what you call a fast, a day acceptable unto the Lord?" (Isa. 58:4, 5)....

Therefore, brothers and sisters, let us nourish our souls with divine food, Jesus Christ the Word. And fasting with both body and soul, as God desires, let us keep this great and saving fast as we should....

Scripture Meditation

Therefore let us keep the Festival, not with the old yeast, the yeast of malice and wickedness, but with bread without yeast, the bread of sincerity and truth.
— 1 Corinthians 5:8

Thought for the Day

To enter truly into the Easter season is to be transformed by the Lord of Easter.

Prayer

Lord, I seek you with all my heart, with all the strength you have given me. I long to understand that which I believe.
—AUGUSTINE OF HIPPO

TUESDAY BEFORE EASTER: KEEPING THE PASSOVER RIGHTEOUSLY

Athanasius continues with his fourth Easter letter of AD 332. He was delayed in writing this by his visit to Constantinople to answer his false accusers and then by illness. The letter was sent ahead of him, but he only arrived personally in Alexandria midway through the Easter fast.

know this letter is late, dear brothers and sisters. Forgive my delay, caused by my being so far from home, and my long subsequent illness. Unusual storms further delayed the letter, but be assured you were not forgotten in spite of these circumstances. For it is my duty to announce the date of the Easter Feast. Nor should you think the letter is ill-timed for our enemies have been put to shame and reproved by the church, because they persecuted us unjustly. So we can sing the triumphant song Israel sang against Pharaoh: "We will sing unto the Lord, for he has triumphed gloriously; the horse and his rider he has thrown into the sea" (Ex. 15:1). So we progress as usual, from feast to feast. And once again it is holy self-examination that stirs up our minds, and which keeps our consciences on guard to dwell on good things....

Our Feast does not relate only to time, but to eternity. It is a heavenly Feast! We do not announce it as a shadow, or a symbol, or a type, for it is the real thing. Israel ate the meat of a dumb lamb to complete the Passover, and having done so, smeared the doorposts with the blood, laughing at their destroyer. But we eat of the Word of the Father, the Son our Savior. We have the lintels of our hearts sealed with the blood of the New Covenant (Matt. 26:28).... Death does not reign anymore! Instead of death there is life, as our Lord has now said: "I am the life"! (John 14:6) ... now death and the devil's kingdom are conquered, filling us with joy and gladness....

What follows, my dear brothers and sisters, is that we do not come to such a feast with filthy garments, but with our consciences clothed now with pure garments. We put on the Lord Jesus Christ, so we can celebrate the Feast with him. This we demonstrate by loving and actively engaged in virtue ... and righteousness ... having strength of mind ... not forgetting the poor, with doors open to all, promoting humility by the hatred of pride, and putting all erotic fantasies to death.... No longer is the Feast kept figuratively only in Jerusalem.... For the New Feast is held wherever God wishes it, for "in every place incense and a sacrifice might be offered to Him" (Mal. 1:11). Likewise, when our Savior made the change from type to reality, He gave them the promise of the New Covenant, that they would no longer eat the flesh of a lamb, but His own: "Take, eat, and drink; this is My body and My blood" (Matt. 26:26–28). So when we are nourished by his body and blood, properly, we keep the Feast of the Passover.

Scripture Meditation

For whenever you eat this bread and drink this cup, you proclaim the Lord's death until he comes.

— I CORINTHIANS 11:26

Thought for the Day

Let us eat and drink worthily by a life lived for Christ.

Prayer

Let me always remember you, love you, meditate upon you, and
pray to you, until you restore me to your perfect image.
— AUGUSTINE OF HIPPO

WEDNESDAY BEFORE EASTER: KEEPING THE FEAST APPROPRIATELY

Athanasius wrote this, his sixth Easter letter, in AD 334.

*O*nce again, dear friends, God has brought us to the Easter season. By
his covenant love we are gathered for that purpose. For the same God
who brought Israel out of Egypt, now calls us to the Feast, as he called
Moses to celebrate it (Deut. 16:1), and as the prophet called Israel, saying "Celebrate your festivals, O Judah, and fulfill your vows" (Nah.
1:15). So if God himself loves the Feast, and calls us to it, it is wrong for
us to postpone it, or to observe it thoughtlessly. Rather we should come
to it eagerly and zealously so that we make a joyful beginning, as a
foretaste of the Heavenly Feast that is to come.... As our Lord says: "I
have eagerly desired to eat this Passover with you before I suffer. For
I tell you I will not eat again until it finds fulfillment in the kingdom of
God" (Luke 22:15–16).

There are three ways in which we "keep the Feast." Firstly, when we
truly know what it is all about. Secondly, when we acknowledge the
Deliverer. And thirdly, when we respond to his grace. As the Apostle
Paul exhorted us: "Therefore let us keep the Festival, not with the old
yeast, the yeast of malice and wickedness, but with bread without yeast,
the bread of sincerity and truth" (1 Cor. 5:8). Our Lord has died so that
we could be freed from doing those things that lead to death. He gave

us his life so that our own might be rescued from the devil's traps. The Word became incarnate so that we could be freed from the control of sin, enabled to worship truly, God who is a spirit, in the Spirit (Rom. 8:9–13).... In our Lord's time the Jews thought they were celebrating the Passover, but they did so in vain when they persecuted the Lord himself. So by their own testimony they called it the Passover of the Jews, not the Lord's Passover (John 6:4). Yes, it was so-called because they denied the Lord of the Passover, and that is why the Lord turning his face from them, declaring: "My soul hates your new moons and your Sabbaths" (Isa. 1:14).

The Lord would rebuke us also, if like the ten lepers who were healed, we remain thankless ... thinking more about the cure they were given, than about the One who had healed them. "But one of them when he saw he was healed, came back, praising God in a loud voice" and falling at the feet of Jesus. He was a Samaritan (Luke 17:19). You see those who give thanks and who glorify God have the same feelings—they bless their Helper for the benefits they have received.... So let us remember these things and not be preoccupied with food, but with praise to our Lord.... Accordingly, we should not live for ourselves any longer, but live as servants of the Lord. For our sakes the immortal, indestructible Word came down and took on mortal humanity for the salvation of all.... Our Lord was sacrificed so that by the shedding of his blood he might abolish death.... Thus when we have learned and realized these things, we properly will keep the Feast, having learned what we should from them, and then we will be ready to enter into the joy of our Lord in the kingdom of heaven....

Scripture Meditation

Now the Feast of Unleavened Bread, called the Passover, was approaching, and the chief priests and the teachers of the law were looking for some way to get rid of Jesus.
—LUKE 22:1–2

Thought for the Day

We worship in spirit and in truth when we appreciate the unique beauty of Jesus Christ, and do so by his Spirit, not our own best effort.

Prayer

Lord, let me hold fast to you, beautiful Lord, whom the angels
themselves yearn to look upon. Wherever you go, I will follow you.
—BERNARD OF CLAIRVAUX

HOLY (MAUNDY) THURSDAY: REGULAR SPIRITUAL SUSTENANCE

*Geert Groote (1340–1384) of Deventer, founder of the New Devotion in the
Low Countries, may have written the following instructions for his followers
to practice as devotional exercises. Later variations of his writings and others
were collected as "On the Life and Passion of Our Lord Jesus Christ." Groote
argued it is invalids who need to eat three meals daily. Likewise the devout
need three "spiritual meals" daily: Think of the basic realities of Christian faith
first thing in the morning; then dwell on the humanity of Jesus throughout the
day; then dwell upon his passion and death each evening. Likewise, each day
of the week can be given specific aspects of faith to meditate upon. So when
Lent and Easter are celebrated, one has dwelt upon these realities as the
daily sustenance of the soul through all the days of the year.
The following excerpt is for "Monday evening."*

*D*early Beloved,

Think about … the beginning of his passion, that is, the last supper
which our Lord had with his disciples: how humbly he washed their feet,
how after eating that paschal lamb he consecrated his own most holy
body and blood, how he gave and instituted the sacrament for his disciples, that meal as a singular testament and his most holy blood in the cup
as a memorial to him, and finally how with his words he instructed and
consoled them most lovingly. Here you should call to memory some of
the special and most loving words from that meal so as to grasp in your

255

heart how much love he showed them there. For instance, "I have eagerly desired to eat this passover with you before I die" (Luke 22:15); or "You will know that you are my disciples if you love one another" (John 13:35); or "You will weep and mourn while the world rejoices; you will grieve, but your grief turn to joy" (John 16:20); or "I will not leave you as orphans; I will come to see you" (John 14:18).

You ought to understand, to break and to chew upon those words with all your strength, and with great sobs you should observe how far you are from them yourself. Then consider the prayer he uttered in agony and his resignation of himself into the hands of his heavenly Father even to bitter death and also that bloody sweat he sweat in fear of the death he was about to suffer. Now throw yourself to the ground and with the loud voice of your heart and folded hands cry out and say, "O grieving Lord, how shall I repay you for all you have given me. I will accept the cup of salvation" (Ps. 116:12).

Scripture Meditation

The LORD remembers us and will bless us: He will bless the house of Israel ... he will bless those who fear the LORD — small and great alike.

—PSALM 115:12–13

Thought for the Day

God's banqueting house is for daily nourishment in the provisions of Christ's love, humility, and forgiveness.

Prayer

Blessed are those who dwell in your house; they are ever praising you.

—PSALM 84:4

GOOD FRIDAY: WHAT IS THE ISSUE AT THE CROSS OF CHRIST?

Karl Barth (1886–1968) was one of the most influential theologians of the twentieth century. He opposed Nazi ideology and gave a new emphasis to the sovereignty of God's Word. He writes this letter to Dr. Louis Glatt of Geneva on September 29, 1967.

The question you put to me regarding the guilt of men for the crucifixion of Jesus ... gives rise to various types of folly and mischief, especially in the relationship between Christians and Jews. Yet I do not think that, because of a wrong understanding of the guilt of men for the crucifixion of Jesus, one can simply draw the conclusion that they were wholly without guilt. I fear that if guilt is totally removed, the crucifixion (and perhaps the whole incarnation) will become a purely fatalistic event. In your letter there is a dubious trace of this. But in this case real man would not be received there by God in his grace, for he, the sinner, would not be really received there by God in his grace.

What is at issue at the cross? That God's eternal election, his good will toward men, even and precisely toward sinful and wicked men, is fulfilled. Indeed, as this good will of God is fulfilled, it is for the first time truly *manifest* that both Jews and Greeks, are all under sin (Romans 3:9). And this is how the story of the crucifixion actually goes. As Jesus did his work for men, the guilt of the Jews and also of the Gentiles (in the form of Pilate and his people), to whom the Jews delivered Jesus, is brought to light. Neither of them, with their acts that are there shown to be sin, could contribute anything at all to the work of God, to the fulfillment of his love. God in his love does not will sin, and therefore they could render no service to him by sinning, but only contradict his work.

On the other hand, neither Jews nor Gentiles in the persons of their representatives could stop God's work with their sin. In their own ways they could only confirm their wickedness, but with it they could not extinguish or evade the fact that God is kind and gracious to them, sinners though they be. If one understands the matter thus, I do not see how one can avoid speaking of the guilt of Jews and Gentiles for the crucifixion of Jesus—of a guilt, be it noted, that one can recall only in the context

257

of the hymn: "Thou hast borne all sin, otherwise we should despair; have mercy on us, O Jesus."

Scripture Meditation

Jews and Gentiles alike are all under sin. As it is written: "There is no one righteous, not even one."
—ROMANS 3:9–10

Thought for the Day

The cross of Christ transforms our lives as nothing else could ever do.

Prayer

O Lord God our Father … Do not allow any of us to remain apathetic or indifferent to the wondrous glory of Easter, but let the light of our risen Lord reach every corner of our dull hearts.
—KARL BARTH

HOLY SATURDAY: THE GOAL OF NEW LIFE

Dr. Murray Rae (b. 1961) trained first as an architect in Auckland, New Zealand, and is now a professor in theology at Otago University, New Zealand. He writes this letter to the editor on August 14, 2003.

ear Jim,

The women who went to the tomb that first Easter morning and found that the crucified one had been raised, were witnesses to the great and final goal of God's creative and redemptive love—the goal of new life! This mystery of God's will, decisively known then, we still cannot know in all its fullness, although the apostle prays we shall go on learning.

It is important, of course, to know that it was the crucified one who was raised. In the agony of crucifixion, culminating in that anguished cry of "godforsakeness," Christ entered the dark valley of human suffering and evil, and thus took upon himself, the agonies of all human history. How often we frail human beings struggle to make sense of suffering. How deeply we are wounded, not merely by physical pain, but by the anxiety that there is no end to it, and ultimately no relief. But that the one who was crucified should be raised, that the one of whom the Creed says, "he descended into hell," should not be left to languish there but be raised again to new life—this is the basis of Paul's words that "neither death, nor life, nor angels, nor rulers, nor things present, nor things to come, nor powers, nor height, nor depth, nor anything else in all creation, will be able to separate us from the love of God in Christ Jesus our Lord" (Rom. 8:38–39).

Through the resurrection of the crucified one the Word of God resounds throughout history calling forth all those who have suffered, all those who have known forsakenness, and all those whose lives are stained by tears. The Word of God resounds after human words have come to an end, after they have uttered their worst—"Crucify him!"—or after speech has been reduced to groans. The Word of God sounds forth from the first Easter morning, and what is heard there is the sound of forgiveness and new life; it is the sound of Christ weaving a new melody into the strains of history that one day will swell into a great oratorio of praise. This is the plan for the fullness of time, that suffering and death will be no more, that every tear will be wiped from our eyes, and that all flesh shall see together the glory and the love of God.

Scripture Meditation

[God] made known to us the mystery of his will ... which he purposed in Christ ... to bring all things in heaven and on earth together under one head, even Christ.

—EPHESIANS 1:9–10

Thought for the Day

Without entering hell, Christ could not have overcome all forces of evil, so his conquest is now absolute.

Prayer

Help us, we pray, to make known to our world that its cause for despair is ended, and that its suffering and its sin will one day be no more. This we ask in the name of the risen Christ, and for his sake. Amen.

—MURRAY RAE

EASTER SUNDAY: AT THE OPEN TOMB

Fränz Jägerstatter [see May 24] writes to his wife
from prison on April 10, 1943.

Christ is risen—Alleluja! So the church rejoices today. And if we must also experience hard times today, we still should and can rejoice with the church regardless. For what is there more joyous than the fact that Christ has risen again and has gone before us as Victor over death and hell? What can give us, as Christians, greater comfort than the knowledge that we need never again fear death?

Dearest wife, you can easily imagine what these holy days have been like for me in prison, but with God it is possible to overcome everything. One should not always fix his thoughts on the things he cannot have at the moment. No matter how great our sufferings in this world might become, I believe the poor souls in purgatory would still change places with us in an instant. That is why we help them as much as we can....

I am, I think, always a child of luck. On Holy Thursday morning I asked again about going to church on Easter—but, again, it was not approved for me. Instead, however, I was promised a visit from a priest who arrived that same afternoon. And thus I was able to fulfill my Easter duty even here, for the priest had brought the Blessed Sacrament along. On Friday, then, others asked again for the priest and, as a result, I was able to receive Holy Communion once more on Saturday morning....

One week passes after another; the important thing is that we do not let a single day go by in vain without putting it to good use for eternity.... This Easter day is also slowly coming to an end. How many more will go by before another peaceful Easter Sunday will be ours? It is good that man cannot see into the future. This way we can take each day just as God sends it to us.

Scripture Meditation

If Christ has not been raised, our preaching is useless and so is your faith.... But Christ has indeed been raised from the dead.
—1 CORINTHIANS 15:14, 20

Thought for the Day

This day reinterprets human history and indeed my own life.

Prayer

Lord, you have passed over into new life, and you now invite us to Passover also. In these past days we have grieved at your sufferings and mourned at your death.... Now at Easter you reveal to us that we have died to sin, passing over to your risen life.
—BERNARD OF CLAIRVAUX

EASTER MONDAY: IS THE RESURRECTION OF CHRIST
TRULY OUR BOTTOM LINE?

Gerard Zerbolt of Zutphen (1367–1398) was the most intellectual and influential leader of the "New Devotion" or renewal movement of the Devotio Moderna after Geert Groote. He composed a treatise titled "The Reformation of the Soul," based on both his own reflections and those of the fathers. Though he died of the plague while still young, he writes the following in "The Spiritual Ascents."

*M*y dear One ...

On the third day Christ rose a victor over death and showed that we too would rise. If you suffered with Christ's passion, rejoice now with his resurrection. Think devoutly on how Christ's soul descended to hell, what he did there, the joy of the holy fathers, the sadness of the demons, and the fear of the guards. Think of the angels' watch over the grave, of whom we are told that one sat alone, then stood, then sat upon a stone, then was in the tomb, and then of two in various positions—all of which shows a multitude of angels all around the tomb and several visits of the women. Think what love and desire compelled Mary Magdalene and the other women to run frequently to visit the Lord's tomb.

Think of Christ's various appearances, his sweet conversations with his disciples. Think why Christ wanted to appear in Galilee, namely to show that you too should move beyond your vices, whence "pasch" equals Easter, means a transition. In Galilee we see the passing over and changing of our bodies, like Christ's, after the general resurrection.

Scripture Meditation

He who descended is the very one who ascended higher than all the heavens, in order to fill the whole universe.

—EPHESIANS 4:10

Thought for the Day

How closely do we really want to identify with Christ?

Prayer

> *I will extol the LORD at all times; his praise will always be on my lips.*

—PSALM 34:1

THE TEMPTATIONS OF "THE FLESH" ARE MORE THAN THOSE OF THE BODY

C. S. Lewis [see letter for December 13] has been called a "Christian Neo-Platonist." But he was shrewd enough to spot the Neo-Platonic tendency in the asceticism of the early and medieval church. He writes this letter to his former student, Dom Bede Griffiths, on January 17, 1940.

Thanks for letter and article. I believe I found myself in agreement with every point you made in the latter. The Platonic and neo-Platonic stuff has, no doubt, been reinforced. (a) By the fact that people not very morally sensitive or instructed by trying to do their best recognize temptations of appetite as temptations but easily mistake all the spiritual (and worse) sins for harmless or even virtuous states of mind: hence the illusion that the "bad part" of oneself is the body. (b) By a misunderstanding of the Pauline use of *sarx*, which in reality cannot mean the body (since envy, witchcraft, and other spiritual sins are attributed to it) but, I suppose, means the unregenerate manhood as a whole. (You have no doubt noticed that *swma* is nearly always used by St. Paul in a good sense.) (c) By equating "matter" in the ordinary sense with *ulh* or *materia* in the scholastic and Aristotelian sense, i.e. equating the concrete corporeality of flesh, grass, earth or water with "pure potentiality." The latter, being nearest to not-being and furthest from the Prime Reality can, I suppose, be called the "least good" of things. But I fear Plato thought the concrete flesh and grass bad, and have no doubt he was wrong. (Besides these two sense of "matter" there is also a third—the thing studied in physics. But who would dare to vilify such a miracle of unceasing energy as *that*?—it's more like pure form that is potentiality.)....

Scripture Meditation

Our struggle is not against flesh and blood, but against the rulers, against the authorities, against the powers of this dark world and against the spiritual forces of evil in the heavenly realms.
—Ephesians 6:12

Thought for the Day

Asceticism has had a bad press because of Neo-Platonism, so have we relaxed too easily into "cheap grace"?

Prayer

Lord ... there is no one that can seasonably help me in my necessities, but only you, my God. You are my hope, my confidence, my Comforter, and in all things most faithful to me.
—Thomas à Kempis

The Mystery of Christ's Passion

C. S. Lewis's friendship with his former student, Owen Barfield, who was a
theosophist, lead Lewis to answer some of the questions raised by Barfield in
this letter of April 1932, some months after Lewis had become a Christian.
Once more, Lewis identifies the influence of Neo-Platonism
within the long history of religious "perfection."

As regards our argument about Gethsemane, I quite see that it
sounds odd to attribute to a perfect man a fear which imperfect men
have often overcome. But one must beware of interpreting "perfect
man" in a sense which would nullify the temptation in the wilderness: a
scene on which, at first, one would be tempted to comment (a) As
regards the stone and bread "Imperfect men have voluntarily starved"
(b) As regards Satan's demand for worship "Most men have never sunk
so low as to feel this temptation at all."

If we are to accept the Gospels however, we must interpret Christ's
perfection in a sense which admits of his feeling both the commonest and
most animal temptations (hunger and the fear of death) and those temptations which usually occur only to the worst of men (devil worship for
the sake of power). I am assuming that the stones and bread represents
hunger: but if you prefer to regard it as primarily a temptation to *thau-
maturgy* ("If thou be the Son of God, command these stones") then it
falls into my second class....

Death for Him also is the final defeat, but the time of *real* Freedom
(I am taking it for granted that the spiritual essence of death is "the
opposite of Freedom": hence the most mortal images are rigidity, suf-
focation, etc.) ...

What is it to an ordinary man to die, if once he can set his teeth to bear
the merely animal fear? To give in—he has been doing that nine times out
of ten all his life. To see the lower in him conquer the higher, his animal
body turning into lower animals and these finally into the mineral—he has
been letting this happen since he was born. To relinquish control—is as
easy for him as slipping on a well-worn shoe. But in Gethsemane it is
essential Freedom that is asked to be bound, unwearied control to throw
up the sponge, Life itself to die. Ordinary men have not been so much in

love with life as is usually supposed; small as their share of it is they have found it too much to bear without reducing a large portion of it as nearly to non-life as they can: we have drugs, sleep, irresponsibility, amusement, are more than half in love with easeful death—if only we could be sure it wouldn't hurt! Only He who really lived a human life (and I presume that only one did) can fully taste the horror of death....

Your idea of Christ as *suffering* from the mere fact of being in the body, and therefore tempted, if at all, to hasten rather than postpone his death, seems to imply that he was not (as the Christian mystery runs) "perfect God and perfect man" but a kind of composite being, a *daimon?* or archangel imprisoned in a vehicle unsuitable to it (like Ariel in the oak) and in constant revolt against that vehicle. This is mythological in the bad sense. The Son was certainly not incarnated in such a sense as not also to remain God (if He had been, the universe would have disappeared).

Scripture Meditation

Being in anguish, he prayed more earnestly, and his sweat was like drops of blood falling to the ground. When he rose from prayer and went back to the disciples, he found them asleep, exhausted from sorrow.
—LUKE 22:44, 45

Thought for the Day

Gethsemane finds us asleep in its mystery, but let us always be awake to its remembrance.

Prayer

Most high, glorious God, enlighten the darkness of my heart. And give me, Lord, a correct faith, a sure hope, a perfect love, that I may carry out your holy and true commands.
—FRANCIS OF ASSISI

WALK THE TALK

Robert Leighton (1611–1684), principal of Edinburgh University,
then Archbishop of Glasgow, would only accept one-fifth of the emoluments
of his office. His ruling passion was to see the unity of the church, signing the
Solemn League and Covenant, yet seeking the best features of both Presbytery
and Episcopacy. His Practical Commentary on First Peter *is a classic.*
This letter is possibly written early in 1659.

Some days ago I received some lines from you, and they were very welcome. For I know no better news can come from any corner of the earth, than of a soul attempting to overcome the world and its own self, and in any degree prevailing and resolving to move still further forward. All the projects and conquests of the world are not to be compared to it.

Oh! What a weariness is it to live among people and find so few real people, or among Christians and know so few real Christians. There is so much talk, and so little action. Religion is turned almost into a popular tune, and so much hot air. And, amid all our petty discourses, pusillanimous and base, so readily dragged into the mud of self and the flesh, dominated by pride and passion, we are called to speak of being "in Christ," clothed with him, believing it because we speak of it so often and so confidently!

Well, I know you are not willing to be thus gulled, since you have glimpses of the beauty of true holiness, and aim at no less than spiritual maturity, which we ultimately aspire to attain. Meanwhile, the smallest advances towards it are worth more than crowns and scepters. I believe you often think of the words of the blessed champion Paul, in 1 Corinthians 9:24, etc. There is a noble guest within us, let it be our business to entertain him honorably! For living with celestial love within us, will make all things contemptible in our vision compared with this. But I must stop, for it is time for me to post this, for whatever time of day you receive this, both of us know it is still night. But the comfort is the bright morning will soon be here to make amends.

—Your weary fellow pilgrim, R. L.

Scripture Meditation

*Do you not know that in a race all the runners run, but only one
gets the prize? Run in such a way as to get the prize.*
— I CORINTHIANS 9:24

Thought for the Day

In our "information society," talk is cheaper than ever, and so the
Christian walk is costlier than ever!

Prayer

Lord, may my desires change to your desires.
—THOMAS À KEMPIS

THE PATH OF THE JUST IS UPWARD AND DIFFICULT

---

*Huevelin (1838–1910), the Abbe de Tourville, trained at the seminary of Saint-
Sulpice in Paris, was forced by ill health to retire early from the priesthood
and on his family estate, the Castle of Tourville, wrote many letters of spiritual
direction during the last twenty years of his life. His message is that it is in the
humble circumstances of our human existence that our spiritual
life grows gradually, but effectively so.*

Perfection never exists apart from imperfection, just as good health
cannot exist without our feeling effort, fatigue, heat or cold, hunger or
thirst; yet none of those prevent the enjoyment of good health.

If you attempt to do all that is possible, all that is desirable, all that might be edifying, you will never succeed. Such an aim would indeed lack simplicity, humility, and frankness; and those three qualities are worth more than everything else to which you might aspire, however good your motives.

Perfection consists not in taking the safest course (sometimes quite the opposite) but in doing the least possible evil, having regard to our state of mind at the time and to the difficulties of our nature. It consists also in modestly holding fast to a very great simplicity, renouncing any course of action which although it either is, or appears to be more perfect in itself, would strain our powers.

I wish so much that you could get hold of the idea of what perfection in this world consists of. It is not like going up a great hill from which we see an ever-widening landscape, a greater horizon, a plain receding further and further into the distance. It is more like an overgrown path which we cannot find; we grope about; we are caught by brambles; we lose all sense of the distance covered; we do not know whether we are going round and round or whether we are advancing. We are certain only of one thing; that we desire to go on even though we are worn and tired. That is your life and you should rejoice greatly because of it, for it is a true life, serious and real, on which God opens His eyes and His heart.

We are far too apt to think of virtue as a broad, smooth road, whereas it is really a very rough and narrow one. It never becomes smooth or less uneven, until we observe that, in spite of all the jolting, we do manage to stay on it and even to advance a little, thanks to our Lord who holds us. Our confidence in Him, gained by experience, gives us a certain inward tranquility in spite of the jolting. That is what is meant by the smooth road.

Scripture Meditation

Not that I have already obtained all this, or have already been made perfect, but I press on to take hold of that for which Christ Jesus took hold of me.

—PHILIPPIANS 3:12

Thought for the Day

Perfection is not our achievement; it is our obedience to God's loving direction.

Prayer

> *Almighty God, to whom all hearts are open, all desires known,*
> *and from whom no secrets are hid; cleanse the thoughts of our*
> *hearts, by the inspiration of thy Holy Spirit: that we may perfectly*
> *love Thee, and worthily magnify thy holy name.*
> —BOOK OF COMMON PRAYER

RETURNING TO THE CITIES OF MEN

Rene Voillaume [see entry for February 16], founder of the Little Brothers,
writes another pastoral letter on the vicissitudes of our lives.

Our life is marked by an alternating rhythm, a movement in opposite directions, imposed by our vocation. We turn away from the world to solitude, for the prayer that will equip us for our work with men. We turn away from men with their pressing need for friendship, to the desert, in order to find God there. No doubt it would have been simpler to have remained in the desert, and there maintained the ideal of poverty, prayer, and love, of which we have spoken. Had we done this we should have followed the footsteps of St. Teresa and many other friends of God.

We know, however, that God asks us to live among men, and in doing so he understands the risks to which he exposes us and all the problems that are bound to arise....

A prophet is brought back from the desert into the public arena only when there is a mission for him to fulfill. *Nothing less than an urgent call to evangelize the world can justify the pursuit of a contemplative vocation of intercession outside the desert.* We should hold this with absolute conviction. We are called to a mission of intercession through prayer and the offering of our life as a sacrifice, but we are also called, in so far as our lives are spent among men, to an outward mission of evangelization. These are the aspects of our mission to which we must now give definition.

We have shown how wrong it would be to make the exclusive and as it were literal imitation of a limited period of our Lord's life, even if this includes the long years he spent in Nazareth, the sole purpose of a religious way of life....

The imitation of our Lord in his journeying along the roads of Palestine, amidst the crowds who thronged around him and would not let him go, in no way implies that the *Petits Freres* are called to be responsible for the ministry of preaching and of the sacraments, or to devote themselves to works that alleviate human suffering. Our Lord had compassion on the multitude who are like sheep without a shepherd, like starving men to whom nobody gives bread, and yet he did nothing to accelerate the slow growth of the mustard seed which he planted deeply in the earth, without apparently worrying about the intervening generations that were bound to follow each other before this tree had grown large enough for its shade to cover the world.

Scripture Meditation

As Jesus approached Jericho, a blind man was sitting by the roadside begging. When he heard the crowd going by, he asked what was happening. They told him, "Jesus of Nazareth is passing by."
—LUKE 18:35–36

Thought for the Day

In the daily press of life and its heavy claims upon us, we can walk with Jesus as intimately in the crowds as in the prayer chamber.

Prayer

Jesus, Son of David, have mercy upon me!
—THE "HESYCHASTIC" PRAYER (LUKE 18:38)

PRAYER IN THE CHRISTIAN'S LIFE

MAY 5: PRAYING TRULY, BY THE EXPERIENCE OF WIDOWHOOD

*This letter from Augustine of Hippo [see entry for December 19] was
destined to become a classic on prayer. He writes to Faltonia Proba, widow
of the wealthiest man in the Roman Empire. After a Gothic army pillaged
Rome in 410, Proba and a retinue of other widows and younger women
fled Rome to take refuge in Carthage in North Africa, where they
established a religious community. Faltonia Proba asked Augustine of
Hippo about prayer for the community. Here begins a paraphrased
series of selections from his long response.*

I haven't forgotten your request, and what I promised you, to write you about praying to God.... I can't tell you what great joy your request gives me, for I see what real concern you have about prayer. Can you not realize that there can be no worthier occupation as a widow than prayer? As the Apostle admonishes: "a woman who is a true widow in her desolation, wholly trusts in the Lord, giving all her days and nights to prayer." It might seem strange to have prayer as your first priority, when you are noble and rich from a worldly perspective, and indeed the mother of so many children. But you are spiritually wise enough to recognize living in this world, with this kind of life, no heart can be free from anxiety.

The One who has inspired you with this good desire [to pray], is the Lord who entered into the grief of the disciples, as they despaired not just for themselves, but for the whole world, how anyone could be saved. They heard the Lord say it was easier for a camel to pass through the eye of a needle than for a rich man to enter the kingdom of heaven. But what is impossible for humanity, is easy for God in his wonderful and full mercy. So it is he, who can so easily enable the rich to enter the kingdom of God, also gives you the holy desire to pray.

When Jesus was here in this world, Our Lord enabled a rich man, Zaccheus, to enter the kingdom of heaven. Then after being glorified by his resurrection and ascension, he imparted his Holy Spirit, which has brought many of the rich to despise this world. In fact he made them richer [spiritually] by healing them from their addiction to wealth. For would you really desire God, if you had not set all your hope upon him? Would you be trusting in him, if your trust was in uncertain riches? Such would despise the Apostle's salutary admonition: "Command those who are rich in this present world not to be arrogant nor put their hope in wealth, which is so uncertain, but to put their hope in God." Rather they are to be rich in good works, generous and willing to share, and so laying up for themselves a firm foundation for their true future in the real life. So because of your love for the true life, you have to see yourself as desolate in this passing world, regardless of how much good fortune you seem to possess....

Thus a Christian heart has to feel the desolation of our present existence in the world, living indeed as exiles from the Lord. For we walk by faith and not by sight. Without this disposition we will not, nor want to, pray. So we must learn to fix our eyes of faith upon the word of the divine Scriptures, as on a lamp in the darkness, until the day dawns and the Morning star arises in our hearts. For the source of that lamp's light is the Light who so shines in the darkness, that the darkness cannot overpower it. To see it, our hearts have to be purified by faith: "Blessed are the pure in heart, for they shall see God." ...

So strive in your prayer to overcome this world. Pray hopefully, trustingly, lovingly, earnestly, and patiently. Indeed, pray as a widow belonging to Christ [Augustine cites Hanna, a barren woman by whose prayers her own child of grace, Samuel, became a man of prayer; and of Anna, who as a prayerful widow recognized Mary's babe as the Savior of the world.] For the destitution and desolation that widows experience make them the true archetype of the true prayer. So long as the human heart is on a pilgrimage in this world, and thus destitute and desolate, unceasing, wholehearted prayer will then be the committal of our "widowhood" to God. You must then, pray as a "widow of Christ," one who doesn't yet see him whose help you implore ...

Scripture Meditation

The widow who is really in need and left all alone puts her hope in God and continues night and day to pray and to ask God for help.
— 1 TIMOTHY 5:5

Thought for the Day

Being a "widow of Christ" refers not to gender, but to those who allow their circumstances to drive them to deeper prayer.

Prayer

O Lord, I have seen you! O Lord, let me see you!
—SIMEON THE NEW THEOLOGIAN

MAY 6: WHAT SHOULD WE PRAY FOR?

Augustine of Hippo [see previous entry] continues his letter to Proba to deal
with her basic request: How do we spend our time praying?

So you have now read about what kind of person we should be, when we desire to pray. But your main concern was about the subject matter of prayer. For the Apostle's words have disturbed you: "We don't know what to pray for as we should." You were afraid it might be a worse condition to pray wrongly, than not to pray at all!

Briefly, let me tell you: pray for a happy life [what all the classical philosophers sought to attain]. But don't believe in the notion that if you can live just as you want, then you will be happy! Even pagan philosophers didn't buy this.... For to wish for something that is wrong, doesn't make it right.... But there are many natural desires that are not wrong, like wishing you were married, or desiring to have children, or having good health, or concern for the temporal well-being of those who are dear to us. We may desire also to enjoy successes and given honors for ourselves and for our dear ones. Provided we don't pursue these desires in arrogance and pride, we are not wrong to have such desires that we may pray for. Of course, we're wrong to want to be self-sufficient in our requests ... or indulge in avarice.... For as the Apostle has said: "Godliness with contentment is great gain. For we brought nothing into this world, and we cannot take anything out of it."

Those who desire this "sufficiency" of God, and nothing else, will live properly. This is what is desired and prayed for by the wise man who said: "Give me neither poverty nor riches, but give me my daily bread" (Prov. 30:2).... I'm sure you will recognize that he was not asking for self-sufficiency, but a sufficiency for the right things, ... of personal well-being such as health, or an extension of friendships, or even the spirit to pray for our enemies.... Yes, even what we think of as our own well-being even extends to our enemies, since there is no member of the human race, whom we are not to love, even when there is no response of love.... And is this all? ... The "sufficiency" of what we need, that of ourselves and of our friends, if it still refers only to the present life it is not enough; it must be displaced, so that we focus more upon eternal life. A healthy body is not enough, when we need a mind set upon eternity.... Our temporal existence is wasted if we do not spend it upon becoming worthy to live in eternity. All that really counts is how we live before God, and of what comes from God.... So why do we scatter our attention in so many directions, asking what we should pray for, when the psalmist tells us what it is....

Scripture Meditation

One thing I ask of the LORD, this is what I seek: that I may dwell in the house of the LORD all the days of my life, to gaze upon the beauty of the LORD and to seek him in his temple.
—PSALM 27:4

Thought for the Day

He who bends to himself a joy
does the winged life destroy
but he who kisses the joy as it flies
lives in eternity's sunrise.
—William Blake

Prayer

> Let me always remember you, love you, meditate upon you, and
> pray to you, until you restore me to your perfect pattern.
>
> —AUGUSTINE OF HIPPO

MAY 7: WHAT ARE THE WORDS OF TRUE PRAYER?

Augustine of Hippo [see entry for May 5] in his letter to Proba continues to
explore the implications of true prayer.

You may think it strange that when Jesus forbids us to indulge in much-speaking … when he knows what we need beyond what we think we "need," yet he urges us to pray. Our Lord even says: "You ought always to pray and not faint." So Jesus teaches us in parables, such as the widow wanting vindication from her adversary, keeping constantly visiting the unjust judge to hear her case. Or the householder desperately needing bread from his neighbor to entertain his guest, even wakes him up in the middle of the night. But God is not unjust, nor is he a sleeping God, so he told us: "Ask, and you shall receive; seek, and you will find; knock, and the door will be open to you." … Of course, we should realize that our Lord does not want us to let him know what we want, since he is not ignorant of it. But he wants us to exercise our desire for himself in our prayers, so that actually we become capable to receive what he wants to give us for our own well-being!

His is a great gift, so he asks us to "widen our hearts" to receive it. So we always pray in faith, hope, and love. We are to "pray constantly," that is to pray for the truly happy life…. Many words are one thing, but a prolonged disposition to prayer is another. For we learn of our Lord that he would spend all night in prayer.... So much-speaking in prayer is to do what we think we have to do, but much-praying is having our hearts pulsing with prolonged and fervent desire directed to the One to whom we are praying. This could be more like sighing than in speaking, more in tears than in words....

Yet we do need words. They help to recall to our minds what we are praying about.... So when we say, "Hallowed be Thy name" we are admonishing ourselves to desire his name, which is always holy, may be kept holy among us, and not be treated with contempt.... And when we say, "Thy kingdom come"—which by the way is His, not ours—so it will certainly come, whether we wish it or not, we are really arousing our desire that it will happen. It is we who need to be worthy to reign there with Him. When, too, we pray, "Thy will be done on earth, as it is in heaven," we are asking him for obedience for ourselves, that his will may be accomplished within us, as it is done by the angels in heaven.

When we say, "Give us this day our daily bread," by "this day" we mean the present time. Either we are asking for "a sufficiency" of what we need, as a basic need like "bread," or else we asking eucharistically for that eternal happiness, this world cannot give, but God alone. When we say, "Lead us not into temptation," we remind ourselves in warning, that we dare not deprive ourselves of God's help when placed in tempt-able situations.... When we say, "deliver us from evil," we again remind ourselves, we are not yet in the state of bliss when we shall no more experience any evil.... So you see how comprehensive is the Lord's Prayer. It is about praying "right" in the presence of God.... Look through so many prayers in Scripture, and you will find nothing that is not already included and summed up in the Lord's Prayer....

Scripture Meditation

When you pray, do not be like the hypocrites.
—Matthew 6:5

Thought for the Day

Christian theologian Origen said, "When you have prayed the Lord's Prayer you have expressed all there needs to be said."

Prayer

Lord, teach us to pray.

—LUKE 11:1

MAY 8: THE PRAYERFULNESS OF "LEARNED IGNORANCE"

A final aspect of Augustine of Hippo's letter to Proba [see entry for May 5]
explores the role of prayer in our sufferings.

Having said all this, perhaps you are still wondering why the Apostle then goes on to say that "We do not know what we ought to pray for, as we should." We can't believe he, or his people, did not know about the Lord's Prayer! ... Was it perhaps because we do not know how profitable our temporal troubles and temptations can actually be? They can help to reduce our pride, to test and exercise our patience, to chastise and destroy some of our weaknesses. But we, ignorant of their beneficial effect upon us, want to be free of all trials. Even the Apostle himself exhibited this "learned ignorance," when he beseeched God three times to take his affliction from him. When he did receive God's answer, he was shown that it was expedient that he did not receive his request. Instead, he was assured "my grace is sufficient for you, for my power is made perfect in weakness."

Thus in these trials which can either benefit or destroy us, we don't know what we should pray for as we should. Precisely because they are hard, negative, painful things that go against the sensitive feelings of our weak nature, we naturally want to pray that they be removed from us. This is what every human being wants. But if the Lord does not take them away, we must not interpret that to be that God is indifferent to us. Rather we should seek to interpret that to mean God is going to bless us in ways we don't yet understand. For that is how God's power is made perfect in weakness.

There are instances of how it was in anger that God granted his people what they had asked for in impatience … as we read in the book of Numbers how the Israelites asked, and received, what they wanted, but their impatience was severely punished. So they asked for a king—a king after their own heart—so they got what they deserved, a bad king indeed! … These are all object lessons for us … never to doubt that it is right to accept God's will, and not ours. For Jesus Christ, our Mediator, has given us an example of this. Humanly he prayed, "Father, if be possible, let this cup pass from me," but then he transformed that human will by adding immediately, "nevertheless, not as I will, but as you will."

Those then, who ask only for the "one thing" of the Lord, and who "seek" it, ask without doubt or anxiety…. The only one and true happy life comes when we contemplate the beauty of the Lord, as our primary, basic desire. Then for the sake of his "one thing," we will seek and pray rightly about everything else…. Thus we have within us something we can only call "learned ignorance," the ignorance we have learnt from the Spirit of God, who helps us in our weaknesses….

Scripture Meditation

We do not know what we ought to pray for, but the Spirit himself intercedes for us with groans that words cannot express.
—Romans 8:26

Thought for the Day

The modern world, full of "explanations," cannot appreciate the depth of our desires before God.

Prayer

Remember O Lord, what has happened to us … joy is gone from our hearts.
—Lamentations 5:1, 15

MAY 9: THE PRAYERFUL EXERCISE OF "CONSIDERATION"

---

*Bernard of Clairvaux [see entry for December 1] wrote "five books of
Consideration" to his former pupil, Pope Eugene III. Excerpts from these
"books" are here shaped as a long personal letter, since they were addressed
personally to the pope. "Consideration" here is used to mean godly piety,
which is the worship of God. In turn, it requires us to reflect upon our self-
understanding in the light of the knowledge of God. Bernard is writing this
toward the end of his life.*

I ask you, what is the point of wrangling and listening to litigants
from morning to night? … Your administrative chores are choking the
charisma of your office.… Is there no wise man among you, asks the
apostle, who can judge between brothers? (1 Cor. 6:5) … "No one who
fights for God entangles himself in secular affairs" (2 Tim. 2:4).… It is
one thing to run headlong into these affairs when there is an urgent
reason, but it is quite another matter, when you dwell on them as if they
were worthy of papal attention all the time.… Now the essence of "consideration" is what the Psalmist urges we should be: "Be still, and know
that I am God" (Ps. 46:10).

The primary importance of "consideration" is that it clears and puri-
fies the mind. So it controls the emotions, guides actions, corrects
excesses, improves behavior, confers dignity and order in life's affairs,
and even imparts knowledge, human and divine. It puts an end to confusion, integrates what has been scattered, roots out secrets, hunts down
truth, scrutinizes appearances of reality, and exposes lies and deceit.… It
stands firm in adversity.… So you will spare a good deal of time to "consideration," if you learn to delegate to others, and select what you think
best you can do yourself.…

Now you well know that we have entered a very difficult time, which
appears to herald an end to our very existence [i.e of Christendom with
the failure of the Second Crusade].… For are they not saying, "where is
their God?" (Ps. 114:10).… Strife has spread among the princes and the
Lord makes them wander in trackless wastes (Ps. 107:40).… How confused are the feet of those announcing peace, and of good news! We said,
"Peace," when there is no peace (Ezek. 13:50); we promised good news,

and behold there is disaster.… Humility restrains me from writing to you that something should be done in this way or that.… For all this we need "consideration." …

Now while "contemplation" means having sure and certain intuitive knowledge of the truth, "consideration" is the opposite, as the search for the truth. For this four things are required. The first is yourself: let your "consideration" begin and end with yourself … think of nothing which is contrary to your own salvation.… Knowing who you are implies knowing your own natural temperament, knowing what you are publicly as the Pope, knowing your own personality—whether kind, gentle and so on. All this will help you know your own limitations, your opportunities and gifts, as well as where you need the help of the Lord, his grace, and sufficiency.… The result will be your focus upon who you are, rather than on what greatness you may have.… Then in turn you will allow "consideration" of others under your service too … as well as those in error around you … so that you know who to choose well for office.

Scripture Meditation

Be still, and know that I am God … the LORD Almighty is with us.
—PSALM 46:10–11

Thought for the Day

Prayerful "consideration" in the pragmatic activism of our time requires a new state of being for our daily walk with God.

Prayer

Lord Jesus Christ, the Truth and the Life, you said that in the time to come the true worshippers of your Father would be those who worshipped you in spirit and in truth. I beseech you therefore to free my soul from idolatry.
—WILLIAM OF ST. THIERRY

MAY 10: THE LIFE OF CONTEMPLATION

The anonymous author of the fourteenth century classic The Cloud of
Unknowing *follows the mystical theology of the pseudo-Dionysius in teaching
the way of the contemplative life. In a more specific way he writes* A Letter of
Private Direction *to a young religious, whom he calls Timothy.*

*M*y spiritual friend in God,

It is personally to you I am writing, about the work of contemplation to which you seem disposed. For if I were to write to all and
sundry, I would have to write what suited them all. But I am writing to
you privately, with you in mind, for what is profitable to you personally. [But for other readers, we need to explain that "contemplating
God" is not about the pursuit of knowledge, since God is ineffable.
Rather it is about "knowing Him through love," which is the meaning
of "contemplation."] So when you begin the first stage, that is to recollect yourself, turn away from mental activity, even if they are good
thoughts. Likewise do not pray with words, unless you feel you really
have to. Likewise be unaware of how long you are in prayer, long or
short, nor be mentally conscious about whether you are using a collect
to pray, or a psalm, hymn, or antiphon.... So don't give your mind the
chance to distract you ... rather speak inwardly to God and say: "What
I am, Lord, I offer it to you without regard to any quality of your
being, other than you are and nothing else." This humble darkness is
to fill your consciousness and is to be the mirror of yourself. So again
don't get curious about your self anymore than you are with God, so
that you become one in spirit with him....

So take the good gracious God, just as he is, and without qualification
bind him to you ... indeed touching him as the woman in the Gospel
touched the hem of his garment ... safe ... and healed of one's sickness.... Lift up your sick self, just as you are, to the gracious God, as he
is, without speculation or special probing.... For he is your being and you
are what you are in him, not only because he is your cause and your
being: but he is also in you as your cause and your being.... So come
down to the lowest point of your being ... not what you are, but that you
are....

My spiritual friend in God, see to it that you leave behind all the speculative reflections of your natural faculties and give complete worship to God, offering your own self simply and entirely to him, all that you are, and just as you are....

The evidence you have that you are being called into this contemplative life is twofold. The first is the internal evidence that you are given strong inner convictions. These may be the consciousness of your own sinfulness, or the passion of Christ, or any other such conviction of the life of faith. You are also given patience to wait, to endure further desolations or consolations, and experience greater graces of God. The external evidence is the strong appeal you receive whenever the contemplative life is spoken of, or what you read about, or that is constantly in your own consciousness when you wake up or go to sleep. So that it accompanies you wherever you are, whatever you do, and that you would run a thousand miles to meet someone with the same experience and convictions. So if your silence is peaceful, your prayer secret, your speech edifying, your behavior modest, your laughter restrained gently, and you love to be alone ... then these are signs you are entering the delights of the contemplative life.... Then you can pass to a state whether consoled or desolate, they neither really matter, for the spirit of love can transcend them both.

Scripture Meditation

He who dwells in the shelter of the Most High will rest in the shadow of the Almighty.

—PSALM 91:1,2

Thought for the Day

The contemplative life of the Christian is celebrating the Sabbath day as a way of life.

Prayer

Lord, how much juice you can squeeze from a single grape.
My soul is so dry that by itself it cannot pray;
Yet you can squeeze from it the juice of a thousand prayers.

—GUIGO THE CARTHUSIAN

MAY 11: PRAY AS IF YOU MIGHT DIE BEFORE YOU
HAVE FINISHED YOUR PRAYER

Like the previous letter, this is also written in the fourteenth century when the
contemplative tradition was strong. It was a period also terrorized by the
plague and other catastrophes. The writer of this letter is considered to be the
author of The Cloud of Unknowing, *probably a Carthusian recluse*
living in the East Midlands of England.

*M*y spiritual friend in God:

In response to your query how best to keep your heart as you pray, I can only do so from my own inadequacy. But I believe, regardless how long or short your prayer is, there is one thing to remind your heart — that you might be dead before you have finished praying! Mark this — for this is no whimsy — for no one can believe otherwise, when we are realistic about our own mortality. If you do so — indeed it is salutary to do so — you will begin to take your sinfulness seriously, and realize the short time there may be left to amend your ways.... For even if you live longer than you anticipate, you will be purged of false optimism about yourself.... It will promote a godly fear, knowing that "the fear of the Lord is the beginning of wisdom." However fear, *per se* is not a solid foundation to build upon, but God is, so let it only be qualified as "the fear of the Lord." ...

This short prayer you make, little as it may be, will then be acceptable to God, even if you die in the meantime. While if you go on living, it will be with growing spiritual maturity, since you are looking for amendment of life. For on the one hand the fear of death is indeed salutary to rid yourself of sinful inclination, while what motivates you to move forward is a sure hope in God's mercy.... Like the "rod and staff" of the psalmist [Ps. 23:4], the one defends you against evil, while the other guides you in divine hope. Indeed, the latter is also the "staff of hope," upon which you can lean as you ascend upwards in the life of contemplative prayer....

The spiritual effect of this exercise of prayer then consists of a reverent affection for God, in an upsurge of love, which arises from spiritual steps of mingling fear with love, and taken upwards with the staff of hope. The effect of this spiritual exercise is what the good Doctor,

Thomas Aquinas, would call devotion. This is nothing else but the readiness of a person's will to do what belongs to the service of God ... I believe St. Bernard takes the same view of this exercise, doing it swiftly and gladly. For out of fear it is done swiftly, and out of loving hope it is done gladly.

I tell you, I would rather be rewarded for perseverance in this exercise, than doing all the penance in Christendom ... fasting, keeping vigil in sleepless nights, wearing a hair-shirt, and all the rest of such ascetic practices. These can only be as good as they direct me towards this spiritual exercise ... but there is much ignorance in their unreflective usage....

I see then this way of life like a garden planted with fruit trees. The trunk and root system may be likened to this godly fear, but the branches and their fruits are like this loving hope.... See it all as God's gracious goodness, not as yours by right, which is sin indeed, but a gracious gift of God.... If then, you think you are doing all right, thank God heartily. And for God's sake, pray for me ... now no more but God's blessing to you, and mine too! In the name of Jesus. Amen.

Scripture Meditation

If you call out for insight, and cry aloud for understanding ... then you will understand the fear of the LORD and find the knowledge of God.
—PROVERBS 2:3, 5

Thought for the Day

Exercise gratitude then hope will flow.

Prayer

Lord, there is none whom I can fully trust to, none that can seasonably help me in my necessities, but only thou, my God.
—THOMAS À KEMPIS

MAY 12: LIVING WITH MARTHA AND MARY—THE "MIXED LIFE"

Walter of Hilton (d. 1396) was an Augustinian canon in the Midlands of
England who wrote several classics, chiefly what came to be known as The
Scale of Perfection. *Here he writes to a layman described as "a great lord,"*
a man of affairs, assuring him that his new commitment in faith does not
mean he need abandon his family and social responsibilities. So he is
given practical advice on how to balance one's spiritual growth
(including works of charity) with one's contemplative life.

*Y*ou ought to mingle the works of an active life with spiritual endeavors of a contemplative life, and then you will do well.

For you should at certain times be busy with Martha in the ordering
and care of your household, children, employees, tenants, or neighbors.
If they do well, you ought to comfort and help them in this; if they do
badly, teach them to amend themselves and correct them. And you
should regard and wisely know how your property and worldly goods are
being administered, conserved, or intelligently invested by your employees, in order that you might, with the increase, the more bountifully fulfill
deeds of mercy to your fellow Christians.

At other times you should, with Mary, leave off the busyness of this
world and sit down meekly at the feet of our Lord, there to be in prayer,
holy thought, and to contemplate him as he gives you grace.

And so you should go from the one activity to the other, fulfilling both
aspects of the Christian life, to balance love of God and love of neighbor.
So let me explain this further. For you can distinguish three ways of living: active, as in business; prayerful, as in spiritual service; and both
together, "the mixed life."

Active life by itself is the province of laymen and women living in the
world, and who tend to be spiritually superficial.... None the less, they
fear God, dread hell, flee from sin, desiring to please God ... and generally intend well towards their fellow Christians. Thus limited, they live as
actively as they can in a positive way... A wholly contemplative life is the
choice of some, who for the love of God, forsake everything else.
Reduced to the barest necessities of life, they abandon everything to
serve God.... The third or "mixed life," is appropriate to ministers of the

Holy Church such as priests and others with pastoral responsibilities, who have care and governance over others…. But it is also generally appropriate to certain laymen who have positions of leadership and responsibility, by virtue of wealth and public office….

Our Lord, in directing us toward this "mixed life," himself exemplified such a life … for he mingled publicly, in showing them his deeds of mercy. He taught the simple by his preaching, he visited the sick and healed them of their illnesses, he fed the hungry, and he comforted those that were in sadness. Then on other occasions he broke away from public discourse to be alone into the desert or upon the hills, and to pray there all night as the Gospel tells us (Luke 6:12). In such a "mixed life" he exemplified … how we can mix business with the active life of charity of those under our care. His life also models how we can also give ourselves devotedly … to prayer, meditation, and contemplation.

Scripture Meditation

This service that you perform is not only supplying the needs of God's people but is also overflowing in many expressions of thanks to God.

—2 CORINTHIANS 9:12

Thought for the Day

Exercise God's love in every level of your existence and relationships as expressive of the "mixed life"!

Prayer

Lord! What a busy restless thing
Hast thou made man! … Ah! Lord!
And what a purchase will that be
To take us sick, that sound would not take thee!

—HENRY VAUGHAN

MAY 13: MAKING PRAYER THE FIRST ORDER OF BUSINESS

During the upheavals of the Reformation, the practice of pastoral counseling
grew to provide courage and comfort to those persecuted as well as to be a
reminder to others of the central tenets of faith in an age of confusion. Martin
Luther [see entry for December 30] wrote many letters of spiritual counsel,
both to ordinary people as well as to princes. This entry and the one that
follows are excerpts of a longer one written in early 1535 to his barber, Peter
Beskendorf. It describes the threefold basis of devotion Luther advocated,
which developed into a tradition in subsequent centuries: meditations on the
Lord's Prayer, the Ten Commandments, and the Apostle's Creed.

*D*ear Master Peter:

I shall tell you as well as I know how what I myself do when I pray.
May our Lord God help you and others to do it better. Amen.

To begin with, when I feel that I have become cold and disinclined to
pray on account of my preoccupation with other thoughts and matters
(for the flesh and the devil always prevent and hinder prayer) I take my
little Psalter, flee to my room, or, if … there is occasion to do so, join the
people in church, and begin to repeat to myself the Ten Commandments,
the Creed, and if I have time, some sayings of Christ or verses from Paul
and the Psalms. This I do in all respects as children do.

It is a good thing to make prayer the first business of the morning and
the last at night. Diligently beware of such false and deceptive thoughts
as suggest: "Wait awhile. I shall pray in an hour or so. I must first take
care of this or that." Such thoughts will lead away from prayer and will
involve you in other affairs that will so occupy your attention that nothing will come of your prayers that day.

It is true that some tasks may confront you that are as good or better than prayer, especially if they are required by necessity. A saying is
ascribed to Saint Jerome to the effect that every work of the faithful is
prayer, and a proverb declares, "He prays double who works faithfully." This is undoubtedly said because the believer, when he is
working, fears and honors God and remembers God's Commandments
so that he doesn't deal unjustly with his neighbor, steal from him, take
advantage of him, or misappropriate what belongs to him. Such

thoughts and such faith undoubtedly make his work prayer and praise as well....

Yet we must also see to it that we do not grow away from true prayer, so go as far as to imagine that busyness is more essential, and so ... become too careless, lazy, cold and listless to pray. The devil, who hounds us, is not lazy or careless, and our flesh is still all too active and eager to sin and inclined to oppose the spirit of prayer. So when your heart is warmed by such meditation ... kneel down or stand with folded hands, lift up your eyes toward heaven, saying to yourself briefly: "Dear God, Heavenly Father, I am a poor, unworthy sinner. I do not deserve to lift up my eyes or hands to thee in prayer. But since you have commanded us all to pray, promising to hear our prayers, and teaching us through thy dear Son, our Lord Jesus Christ, both how and what to pray, I come to you in prayer. I do so obediently, relying on your gracious promises ... and praying with all your saints ... "Our Father which art in heaven."

Scripture Meditation

When you pray, go into your room, close the door and pray to your Father, who is unseen. Then your Father, who sees what is done in secret, will reward you.
—Matthew 6:6

Thought for the Day

"Centering prayer," as we now call such preparation, requires us to be morally transparent before God.

Prayer

I am certain that you, God, are true and cannot lie. Enable me to be steadfast in faith, never doubting, not because of the merits of my prayer but because of the certainty of your truth.
—Martin Luther

MAY 14: "WARM FEELINGS" ARE NOT ENOUGH IN OUR PRAYERS

Teresa of Avila (1515–1582) was the reformer of the Carmelite order in Spain. She spent her first eighteen years in a convent, removed from God and feeling incapable of a genuine life of prayer. Then she was transformed by a vision of Christ during an illness and wrote her classic on prayer, The Interior Castle, *as well as her* Life, *which elaborates autobiographically her personal growth and experiences of prayer. Some 458 of her letters have been edited. The following was written on October 23, 1576, to her friend and coreformer, P. Jeronimo Gracian, in Seville.*

May the grace of the Holy Spirit be with your Paternity, my Father.

I have received three letters from you today! ... The Lord has amply repaid me for the long time I have had to wait for them....

The whole matter in a nut-shell is that the prayer which is most acceptable to God is that which leaves the best results. Results, I mean, in actions. That is true prayer. Not certain gusts of "feely-touchy," and nothing more. For myself, I wish no other prayer but that which improves me in virtue. I would rather live more integrated to how I pray. So I esteem a 'good prayer' as one which leaves me more humbled, even if it is still best with great temptations, sufferings, and aridities. For it must never be thought that because one has much suffering, therefore one cannot have prayed effectively enough. For one's suffering should be as incense offered before God. So I tell my daughters that they must work and suffer as well as pray, and that it is the best prayer which is associated with the most work and the utmost suffering.

Scripture Meditation

I trust in the Lord. I will be glad and rejoice in your love, for you saw my affliction.

—PSALM 31:6–7

Thought for the Day

Real prayer, whether born of happiness or suffering, leads us to honor God with our actions.

Prayer

Make me serve Thee faithfully, and in all else, do with me what you will.

—TERESA OF AVILA

MAY 15: PREPARING FOR EVERLASTING REST

Richard Baxter (1615–1691), one of the great Puritan Anglican pastors, was an intensely productive author, writing nearly two hundred books. So he apologizes in this pastoral letter to his Kidderminster flock that by writing he should ever "have become thus public, and burden the world with any writings of mine." He explains how he came to write The Saints' Everlasting Rest, *a unique classic on the prayerful life, i n this dedicatory letter of January 15, 1649.*

*M*y dear Friends,

… The Lord has forced me quite beyond my own resolution to write this treatise and leave it in your hands.… Being in my (military) quarters far from home, cast into extreme languishing (by the sudden loss of about a gallon of blood), after many years suffering weakness (of general health), and being without companionship, and no books except the Bible, living in continual expectation of death, I turned my thoughts to my Everlasting Rest. Through extreme weakness, my memory being imperfect, I took up my pen and began to draft my funeral sermon, with some personal helps for my own meditations of heaven. In this condition, God was pleased to presence himself to me for about five months away from home, where having nothing else to do, I pursued this work, which grew to what it has now become [i.e. over a thousand pages, instead of one or two sermons! Baxter then enumerates ten directions given to his parishioners.]

1. Labor to be people of knowledge and sound understanding [i.e. of the faith] as being much conducive to the soundness of heart and life. A weak judgment is easily corrupted ... so read much of the writings of the old divines....

2. Do your utmost to get a faithful minister, when I am taken from you....

3. Let all your knowledge turn into affection and practice; keep open the passage between your heads and hearts, that every truth may go the quick. Spare no pains in working out your own salvation....

4. Be sure you make conscience of the great duties you have to perform in your families. Teach your children and your servants the knowledge and fear of God. Pray with them daily and fervently....

5. Beware of extremes in the controversial points of religion. When you avoid one error take heed not to run into another error.... There is a true mean in the doctrines of justification and redemption.

6. Above all, see that you are followers of peace and unity, both in the church and among yourselves ... He who is not a son of peace is not a son of God....

7. Above all, be sure you get rid of pride in your hearts. Don't forget all the sermons I have preached to you against this sin. For there is no sin more natural, more common, or more deadly....

8. Be sure to keep the mastery over your flesh and the senses. Few ever fall away from God but the cause is pleasing the flesh ... "Make no provision for the flesh, to satisfy its desires" (Rom. 8:5–7; 13:4)....

9. Accept the great duty of reproving and exhorting those around you ... yet don't punish without due process.

10. Lastly, be sure to maintain a constant delight in God, and spirituality in all your worship. Think it not enough to delight in duties, if you do not take delight in God ... Live a constant readiness and expectation of death; and be sure you get acquainted with this heavenly conversation, which this book I have written to direct you ... until we may together enter into Everlasting Rest.

Your most affectionate, though unworthy teacher, Rich. Baxter

Scripture Meditation

The Lord is my strength and my song; he has become my salvation.
—PSALM 118:14

Thought for the Day

In a culture that seeks to escape the painful realities of death and dying, how much we have to learn from the great Puritans like Baxter, who faced death with courage and clarity.

Prayer

To the God of mercy, do I offer my most hearty thanks, … who has supported me in these fourteen years in a languishing state, in which I scarcely ever had an hour free from pain, and who has over twenty times delivered me, when I was near death…. My flesh and my heart failed, but God is the strength of my heart for ever.
—RICHARD BAXTER

BASIC ISSUES OF CHRISTIAN LIVING

MAY 16: WHAT IS SPIRITUAL PRIDE?

*John Ilyitch Sergieff [see entry for March 9], better known as John of
Kronstadt, was a Russian Orthodox priest who resigned after six years as
bishop of St. Petersburg to devote himself for the rest of his life to spiritual
counsel and letter writing to thousands of unknown inquirers throughout
Russia. His work,* My Life in Christ, *is a collage of the many letters he wrote,
an excerpt of which follows.*

Spiritual pride reveals itself by the fact that a proud man dares to
make himself a judge of religion and of the Church, saying: "I do not
believe in this, and I do not acknowledge this; this I find superfluous, that
unnecessary, and this strange or absurd." Spiritual pride also manifests
itself in boastfulness, in the proud man's pretended knowledge of everything, whilst in reality he knows very little or his spiritual eyes are
entirely blind. "That is not worth reading," he says, "it is all well known;
these sermons are not worth reading; they contain the one same thing
which I already know."

Human pride also shows itself to a great extent when an ordinary
mortal dares to compare himself with God's saints, and does not see their
great and wonderful perfections acquired with the assistance of the grace
of God; perfections which God Himself has crowned and glorified in
them. Such a man says: "Why should I reverence them, and especially
why should I pray to them; they are men like me; I pray to God alone?"
And he does not consider that God Himself commanded us to ask the
prayers of the righteous for ourselves. "For him will I accept."

Spiritual pride also exhibits insensibility to our sins, by the Pharisee's
self-justification and self-praise, by unawareness of God's mercies, by
ingratitude to God for all that is good, by not feeling the need to praise
God's greatness. All those who do not pray to the Almighty God, "to the
God of all spirits and of all flesh," to the Life, do not pray because of
their secret pride.

Scripture Meditation

God opposes the proud but gives grace to the humble.
—James 4:6

Thought for the Day

Pride settles in when we lose knowledge of self and of God's grace.

Prayer

Lord, bring me low; for you were lowly in your blessed heart:
Lord keep me so.
—Christina Rossetti

MAY 17: THE RICH MAN AND LAZARUS

---

*Peter Damian (1007–1072), bishop of Ostia, worked closely with the papal
authorities as a reforming legate and diplomat. He wrote many pastoral
letters. Here he replies to the queries of a monk named Peter in 1045
concerning Gregory the Great whose writings remained influential
throughout the Middle Ages.*

My dear son,

You ask me for the meaning of blessed Gregory's statement in his
homily on the rich man, when he said: "Some think that the precepts of
the Old Testament are more severe than those of the New, but these
people are in error because they interpret rashly. In the Old Testament it
is not niggardliness [to give grudgingly or petty in giving or spending]

that is punished, but plundering; and when something is taken unjustly it is penalized by fourfold restitution [2 Sam. 12:6].

Here, however, this rich man is not censured for having taken things that belonged to others, but for not having given what was his. In these words the celebrated doctor seeks only to establish that if the rich man had lived in Old Testament times he would not have been consigned to the punishment of hell. Therefore, according to this statement, he perished because in living under the new dispensation of grace, he refused to observe the Gospel....

With all due respect to the doctors, let me reply briefly to this question, using the ideas that now come to mind. The Lord says in the Gospel: "The law and the prophets obtained until John appeared." But John commanded: "The man with two shirts must share with him who has none, and anyone who has food must do the same." But as there are two precepts in this statement of John, so there are two sins committed by the rich man. John indeed said: "The man with two shirts must share with him who has none," but the latter "was dressed in purple and the finest linen." John added: "Anyone who has food must do the same," but the rich man "feasted in magnificence every day," and in both cases he was clearly shown to be insensitive and inhumane by not clothing the naked Lazarus, whom the dogs licked, and by absolutely denying food to him who would have been glad to satisfy his hunger with the crumbs that fell from the table. This is an important matter, and one need not wonder that it had extensive antecedents....

If one were to object to my explanation by stating that Abraham said to the rich man: "They have Moses and the prophets, let them listen to them," but did not say, "they have Christ, they have John," ... this statement of John's is not out of line with the pronouncements of the earlier prophets: "Share your food with the hungry, take the homeless poor into your house, clothe the naked when you meet them." Moses also says: "God will raise up a prophet for you, one of your own race, to whom you should listen as you would to me." And the Lord himself says: "If you believed Moses you would believe what I tell you, for it was about me that he wrote." Therefore whatever is written of Moses and the prophets can surely also be said of John and of Christ.

Scripture Meditation

If they do not listen to Moses and the Prophets, they will not be
convinced even if someone rises from the dead.

—LUKE 16:31

Thought for the Day

Humans cannot think of eternal punishment without bias; we should
leave the concept in the hands of God, who is righteous and just.

Prayer

Pardon us, O Lord, pardon us.... May your judgment give new
shape to our souls. May your power mould our hearts to reflect
your love. May your grace infuse our minds, so that our thoughts
reflect your will.

—WILLIAM OF ST. THIERRY

MAY 18: JESUS' WORST ENEMIES WERE THE RELIGIOUS LEADERS

*Mark Davis (b. 1957), associate professor of pastoral studies at Carey
Theological College, Vancouver, Canada, often discussed with the editor his
struggles with professionalism within contemporary Christianity. In this
letter of April 1, 2002, he expresses courageously what others may feel but
dare not express. For him, his conversion as a youth and his call into
ministry occurred at the same time, leading to a subsequent
confusion about his Christian identity.*

*D*ear Jim,

Like the Pharisee in the parable of the Publican and Pharisee, our faith can move from God to our own intelligence, or to our own giftedness or to the latest new program that is "guaranteed to revolutionize your ministry!" We move from being servants to CEO's, from being ministers to being managers, from being sojourners to being travel guides.

In my position of teaching in a Christian institution I am struck by how much we as Christians put our faith into our own devices, cleverness, and brilliance. Academic achievement supersedes the fruit of the Spirit, cleverness eclipses humility and programs replace relationship. The results are that ministry becomes a game of our own invention: One that we play to win, or at least to impress. Sadly the authentic ones among us are often then unnoticed.

I don't write this pejoratively. I write it as one who has struggled with my own "professionalism." I know in my own life what it is to minister out of *my* strength, *my* skill, *my* initiative. As I look back over the years I am convicted by how much of my ministry was born out of my own ego needs. So much of my ministry was motivated by me trying to win the praise of others and of God. The goals overshadowed the means. Time spent in the Word was replaced by time spent in my day timer. Time spent in prayer and meditation was replaced by time spent in busyness. Over time ministry became less and less about meeting with God and what He was doing in the lives of others and in the life of the church, and more and more about me taking God to others and to the Church.

That, I believe, is the line where one loses one's amateur status as a lover of God. It's when you stop seeking God and believe He is yours to take. Once that line is crossed, the silent Pharisee that resides in all of us begins in ways subtle and not so subtle to seek out the places of honor. We focus on power, popularity and position. I know what it is to be more focused on what it is I can get out of ministry rather than what it is ministry is asking of me. Yet the disguise is so perfect, few challenge it. When they do, we protest, a little too loudly, "this isn't about me, it's about the kingdom!" I know what it's like to minister in the name of the Lord, knowing that His Spirit is quenched within me. At times I have glimpsed behind my own denial, to see my own spiritual emptiness. I know only all too well how often I "fake it." More than once I have thought of leaving the Christian vocation, for the sake of my own integrity and my own soul....

For me, vocational ministry has not been an easy setting in which to grow in Christ. It has its own "danger, toils, and snares." The problem is that they are camouflaged, and not easily recognizable. In fact many of the things that have taken me away from Christ are the very things the Christian community supports. Performance and busyness are two of the more significant snares encouraged by the church today. Looking back, if there was one thing I would do differently it would be I would spend more time guarding my heart and nurturing my soul. I would be far more intentional about prayer, anonymous service, and allowing myself to be ministered to. I would be more open and vulnerable and less plastic and presentable. I would manage God less, and seek Him more. I continue to struggle.

Grace and peace.

Scripture Meditation

If I have the gift of prophecy and can fathom all mysteries and all knowledge, and … have not love, I am nothing.
—I Corinthians 13:2

Thought for the Day

Is professionalism in the church today a profound distortion of authentic Christian service?

Prayer

I no longer want just to hear about you, beloved Lord, through messengers. I no longer want to hear doctrines about you, nor to have my emotions stirred up by people speaking of you. These messengers simply frustrate and grieve me, because they only remind me how far distant I am from you.
—John of the Cross

MAY 19: THE FORGIVING LOVE OF JESUS IS PERHAPS NEEDED MOST WITHIN CHRISTENDOM

*Around AD 379 Gregory of Nazianzus (329–389), one of the great
Cappadocian Fathers, writes Theodore, bishop of Tyana, when some Arian
adversaries [i.e. those who denied the deity of Christ] began persecuting them
by breaking into their church service and stoning the clergy. Theodore wanted
to prosecute these aggressors but Gregory calls for restraint,
even forgiveness, in the spirit of Christ.*

I hear that you are indignant at the outrages that have been committed on us by the Monks and Mendicants. And it is no wonder, seeing that you never yet had felt a blow, and were without experience of the evils we have to endure, that you did feel angry at such a thing. But we as experienced in many sorts of evil, and as having had our share of insult, may be considered worthy of belief when we exhort Your Reverence, as old age teaches and as reason suggests. Certainly what has happened was dreadful, and more than dreadful—no one will deny it: that our altars were insulted, our mysteries disturbed, and that we ourselves had to stand between the communicants and those who would stone them, and to make our intercessions a cure for stonings; that the reverence due to virgins was forgotten, and the good order of monks, and the calamity of the poor, who lost even their pity through ferocity. But perhaps it would be better to be patient, and to give an example of patience to many by our sufferings. For argument is not so persuasive of the world in general as is practice, than silent exhortation....

"O Ephraim what shall I do unto you," God says. What anger is here expressed—and yet protection is added. What is swifter than Mercy? The Disciples ask for the flames of Sodom to be upon those who drove Jesus away, but He deprecates revenge. Peter cuts off the ear of Malchus, one of those who outraged Him, but Jesus restores it. And what of him who asks whether he must seven times forgive a brother if he has trespassed, is he not condemned for his niggardliness, for to the seven is added seventy times seven? What of the debtor in the Gospel who will not forgive as he has been forgiven? Is it not more bitterly exacted of him for this?

And what says the pattern of prayer? Does it not desire that forgiveness may be earned by forgiveness?

Having so many examples, let us imitate the mercy of God, and not desire to learn from ourselves how great an evil is requital of sin.... And do not let us so quickly destroy so great and glorious a work through what is perhaps the spite and malice of the devil; but let us choose to show ourselves merciful rather than severe, and lovers of the poor rather than of abstract justice.... May God forgive the noble Paulus his outrages upon us.

Scripture Meditation

Father, forgive them, for they do not know what they are doing.
—LUKE 23:34

Thought for the Day

Since only God can forgive sins, we are seeking to have his Spirit in our desire to forgive.

Prayer

Almighty Father, give me ... a meek and gentle spirit, that I may be slow to anger, and easy to mercy and forgiveness.
—JEREMY TAYLOR

MAY 20: SHARING IN THE RING OF FORGIVENESS

A mother (b. 1950) who requested anonymity wrote this letter to her only daughter, one month after the eighteen-year-old girl was killed in a car accident on June 20, 2003.

*M*y dearest little Bumble Bee,

I would like to tell you how immensely proud I am of you! Your teacher sent me the essay you wrote a month before your death. It was a precious gift to me. You said: "Through God I have learnt the intense power of gratitude. Being thankful to God even in hardship is a very powerful weapon that transforms one's very soul. For myself, gratitude to God in its essence helps me to understand and to control my anger."

Yes, we could see the difference in your life; you were no longer angry with us. Now I understand how radical was your change of perspective. The story did not end there, because your dear friend told me you found a box in your father's drawer that contained a love letter and a ring, sent by an acquaintance. You wore the ring to see if your father would ever notice it on your finger, and thereby confess to you about it. I am so impressed that you told your closest friends it symbolized that people are human and make mistakes, and that forgiveness was the most important part of our life. One of your closest friends wears the ring now. After her parents divorced she said you reminded her that to forgive was so important. What a beautiful message to give to others!

I think of two passages when I think of you, my dear one. The first is 1 Thessalonians 5:18. The second is from William Law, an eighteenth century bishop, who said: "If anyone could tell you the shortest, surest way to our happiness and perfection, he must tell you to make it a rule to yourself to thank and praise God for everything that happens to you, for it is certain whatever seeming calamity confronts you, if you thank and praise God for it, you turn it into a blessing!"

Scripture Meditation

Give thanks in all circumstances, for this is God's will for you in Christ Jesus.

—1 THESSALONIANS 5:18

Thought for the Day

Only the transcendent love of Jesus Christ can enable us to have such a spirit of forgiveness for others combined with thanksgiving to God.

Prayer

My dear Heavenly Father, I pray that those who are intertwined in our lives will see your glory in your grace and forgiveness to us all. Amen.

—A WIFE AND MOTHER

MAY 21: EMBRACING IN FORGIVENESS WITHIN A LITIGIOUS SOCIETY

In this letter, a Jewish businessman recounts a significant event on October 5, 2002, within his business operation as manufacturer of hot-air balloons.

This was one of those defining moments in life, when in an instant, a word or gesture can teach you an enormous lesson, if you're open and just go with what is right.

When Angel's mother was about 47 or 48, and almost menopausal, she discovered she was pregnant ... the entire family was thrilled beyond words when Angel was born. She grew up the ideal child, and through her lifetime gave all who knew her joy.... When she 24 she accepted an invitation to take a balloon ride with a friend of a friend, not knowing the pilot was a student pilot who had never flown solo before. During the flight a hurricane swept through the mountains where they were flying, shredding the balloon, falling 1500 feet. Angel's father died of a broken heart.

Some time later a law firm contacted the family, talking them into taking a lawsuit. This was about two years before my wife and I had bought the business. Eventually our insurance company got tired of the harassment, demanded a trial, and the judge dismissed the case. But the attorney managed a retrial, finding some dishonorable people to be witnesses against us, mostly unemployed coal miners, or parents who had loved Angel as their children's teacher. The trial dragged on, placing the wreckage of the balloon on the front lawn of the court house, while I sat in court feeling lower than a snake's belly, and listening to her mother weeping quietly behind me.... Finally the verdict came, 'not guilty'! ... we were pronounced innocent....

Out in the hall there was Angel's mother. I had no bitterness towards her, and felt an overpowering need to go to her. I walked over, and we just looked at each other. I put my arms around her and she put hers around me. We both wept quietly for a longtime, to the astonishment of the onlookers. My attorney went apoplectic, crying out, "What the hell is the matter with you. We won!"

Do you know, Paula, for the life of me, I couldn't understand what we had won. Angel was dead, and this lovely lady had lost a daughter. The family had lost a sister and aunt. My father had always taught me, in relationships we don't win unless everybody "wins." In this case we had all lost a lovely young lady ... the mother and I have now started to write each other regularly....

Scripture Meditation

Who can forgive sins but God alone? ... that you may know that the Son of Man has authority on earth to forgive sins.
—MARK 2:7, 10

Thought for the Day

Arigato Gozaimasu said, "Without the kindness of others, it is difficult to exist."

Prayer

You are forgiving and good, O Lord, abounding in love to all who call to you.
—PSALM 86:5

MAY 22: APPRECIATING THE PERSON OF CHRIST

Ambrose [see entry for January 5] writes to his sister Marcellina in tenderness
and appreciation of her love of Jesus as being like that of
the woman who anointed his feet.

*L*et us consider what is contained in the reading of the Gospel: "One of the Pharisees asked the Lord Jesus to dine with him; so he went into the house of the Pharisee, and reclined at table. And behold, a woman in the town, who was a sinner, upon learning that Jesus was at table in the Pharisee's house, brought an alabaster jar of ointment; and standing behind him at his feet, she began to bathe his feet with her tears." And then I read on to the words: "Thy faith has saved you; go in peace" (Luke 7:36–38, 50). How simple in words, I went on to say, but how deep in meaning is the reading of the Gospel! As these are the words of the great Counselor, let us consider their depth.

Our Lord Jesus Christ decided that human beings could be bound and won over to what is right more readily by love than by fear, and that love does more for correction than does fear. And so ... He came, born of a virgin....

He saw us bound by a heavy debt. No one could pay his debt with his inheritance of innocence; I could not free myself with any I had. But He gave me a new kind of acquittal, enabling me to get another creditor, because I had no means to discharge my debt. But it is sin, not nature which has made us debtors.... Then the Lord Jesus came; He offered His death for the death of all; He poured out His blood for the blood of everyone.

So He says to Simon: "Do you see this woman? I came into your house. You did not give me any water for my feet, but she wet my feet with her tears and wiped them with her hair" (Luke 7:44).... He pours water on the feet of Christ who forgives the lowly their sins, and in setting free the common man, he bathes the feet of Christ....

This is why the Pharisee poured no water on Christ's feet, because he did not have a soul free from the filth of unbelief. And how could he wash his conscience if he had not received the water of Christ? ... Therefore, Simon the Pharisee, who had no water, had, of course, no tears. How could he have tears if he did not do penance, for, not believing in Christ, he had no tears? If he had had them, he would have bathed his eyes so that he could see Christ whom he did not see, although he was at table with Him. If he had seen Him, surely he would never have doubted His power.

"You gave me no kiss, but she, from the moment she entered, has not ceased to kiss my feet" (Luke 7:45). A kiss is a mark of love. How, then, can a Jew have a kiss, who has not known peace, who has not received peace from Christ when He said: "My peace I give you, my peace I leave unto you" (John 14:27)....

The Pharisee, therefore, had no kiss except perhaps that of the traitor Judas. But even Judas did not have a kiss, and when he wished to show the Jews the promised kiss as a sign of betrayal the Lord said to him: "Judas, do you betray the Son of Man with a kiss?" (Luke 22:48) that is, you are offering Me a kiss, and you do not have the love of a kiss; you offer a kiss, and you know not the mystery of a kiss. It is not the kiss of the lips which is sought, but of the heart and soul.

Scripture Meditation

Her many sins have been forgiven—for she loved much. But he who has been forgiven little loves little.
—LUKE 7:47

Thought for the Day

Following the symbolism of Augustine and Bernard of Clairvaux, "the kiss of the feet" is service, "the kiss of the hand" is companionship, but "the kiss of the lips" is intimate communion with our Lord, reserved to those who love much having been forgiven much.

Prayer

O Lord my God! I cannot speak to you at present without tears and sadness and also overwhelming joy. You desire constantly to be present with me ... yet despite your wonderful love, I still often do things which offend and upset you.... Teach me to sing of your mercies.
—TERESA OF AVILA

MAY 23: THE MEANING OF ANOINTMENT (HOLY MURON)

In 2001 Karekin II, the Supreme Patriarch and Cattolicos of the
Armenian Orthodox Church, issued a pastoral communication on the
Holy Muran. The letter was written by two of its theologians,
Hacob Keusseyan and Vardon Devrikian.

*M*uron, a Greek word for "fragrant oil" or "essence flowing from a plant," is derived from the root "to rub," "to anoint." Since ancient times, olive oil has been used, together with various fragrant spices. Reference to it is in the ancient Jewish feast days (Ps. 23:5; Amos 6:6). While in the days of Christ, to pour the ointment on the head or the feet of the guest as a sign of honor was customary (Mark 14:3; John 12:3). Moses was commanded by God to anoint and consecrate in the way the holy Tabernacle and all its utensils (Ex. 30:23–30), while the priests of God also used the olive oil mixed with extensive, precious, incense, and various spices and flowers; the finest and the most precious of these was the ointment of spikenard (Song 1:12, Mark 14:3). Later the kings of Israel were also so consecrated ... as a sign of Yahweh's approval, and as expressive of his grace....

But this act of anointment was changed fundamentally by the coming of the long awaited Messiah, the Only Begotten Son of God. The equivalent of the Hebrew word "Messiah" in Greek is "Christ," which means "Anointed." This name fully qualifies the highest priestly calling to be now that of Christ the Savior (Heb. 6:20), since He is now full of the Spirit and of the power of God; the true image of the invisible God (2 Cor. 4:4). If prior to the coming of Christ only those mortals chosen by God were anointed, now Christ by His essence and divine purpose, is in Himself "the anointed of the Lord" (Luke 2:11; Acts 2:36). Thus it is no chance event, that when Christ first entered the synagogue of Nazareth He read the section from the book of the prophet Isaiah where it is written, "The Spirit of the Lord is upon me, because He hath anointed me to preach the Gospel to the poor; He hath sent me to heal the broken-hearted ..." (Luke 4:18; Isa. 61:1). And now, the words of the prophet have found their full expression in this Divine self-recognition of our Savior.

Scripture Meditation

You know what has happened … how God anointed Jesus of Nazareth with the Holy Spirit and power, and how he went around doing good and healing all who were under the power of the devil, because God was with him.

—ACTS 10:37–38

Thought for the Day

Originally in the Armenian Church, the Holy Muron was replenished on Holy or Maundy Thursday. But like other religious traditions it became mixed with ethnic considerations, as if the essence of being "an Armenian Christian" is now in being so anointed.

Prayer

Through this anointing we are bound with hope to the miracle of your cross, O Christ, for by baptism into your death, O living God, we partake of your divine immortality through you your-self, O God, placing complete trust in you, forever, full, and inseparably.

—GRIGOR NAREKATSI

MAY 24: REMEMBERING PETER'S DENIAL, LET US BE FAITHFUL

Franz Jägerstatter (1907–1943) was a devout Austrian Catholic who in personal isolation opposed the Nazis. He lived as "a relatively untutored man from a remote and isolated village," St. Radegund, 30 km from Hitler's own birthplace. But he made it known that he would refuse to serve in the Nazi army, even when "religious friends" tried to dissuade him of his

decision. Called to active duty in February 1943, he refused, was arrested,
imprisoned, and after a military trial, was beheaded on August 9, 1943. He
writes to his parish priest, Pastor Karabath, on February 22, 1943,
the day of his summons to military service.

everend Father:

I greet you from the bottom of my heart and thank you sincerely for your note. I must tell you that you will probably be losing another of your parishioners soon. Today I received the induction notice and am ordered to report (on the 25th) at Enns. However, since no one can dispense me from what I view as the danger to the health of my soul that this gang presents [i.e. the Nazis], I cannot change my decision, which you already know. As it is, it is so hard to come even one step closer to perfection. Is it even conceivable to try in such an outfit?

Christ did not praise Peter for denying Him merely out of fear of men. How often would I probably have to repeat that denial, serving with this outfit—for if one were not to do so, he could be almost certain that he would never see his dear ones on earth again. Everyone tells me, of course, that I should not do what I am doing because of the danger of death; but it seems to me that the others who do fight are not completely free of the same danger of death.... I believe it is better to sacrifice one's life right away than to place oneself in the grave danger of committing sin and then dying.

From my heart I ask you to pray for me, and to forgive me any trouble I may ever have caused you. May God not abandon me in the last hour! God and the Blessed Virgin will surely not abandon my family when I can no longer protect them myself. Things will be very hard for my dear ones. This leave-taking will be most difficult. Your deeply indebted sexton greets you from his heart. May God protect you and all other priests.

Scripture Meditation

Simon, Simon, Satan has asked to sift you as wheat. But I have
prayed for you, Simon, that your faith may not fail. And when
you have turned back, strengthen your brothers.
—LUKE 22:31–32

Thought for the Day

Without God's grace we cannot withstand the assaults of God's enemies.

Prayer

We beseech you, Almighty God, look upon the hearty desires of your humble servants, and stretch forth the right hand of your Majesty, to be our defense against all our enemies; through Jesus Christ our Lord. Amen.

—COLLECT FOR THE THIRD SUNDAY IN LENT

MAY 25: THE FINAL WORDS OF A HUMAN BEING
BEFORE ENTERING ETERNITY WITH CHRIST

Helmuth James von Molke (1907–1945) came from a proud Prussian family and was the great-great nephew of Bismarck's chancellor. Betrayed and arrested for the plot to assassinate Hitler on January 19, 1944, he found facing death at the age of thirty-eight years "a hard bit of the road ahead of me." In court he testified, "I stand before you, not as a Protestant, not as a big landowner, not as a nobleman, nor as a German ... but as a Christian and nothing else." He wrote some 1,600 letters to his wife, Freya—this one on January 11, 1945, the day he was hanged in Tegel prison.

My love,

I just feel like chatting with you a little. I have really nothing to say.... Just don't let anything trouble you. It really isn't worth it.... I think with untroubled joy of you and the boys, of Kreisau and everybody there; the parting doesn't seem at all grievous at the moment. That may still come.

But it isn't a burden at the moment. I don't feel like parting at all. How this can be so, I don't know. But there isn't any trace of the feeling that overwhelmed me after your first visit in October, no, it must have been November. Now my inner voice says (a) God can lead me back there today just as well as yesterday, and (b) if he calls me to himself, I'll take it with me. I haven't at all the feeling which sometimes came over me: Oh, I'd like to see it all again just once more. Yet I don't feel at all "other-worldly." You see that I am quite happy chatting with you instead of turning to the good God. There is a hymn—2,084—which says "for he to die is ready who living clings to Thee." That is exactly how I feel. Today, because I live, I must cling to him while living; that is all he wants. Is that pharisaical? I don't know. But I think I know that I only live in his grace and forgiveness and have and can do nothing by myself....

The decisive phrase of the trial was: "Herr Graf, one thing Christianity and we National Socialists have in common, and only one: we demand the whole man." I wonder if he realized what he was saying? Just think how wonderfully God prepared this, his unworthy vessel. At the moment when there was danger that I might be drawn into active preparations of a putsch—it was in the evening of the 19th that Stauffenberg came to Peter—I was taken away, so that I should be and remain free from all con-nection with the use of violence. —Then he planted in me my socialist leanings, which freed me, as big landowner, from all suspicion of represent-ing interests. —Then he humbled me as I have never been humbled before, so that I had to lose all pride, so that at last I understand my sinful-ness after 38 years, so that I learn to beg for his forgiveness and to trust to his mercy. —Then he lets me come here, so that I can see you standing firm and I can be free of thoughts of you and the little sons, that is, of cares; he gives me time and opportunity to arrange everything that can be arranged, so that all earthly thoughts can fall away. —Then he lets me experience to their utmost depth the pain of parting and the terror of death and the fear of hell, so that all that should be over, too. —Then he endows me with faith, hope, and love, with a wealth of these that is truly overwhelming....

Dear heart, my life is finished and I can say of myself: He died in the fullness of years and of life's experience. This doesn't alter that fact that I would gladly go on living and that I would gladly accompany you a bit further on this earth. But then I would need a new task from God. The task for which God made me is done. If he has another task for me, we shall hear of it. Therefore by all means continue your efforts to save my life, if I survive this day. Perhaps there is another task.

I'll stop, for there is nothing more to say. I mentioned nobody you should greet or embrace for me; you know yourself who is meant. All the texts we love are in my heart and in your heart. But I end by saying to you by virtue of the treasure that spoke from me and filled this humble earthen vessel:

The Grace of our Lord Jesus Christ
and the love of God and the fellowship
of the Holy Spirit be with you all.
Amen. J.

Scripture Meditation

It was just before the Passover Feast. Jesus knew that the time had come for him to leave this world and go to the Father. Having loved his own who were in the world, he now showed them the full extent of his love.

—JOHN 13:1

Thought for the Day

Facing death is the opportunity for the greatest clarification of truth.

Prayer

*Thou, O Christ art all I want
More than all I find in Thee.*

—CHARLES WESLEY

MAY 26: A ROMANTIC VIEW OF RELIGIOUS LEISURE

*Hannah More (1745–1833) would be a remarkable lady in any century. A
close friend of the celebrities of her day—Samuel Johnson, Sir Richard
Burke, Joshua Reynolds, David Garrick—she became the leading
pamphleteer for the abolition of slavery, founder of the National Sunday
Movement, and other causes. She wrote this letter to John Newton in 1787 at
age thirty-two, when she was frustrated with her slow
spiritual growth as a Christian.*

Dear Sir,

In this pretty quiet cottage, which I built myself two years ago, I have
spent the summer. It is about ten miles from Bristol, on the Exeter road,
has a great deal of very picturesque scenery about it, and is the most perfect little hermitage that can be conceived. The care of my garden gives
me employment, health and spirits.

I want to know, dear sir, if it is peculiar to myself to form ideal plans
of perfect virtue, and to dream all manner of imaginary goodness in
untried circumstances, while one neglects the immediate duties of one's
actual situation. Do I make myself understood? I have always fancied
that if I could secure to myself such a quiet retreat as I have now really
accomplished that I should be wonderfully good; that I should have
leisure to store my mind with such and such maxims of wisdom; that I
should be safe from such and such temptations; that, in short, my whole
summers would be smooth periods of peace and goodness.

Now the misfortune is, I have actually found a great deal of the comfort I expected, but without any of the concomitant virtues. I am
certainly happier here than in the agitation of the world, but I do not find
that I am one bit better: with full leisure to rectify my heart and affections, the disposition unluckily does not come. I have the mortification to
find that petty and (as they are called) innocent employments can detain
my heart from heaven as much as tumultuous pleasures.

If to the pure all things are pure, the reverse must be also true when I
can contrive to make so harmless an employment as the cultivation of
flowers stand in the room of a vice, by the great portion of time I give up
to it, and by the entire dominion it has over my mind. You will tell me

313

that if the affections be estranged from their proper object it signifies not much whether a bunch of roses or a pack of cards effects it. I pass my life in intending to get the better of this, but life is passing away, and the reform never begins. It is a very significant saying, though a very old one, of one of the Puritans, that "hell is paved with good intentions." I sometimes tremble to think how large a square my procrastination alone may furnish to this tessellated pavement.

I heartily commend myself to your prayers, and am, with the most cordial esteem, dear sir, your much obliged and faithful, H. More.

Scripture Meditation

I have the desire to do what is good, but I cannot carry it out.
—ROMANS 7:18

Thought for the Day

An ideal environment does not, by itself, change our hearts.

Prayer

God harden me against myself:
This coward with pathetic voice
Who craves for ease, and rest, and joys.
—CHRISTINA ROSSETTI

MAY 27: JESUS CHRIST—RISEN FROM THE DEAD

Pope Leo I, the Great, (d. 461) dominated the orthodox findings of the Council of Chalcedon in 451, the Fourth Ecumenical Council, which settled

the church's confession that "we should confess that our Lord Jesus Christ
is one and the same Son, the same perfect in his divinity, the same perfect
in his humanity, truly God and truly man." He writes this
undated pastoral letter to his flock.

*D*early beloved,

Those days between the Resurrection and Ascension of our Lord, did not pass away in an inactive course: for in them great and sacred truths were confirmed, and mysteries were revealed. In them the fear of terrible death was taken away, and the immortality not only of the soul, but also of the flesh, was displayed. In them, by means of the Lord's breathing, the Holy Spirit was poured into all the Apostles; and to the blessed Apostle Peter above the rest, after the keys of the kingdom, was entrusted the care of the Lord's flock. In those days, when two disciples were on their road, the Lord associated Himself as a third with them; and in order to clear away all the darkness of our uncertainty, the tardiness of those who were trembling with fear, was rebuked. Illuminated hearts received the flame of faith, and having been lukewarm, were made to burn while the Lord "opened the Scriptures." Moreover, "in the breaking of bread the eyes" of those who sat at meat with Him were opened: more blessed still, the glorification of their [new] nature was shown to them....

But among these and other miracles, tossed by restless thoughts, the Lord had appeared in the midst of the disciples, saying, "Peace be unto you" ... they supposed they had seen a spirit and not flesh.... He confutes their doubting thoughts, which were discordant with the truth, by presenting visually to the eyes, the marks of the Cross in His hands and feet, and invites them to handle Him carefully. Indeed, it was to heal the wounded hearts of unbelievers, that the traces of the nails and spear were retained. So they could hold fast, no longer in doubt, but by a most assured knowledge, the corpse lain in the sepulcher, would be seated on the throne with God the Father.

Scripture Meditation

In the presence of God and of Christ Jesus, who will judge the living and the dead, and in view of his appearing and his kingdom, I

will give you this charge: Preach the Word … correct, rebuke, and encourage.
—2 TIMOTHY 4:1–2

Thought for the Day

Let our faith be grounded in God's word not in our emotions.

Prayer

Whom have I in heaven but you? And earth has nothing I desire besides you.
—PSALM 73:25

MAY 28: THE RESURRECTION OF JESUS CHRIST IN OUR DAY-TO-DAY LIFE

Dr. Paul Spilsbury (b. 1966) is a professor of New Testament at Canadian Bible College, Calgary. He writes to an inquirer on August 14, 2003.

Dear Gavin,

I have been thinking about what the resurrection of Jesus means for us in our day-to-day lives. This event was, after all, the very essence of the first Christians' faith. Their belief that Jesus had been raised from the dead was what distinguished them from everyone else in the ancient Mediterranean world, and I think that it should be what distinguishes us from those who do not believe in Christ today. The ancient Greeks did not think resurrection was possible. For them, Hades—the place one goes after one dies—was an inescapable place of shades and ghosts in the nether regions of the earth, cut off from the warmth and hope of the land of the living. Some philosophers speculated about the possibility of a higher kind of life after death. This was not the life of resurrection, though, but a disembodied existence of the immortal soul, available only to the elite few who were truly enlightened. For the average person the outlook after death was a gloomy and dank half-life in the under-side of the world. This meant that you had to make the most of the present, because this life is as good as it gets.

Some of the Jews in the time of Jesus had a far brighter view of the future, for those who belonged to God. They also had a far less optimistic view of the present world. Ever since the time of the prophet Daniel, Jews have believed that the present age, characterized by suffering, pain and oppression, would eventually give way to a new age in which death and dying would be done away with, to enter a life of *shalom*, peace and wholeness made possible by the Holy Spirit himself.

The first Christians believed this too, but with one significant difference: the resurrection had already happened with the resurrection of Jesus! Or, at least it had begun to happen, for the old age of suffering and oppression was still there, and the new age had not fully arrived. So what are we to make of this? Raised from the dead, Jesus was inaugurating the end of the world as we know it, and the beginning of the age of the future, the age of *shalom*. More than that, he was bringing into the present age the first fruits of the age to come, meaning that the life of the future world has begun to take root and to grow in the midst of the present age, giving life here and now a whole new significance. Neither the Greeks who had no hope for the future, nor the Jews who had little hope for the present were quite right. But the resurrection of Jesus now gives us both a meaningful life now, as well as the hope of a better future. For this we need radically to align ourselves by faith with the Spirit of Christ in the world—the Spirit of resurrection—instead of being with the spirit of the age. How this works out in practice is our life task of faith, as we embrace the life of the resurrected Lord Jesus. In his love, Paul.

Scripture Meditation

Jesus said to [Martha], "I am the resurrection and the life. He who believes in me will live, even though he dies; and whoever ... believes in me will never die."
—JOHN 11:25–26

Thought for the Day

Joining to the resurrected Lord Jesus implies loosening our ties to the old dying world and binding ourselves to the life of the world to come.

Prayer

O Lord, listen to my plea
… I die because I do not die …
I long to be taken from this dark earth,
I long to be released from this dark body.
Then I shall cry with ecstatic joy;
I live because I live in you.
—JOHN OF THE CROSS

MAY 29: CELEBRATING THE LORD'S DAY

Augustine of Hippo further writes to Januarius on why we celebrate "the Lord's Day" as the unique weekly day of rest throughout the year.

Why we celebrate Easter, so that it comes after the Sabbath is unique to the Christian faith. The Jews celebrate only the first month, and the phase of the new moon from the fourteenth to the twenty-first. Our forebears judged we needed to distinguish our feast from the Sabbath of the Jews. Moreover, God the author of time is before all time, coming "in the fullness of time," with the power to both lay down his life and to take it again.... Asked about his time, he replied, "My hour has not yet come," for he was not waiting for a time fixed by fate, but for a time appropriate to the mystery he was going to institute. So he did what we cannot do, he fixed the time; instead, we have to go by astronomic time instead!

Now we are sustained by faith, hope and love, in striving to enter into that eternal rest. We make the transition from this life into that "rest," by what our Lord Jesus Christ deigned to reveal and consecrate by his passion. This "rest" is not slothful inaction, but a kind of indescribable peace that comes from effortless action. For the end result is that the labors of this life are exchanged for the sheer delight of another way of acting. It is an activity that consists in praising God, without physical effort or anxiety. Moreover, we don't need to relapse to the old way of "busyness," for we can enter into a new quietude of soul, where there is no weariness in work, nor restlessness of thought.

The "Sabbath" represented that original way of life, prior to the "Fall," on the seventh day. Afterwards, it was reinterpreted as "the Return of the Prodigal" now restored from wandering, accepted, and clothed in "the best robe," the spiritual "First Day of the Week," which we now call "The Lord's day." When you read Genesis on the days of creation, you realize that originally the seventh day had no evening, for it was now rest without end. But for the sinner, the original everlasting life was forfeited. Now "the first day of the week," represents a return to the original life, as everlasting rest, not forfeited but restored! …

Scripture Meditation

Find rest, O my soul, in God alone; my hope comes from him. He alone is my rock and my salvation.
—PSALM 62:5–6

Thought for the Day

The weekly celebration of "The Lord's Day" is the reminder of where our hearts can and should only be, truly at rest in the Lord.

Prayer

You are great, Lord, and greatly to be praised.… You have created us for yourself, and our hearts are restless until they rest in you.
—AUGUSTINE OF HIPPO

MAY 30: BAPTISM AS THE NEW BEING IN CHRIST

Leo the Great (400–461), bishop of Rome, wrote many letters and sermons
that attest to the depth and seriousness of his theological thought. This is one
of his Episcopal letters, dated October 21, 447.

*B*ishop Leo, to all the bishops presiding throughout Sicily, greetings in the Lord....

Although, what pertains to Christ's lowliness and to His glory come together, respectively, in one and the same person. Whatever divine power and human weakness exist in Him, all affect our redemption. But it is especially in the death of the Crucified and in His resurrection from the dead that the power of baptism establishes a new being out of the old [for the Christian]. That is to say, both the death and the life of Christ operate in those being reborn. As the Apostle says: "Do you not know that all we who have been baptized in Christ have been baptized into his death? For we were buried with him by means of baptism into death, so that, as Christ has risen from the dead through the glory of the Father, we also may walk in newness of life. For if we have been united with him in the likeness of death, we shall be also in the likeness of his resurrection." ... Hence it is apparent from such use of analogy in teaching us about our baptism and adoption as "sons of God", the day and season for such a celebration were also chosen, to be in harmony with what was done in Christ, our Head. So in the rite of baptism, death occurs from the slaying of sin; hence is enacted the triple immersion to reflect upon the three days of burial. While our rising out of the water is reflective, of Christ being raised from the tomb. Hence, the very nature of the rite shows that ordinarily the right day for the reception of this grace [i.e. Sunday] is celebrant of the day on which both the power of the gift and the form of the rite had their origin.

What follows helps very much to confirm this point. The Lord Jesus Christ Himself, after He arose from the dead, gave to his disciples (and in them He instructed all those who are in charge of churches) the rite and the power of baptizing, saying: "Go, therefore, and make disciples of all nations, baptizing them in the name of the Father, and of the Son, and of the Holy Spirit." Of course, He could have instructed them about this even before His passion, except that he especially wanted it understood that the grace of rebirth began only with His resurrection.

Scripture Meditation

> *Don't you know that all of us who were baptized into Christ Jesus were baptized into his death?*
> —ROMANS 6:3

Thought for the Day

The paradigm of "death-resurrection" gives the Christian a unique identity.

Prayer

> *Eternal God, who by thy holy breath of power makes us a new creation for thyself, we beseech thee to preserve what thou has created, and consecrate what thou has cleansed.*
> —ROWLAND WILLIAMS

MAY 31: THE MEANING OF ETERNAL LIFE

Karl Barth (1886–1968), among the greatest theologians of the twentieth century, wrote many pastoral letters. Here he replies to Werner Ruegg from Basel on July 6, 1961.

*D*ear Mr. Ruegg,

Is there a state beyond which interaction is possible with the dead? In all honesty I could reply to this question only that I had no knowledge of such a state and that the lady who put the question would do better to consider that in both this life and the next it is with God that she has to do.

Naturally there is much more to say about eternal life than that. I cannot be explicit in this letter, but I can at least give you a hint of my thinking on the issue in the light of Revelation and indeed the whole of holy Scripture.

Eternal life is not another and second life, beyond the present one. It is this life, but the reverse side which God sees although it is as yet hidden from us—this life in its relation to what He has done for the whole world, and therefore for us too, in Jesus Christ. We thus wait and hope, even in view of our death, for our manifestation with Him, with Jesus Christ who was raised again from the dead, in the glory of not only the judgment but also the grace of God. The new thing will be that the cover of tears, death, suffering, crying, and pain that now lies over our present life will be lifted, that the decree of God fulfilled in Jesus Christ will stand before our eyes, and that it will be the subject not only of our deepest shame but also of our joyful thanks and praise. I like to put it in the fine stanza of Gellert in which he speaks of knowing in the light what is now obscure on earth, of calling wonderful and glorious what took place inscrutably, of seeing with our spirit the context of our destiny with praise and thanksgiving.

This is "what the professor thinks" and this is what he should have said briefly last Sunday to the woman who wanted to know about spirit appearances and to all the other listeners.

With friendly greetings, yours, Karl Barth.

Scripture Meditation

The throne of God and of the Lamb will be in the city, and his servants will serve him. They will see his face, and his name will be on their foreheads. There will be no more night.

—REVELATION 22:3–5

Thought for the Day

Eternal life is this life seen from God's perspective.

Prayer

Almighty God, who through your only Begotten Son Jesus Christ has overcome death, and opened unto us the gate of everlasting life ... put into our minds good desires ... through Jesus Christ our Lord. Amen.

—COLLECT FOR EASTER MONDAY

SOURCES

The sources of letters are identified by page numbers; some are excerpts from various pages. Authors are listed alphabetically. Permission has been granted for all personal communications. Most of the prayers are in "public domain"; some are excerpts from *Great Souls at Prayer*.

BIBLIOGRAPHY

à Kempis, Thomas. *Thomas à Kempis and the Brothers of the Common Life*. Vol. 2. London: Kegan, Paul, Trench, & Co., 1882, 165–70.

Abbé de Tourville. *Letters of Direction: Thoughts on the Spiritual Life*. London & Oxford: Mowbray, 1982, 12–13, 28–30.

Adam of Perseigne. *The Letters of Adam of Perseigne*. Vol. 1, Letter 11. Translated by Grace Perigo. Kalamazoo, MI: Cistercian Publications, 1976, 58, 59, 61.

Aelred of Rievaulx. *A Letter to His Sister*. Translated by Geoffrey Webb and Adrian Walker. London: A. R. Mowbray & Co. Ltd., 1957, 60.

— — —. *Jesus at the Age of Twelve*, trans. pp. 26–7, 35, 36, 38.

— — —. *Aelred of Rievaulx: Treatises and Pastoral Prayer*. Kalamazoo, MI: Cistercian Publications, 3–4, 9–16, 26–27, 35–36, 38.

Alexander, Desmond. Personal communication.

Alexandrina of Ricci. *Letters from the Saints*. Compiled by Claude Williamson. London: Salisbury Square, n.d., 149–151.

Alphonsus of Liguori. *Alphonsus de Liguori: Selected Writings*. Edited by Frederick M. Jones. New York: Paulist Press, 1999, 328–29.

Ambrose of Milan. *Saint Ambrose: Letters 1–91*. Vol. 26. Translated by Mary Melchior Beyenka. Washington, D.C.: Catholic University of America, 1954, 386–91.

Anonymous. *The Pursuit of Wisdom and Other Works by the Author of the Cloud of Unknowing*. Translated and edited by James Walsh. New York: Paulist Press, 1988, 166–69, 219–24.

— — —. Mother's letter. April 21, 2003.

— — —. Pastor's letter. October 7, 2002.

— — —. Pastor's letter of resignation. February 11, 2004.

— — —. Hot-air balloon manufacturer letter. April 22, 2001.

Athanasius. *A Library of Fathers of the Holy Catholic Church: Historical Tracts of St. Athanasius*. Translated by members of the English Church. Oxford: John Henry Parker, 1843, 299–300.

— — —. *St. Athanasius: Select Works and Letters*. A Select Library of Nicene and Post-Nicene Fathers of the Christian Church, 4. Edinburgh: T. & T. Clark, 1998, 519–20, 551–52.

— — —. *The Resurrection Letters, St. Athanasius, Bishop of Alexandria, from A.D.*

328–373. Nashville: Thomas Nelson, 1979.

Augustine of Hippo. *Letters 100–155*. Vol. 2. Translated by Sister Wilfrid Parsons. New York: Fathers of the Church, 1953, 56, 78–79, 87–88, 153–155, 177.

— — —. *Letters 211–270*. Vol. 4. Translated by Sister Wilfrid Parsons. New York: Fathers of the Church, 1955, 94–97, 97–100.

— — —. *Letters 1–99*. Vol. 1. Edited by John E. Rotelle. Translated by Roland Teske. New York: New City Press, 2001, 110–11, 114.

— — —. "The Letter to Proba." *Letters of Saint Augustine: The Words of the Most Celebrated Theologian of the Latin Church*. Translated by John Leinenweber. Liguori, MO: Triumph Books, 1992, 120–29.

— — —. *On Christian Belief: The Works of Saint Augustine: A Translation for the 21st Century*. New York: New City Press, 2005.

— — —. *Saint Augustine's Enchiridion*. London: Sheldon Press, 1953, 7–8.

— — —. "Letter 147 to the noble lady Pauline." *The Classics of Western Spirituality*. New York: Paulist Press, 1989, 165.

Averbeck, Richard. Personal communication.

Barnes, M. Craig. Personal communication.

Barnett, Paul. Personal communication.

Barth, Karl. *A Letter to Great Britain from Switzerland*. London: Sheldon Press, 1941, 1, 4–7, 9–11–13, 23–26.

— — —. *Karl Barth: Letters, 1961–1968*. Translated by Geoffrey W. Bromley. Grand Rapids: Eerdmans, 1981, 9, 184, 267–68.

Basil the Great. *St. Basil: Select Works and Letters*. Translated by Blomfield Jackson. Grand Rapids: Eerdmans, 1978, 194–96, 231.

Baxter, Richard. "Advice to a Young Minister," *The Congregational Quarterly* 3 (1952): 232–35.

— — —. Letter to Thomas Wadsworth. Folio 249 of Baxter's Letters. January 1656.

Begbie, Jeremy. Personal communications.

Benincasa, Catherine. *Catherine Of Siena As Seen In Her Letters*. Translated and edited by Vida D. Scudder. London: J. M. Dent, 1906, 25–28, 132–3, 168.

Bernard of Clairvaux. *Five Books On Consideration: Advice to a Pope*. Translated by John D. Anderson and Elizabeth T. Kennan. Kalamazoo, MI: Cistercian Publications, 1976, 29, 37–38, 47–48, 52–53, 56.

— — —. *The Letters of St. Bernard of Clairvaux*. Translated by Bruno Scott James. Kalamazoo, MI: Cistercian Publications, 1998, 137–8, 289–90, 292–93.

Berulle, Cardinal Pierre de. *Berulle and the French School: Selected Writings*. Edited by William M. Thompson, translated by Lowell M. Glendon. New York: Paulist Press, 1989.

Blake, William. *The Portable Blake*. Edited by Alfred Kazin. New York: Penguin Books, 1981, 178–180.

Bockmuehl, Mrs. Elizabeth. Personal communication.

Bonar, Andrew A., ed. *Memoirs and Remains of the Rev. Robert Murray McCheyne*. London: Oliphant, Anderson & Ferrier, 1892, 322–23.

— — —. *The Letters of Samuel Rutherford*. Edinburgh: Oliphant & Ferrier, 1891, 85–87.

Bonhoeffer, Dietrich. "How the Prison Letters Survived." In *Friendship and Resistance:*

Essays on Dietrich Bonhoeffer. Edited by Eberhard Bethge. Grand Rapids: Eerdmans, 1995, 38–57.

– – –. *Letters and Papers from Prison.* London: Canterbury Press, 1971, 278–82.

Bossuet, Jacques-Benigne. *Oeuvres Completes Frédéric de Bossuet.* Edited by F. Lachat. Vol. XXVII. Paris: Librairie de Louis Vives, 1864, 294–95.

Bowen, Stuart C. Personal communication.

Bray, Gerald. Personal communication.

Brooke, Dorothy, ed. *Christian.* London: Earnest Benn Ltd., 1929, 80–82.

Brown, John. *Works of John Brown of Haddington.* Edited by Robert Mackenzie. London: Banner of Truth Trust, 1964, 204–05.

Buxton, Thomas Fowell. *Memoirs of Sir Thomas Fowell Buxton, Baronet.* Edited by Charles Buxton. London: J. Murray, 1848, 366–67.

Cabrini, Frances Xavier. *The Travels of Mother Frances Xavier Cabrini: Foundress of the Missionary Sisters of the Sacred Heart of Jesus.* Exeter: Streatham Hill, 1925, 252–56.

Calvin, John. *Letters of John Calvin.* Edited by Jules Bennett. Carlisle, PA: Banner of Truth Press, 1988, 295–96, 300–1, 411–14.

Camus, Jean Pierre. *The Spirit of Francis de Sales.* Translated by H. L. Sidney Lear. London: Longmans, Green and Co., 1908, 11–12.

Canlis, Julie. Personal communication.

Carus, William, ed. *Memoirs of the Life of Rev. Charles Simeon, M.A.* New York: Robert Carter, 1848, 303–304.

Chalmers, James. *Autobiography and Letters.* Edited by Richard Lovett. London: The Religious Tract Society, 1903, 209–10, 212, 214–15.

Chalmers, Thomas, ed. *Select Letters of the Rev. William Romaine.* London: William Collins Co., 1830, 56–59, 156–58, 276–84, 377–78.

Chan, Grace. Personal communication.

Charles Wesley's papers. Methodist Archives and Research Centre. John Ryland University Library, University of Manchester.

Constantine. "Letter to Bishop Alexander and Arius." In *Private Letters Pagan and Christian.* London: Earnest Benn Limited, 1929, 106, 108.

Cowper, William. *The Letters of the Late William Cowper, Esq. to His Friends.* Edited by J. Johnson. London: Baldwin, Cradock and Joy, 1820, 10–11, 529–30.

Crabb, Larry. Personal communication.

Cyprian of Carthage. *Cyprian Letters 1–81, Fathers of the Church.* Vol. 51. Translated by Sister Rose Bernard Donna. Washington, D.C.: Catholic University of America Press, 1964, 162–3, 167–8.

Daly, Robert, ed. *Letters and Papers of the Late Theodosia A. Viscountess Powerscourt.* London: G. Morrish, undated.

Damian, Peter. *Peter Damian: Letters 1–30.* Translated by Owen J. Blum. Washington, D.C.: Catholic University of America Press, 1989, 109–11.

Davies, Mark. Personal communication.

de Caussade, Jean-Pierre. *Abandonment to Divine Providence.* Translated by E. J. Strickland. Exeter: Catholic Records Press, 1921, 122–25, 268–69; 348–49.

de Foucauld, Charles. *Inner Search: Letters (1889–1916).* Translated by Barbara Lucas.

New York: Maryknoll, Orbis, 1979, 84–85.

— — —. *Soldier of the Spirit: The Life of Charles de Foucauld.* Edited by Michael Carrouges, translated by Marie-Christine Hellin. New York: G. P. Putnam, 1956, 81, 86–87.

— — —. *Spiritual Autobiography of Charles de Foucauld.* Edited by Jean-Francois Six, translated by J. Holland Smith. New York: Dimension Books, 1964, 31–32, 80–82, 108–9.

de la Motte Fenelon, Francois. *Selections from the Works of Fenelon,* London: John Chapman, 1845.

— — —. *Spiritual Letters of Archbishop Fenelon: Letters to Women.* Translated by H. L. Sidney Lear. London: Rivingtons, 1877.

de Paola, Francis. *Tradition Day by Day, Readings from Church Writers.* Compiled by John E. Rotelle. Villanova, PA: Augustinian Press, 1994, 116.

de Sousa, Barbosa. Personal communication.

Derderian, Hovan. *The Lenten Period and the Lord's Prayer,* 1–4.

Devenyi, Eva. Personal communication.

DeVoto, Bernard, ed. *New Uncensored Writings by Mark Twain Letters From the Earth.* San Francisco: HarperCollins, 1991, 15–16, 51, 53.

Diewert, Dave A. Personal communication.

Doherty, Catherine de Hueck. *Dearly Beloved: Letters to the Children of My Spirit.* Vol. 1. Combermere, Ontario: Madonna House Publications, 1988, 171–78, 234–35.

Dostoevsky, Fyodor. *Selected Letters of Fyodor Dostoyevsky.* Edited by Joseph Frank and David Goldstein. Piscataway, NJ: Rutgers University Press, 1987, 420–21.

Dudden, F. Homes. *Gregory the Great: His Place in History and Thought.* Vol. 2. London: Longmans, Green, and Co., 1905, 237.

Dugalescu, Peter. Personal communication.

Elchaninov, Alexander. *The Diary of a Russian Priest.* Translated by Helen Iswolsky. London: Faber & Faber, 1967, 207–8.

Elves, Alberto. Personal communication.

Eudes, John. *En tout la volonté de Dieu: Saint Jean Eudes à travers ses lettres.* Edited by C. Guillon. Paris: Cerf, 1981, 68–69.

Evagrius Ponticus. *The Pratikos: Chapters on Prayer.* Cistercian Studies Series, 4. Translated by John Eudes Bamberger. Kalamazoo, MI: Cistercian Publications, 1978, 12–14, 16–20.

Ferrer, Vincent. *Letters from the Saints.* Complied by Claude Williamson. London: Salisbury Square, n.d., 33–47.

Fitzgerald, Sally, ed. *The Habit of Being: Letters of Flannery O'Connor.* New York: Random House, 1940, 92, 99–100.

Fletcher, John William. *The Posthumous Pieces of the Reverend John William de la Flechere.* Edited by Melville Horne. Albany, NY: T. Spencer and A. Ellison, 1794, 277–9, 288–290, 297–300, 305–9, 327–28.

Foley, Henry. *Records of the English Province of the Society of Jesus.* Vol. 1. London: Burnes and Oats, n.d., 338.

Fulbert of Chartres. *Tradition Day by Day, Readings from the Church Fathers.* Villanova, PA: Augustinian Press, 1994, 23.

Ganss, George E, ed. *Ignatius of Loyola: The Spiritual Exercises and Selected Works.* New York: Paulist Press, Inc., 1991, 332–34.

Gay, Craig M. Personal communication.

George, Timothy. Personal communication.

Gerson, Jean. *Jean Gerson: Early Works.* Translated by Brian Patrick McGuire. New York: Paulist Press, 1998.

Gourevitch, Philip. *Stories from Rwanda.* New York: Farrar, Strauss & Giroux, 1998.

Gregg, Robert C., trans. *Athanasius: the Life of Antony and The Letter to Marcellinus,* New York: Paulist Press, 1980.

Gregory of Nyssa. "Letter XVII, to Eustathia, Ambrosia and Basilissa," in *Select Writings and Letters of Gregory, Bishop of Nyssa.* Translated by William More and Henry Austin Wilson, edited by Henry Wace. Edinburgh: T. & T. Clark, 1994, 542–45.

Groote, Geert. *Devotio Moderna: Basic Writings.* Translated by John van Engen. New York: Paulist Press, 1988, 98.

Grou, Jean Nicolas. "The Hidden Life of the Soul," in *Selections from the World's Devotional Classics.* Vol. 10. Edited by Robert Scott and George W. Gilmore. Unknown binding, 1916, 89–90.

Hacob, Keusseyan and Vardon Devri. *Holy Muron: the Mystery of the Holy Surion (Chrism).* Translated by Lilith Sargissian. St. Etchmiadzin, Armenia: Holy See Press, 2001, 3–4, 11.

Hall, Joseph. *The Works of Joseph Hall.* Vol. 9. Edited by Josiah Pratt. London: Whittingham, 1808, 490–97.

Harris, Joel Chandler. *Letters of the Century.* Edited by Lisa Grunwald and Stephen J. Adler. New York: Random House, 1999, 13–14.

———. *Dearest Chums and Partners: Joel Chandler Harris's Letters to His Children.* Edited by Hugh T. Keenan. Athens: University of Georgia Press, 1993, 350–52.

Hatina, Tom. Personal communication.

Havergal, Frances Ridley. *Memorials by Her Sister.* New York: Anson D. F. Randolph and Co., 1880, 64, 72–73, 217, 229–30.

Hindmarsh, Bruce. Personal communication.

Holt, Helen. Personal communication.

Houston, James M., ed. *The Mind on Fire: Blaise Pascal.* Colorado Springs: Victor, 2005, 235–43, 249–50, 253.

Ignatius of Antioch. "Letter to the Romans," in *The Genuine Epistles of the Apostolical Fathers.* Edited by William, Lord Archbishop of Canterbury. New York: Southwick and Pelsue, 1810, 211–16.

Jacobs, Harriet Ann. *Incidents in the Life of a Slave Girl.* Edited by Jean Fagan Yellin. Cambridge: Harvard University Press, 1987, 242.

Jägerstatter, Franz. *In Solitary Witness: The Life and Death of Franz Jägerstatter.* Edited by Gordon Zahn. Springfield, IL: TempleGate Publishers, 1964, 101–102.

Jeffrey, David Lyle, ed. *English Spirituality in the Age of Wesley.* Grand Rapids: Eerdmans, 1987, 314–15, 441–44.

Jerome. "Letter to Marcellina," in *Private Letters Pagan and Christian.* Edited by Dorothy Brooke. London: Earnest Benn Ltd., 1929, 155–56.

John of Avila. *Letters of Blessed John of Avila*. Edited and translated by the Benedictines of Stanbrooke. London: Burns Oates, 1904.

John of the Cross. *The Works of St. John of the Cross*. Edited by David Lewis. London: Thomas Baker, 1891, 549–50.

John of Kronstadt (John Iliytch Sergieff). *My Life in Christ*. Translated by E. E. Goulaeff. London: Cassell & Company, Ltd., 1897, 8–9, 439.

Johnson, Darrell. Personal communication.

Johnston, J. O. and W. C. E. Newbolt, eds. *Spiritual Letters of Edward Bouverie Pusey*. London: Longmans, Green and Co., 1898, 251–52, 281–83.

Keble, John. *Letters of Spiritual Counsel and Guidance*. Edited by R. J. Wilson. Oxford: Oxford University Press, 1870, 154–57.

Kierkegaard, Søren. *Journals and Papers*. Vol. 5. Edited and translated by Havard and Edna Hong. Bloomington: Indiana University Press, 1978, 83, 148.

Kim, Sang-Bok. Personal communication.

Kreiner-Phillips, Kathy. Personal communication.

Lee, Michelle. Personal communication.

Leighton, Robert. *The Whole Works of Robert Leighton, D. D.* Edited by John Norman Pearson. New York: J. C. Riker, 1852, 762.

Leo the Great. "Letters," in *The Fathers of the Church: A New Translation*. Vol. 34. Translated by Edmund Hunt. New York: Fathers of the Church Inc., 1957, 71–72.

———. *Sermons of Leo the Great on the Incarnation*. Translated by William Bright. London: Joseph Masters, 1862, 64–67, 70–74, 77–79.

Levine, Jerry. Personal communication.

Lewis, C. S. "They Stand Together: Letters between C. S. Lewis and Arthur Greaves," in *The Collected Letters of C. S. Lewis, Volume 1: Family Letters, 1905-1931*. Edited by W. H. Lewis. London: Geoffrey Bles, 1966, 175, 303–306, 335–36.

———. *The Screwtape Letters. London:* Centenary Press, 1942, 136, 138–40.

Long, V. Philip. Personal communication.

Luther, Martin. *Luther: Letters of Spiritual Counsel*. Vol. 18. Edited and translated by Theodore G. Tappert. Vancouver: Regent College Publishing, 1997, 98, 125–27, 129.

Macarius of Optino. *Russian Letters of Direction, 1834–1860*. Crestwood, NY: St. Vladimir University Press, 1975, 30.

MacDonald, Greville. *George MacDonald and His Wife*. London: George Allen & Unwin, 1924, 373–74.

Maid of Madame Guyon. "Letter to Francois Fenelon," in *The Archbishop of Cambrai's Dissertation on Pure Love*. London: Luke Hinde, 1750, 239–49.

Mann, Bart. Personal communication.

Manson, Mary. Personal communication.

Markkula, Juhana. Personal communication.

Martyn, Henry. *Journals and Letters of Henry Martyn*. Edited by S. Wilberforce. London: R. B. Seeley and W. Burnside, 1839, 512–14, 516, 757.

Mason, Mike. Personal communication.

Maximus the Confessor. *Centuria*. Translated by Andrew Louth. New York: Routledge, 1996, 86–87.

Mihoc, Vaslie. Personal communication.

Millard, Allen. Personal communication.

Miller, Perry and Thomas H. Johnson, eds. *The Puritans: A Sourcebook of Their Writings.* Mineola, NY: Dover Publications, 2001, 481–82, 486–88.

Milne, Fred. Personal communication.

Muelle, Karen. Personal communication.

Muggeridge, Malcolm. Personal communication.

Mutch, Barbara. Personal communication.

Nazianzen, Gregory. "Letter to Nicobulus," in *Letter-Writing in Graeco-Roman society.* Edited by Stanley K. Stovers. Louisville: John Knox Westminister Press, 1986.

— — —. "Letter to Nebridus," in *Private Letters Pagan and Christian.* Edited by Dorothy Brooke. London: Earnest Benn, Ltd, 1929, 143.

— — —. "Letter from Cyril of Jerusalem and Gregory Nazianzen," in *A Select Library of Nicene and Post-Nicene Fathers of the Christian Church.* Vol. 7. Edinburgh: T. & T. Clark, 1989, 471–72.

Newton, Isaac. *The Orthodox Churchman's Magazine and Review, a Treasury of Divine and Useful Knowledge.* London: J. G. Barnard, 1806, 199–202.

Newton, John. *The Works of the Rev. John Newton, An Authentic Narrative.* Edited by Richard Cecil. Edinburgh: Thomas Nelson and Peter Brown, 1827, 1–3, 16–18, 39–41, 100–104.

Nigg, Walter, ed. *Gerhard Tersteegen, Eine Auswahl aus seinen Schriften.* Wuppertal: R. Brockhaus Verlag, 1967, 104–105, 111–13, 115, 129–31.

Olier, Jean-Jacques. *Oeuvres Completes de M. Olier, M. L'Abbe Migne.* Paris: J-P. Migne, 1856, 802–804, 951–53, 1050–53.

Olphe-Galliard, Miche, ed. *Lettres Spirituelles: Marguerite du Saint-Sacrement.* Paris: Desclee de Brouwer, 1964, 77–78, 127–30.

Overman, Dean. Personal communication.

Packer, J. I. Personal communication.

Palmer, Earl F. Personal communication.

Pascal, Blaise. *Oeuvres completes.* Edited by J. Chevalier. Paris: 1954, 703–705.

Peers, E. Allison, trans. *The Letters of Saint Teresa of Jesus.* London: Sheed and Ward, 1951, 316–17.

Peterson, Eugene. Personal communication.

Pozapalian, Nerses. Personal communication.

Priddy, Barbara. Personal communication.

Provan, Iain. Personal communication.

Quek Swee Hwa. Personal communication.

Ravier, Andre, ed. *Francois de Sales: Lettres Intimes.* Paris: Le Sarment, Fayard, 1991, 131–33, 147–55, 171–72.

Ridley, Nicholas. *The Works of Bishop Ridley.* Cambridge: The University of Cambridge Press, 1841, 395–418.

Robson, Ellie. Personal communication.

Rogers, Henry. *The Life and Character of John Howe, M.A. with an Analysis of His Writings.* London: The Religious Tract Society, 1863, 201–12.

Romaine, William. *Life Walk and Triumph of Faith: With an Account of His Life and Work by Peter Toon,* Cambridge: James Clarke & Co., 1970.

Rosenstock-Huessy, Eugene. *Judaism against Christianity*. New York: Schocken Books, 1969, 97–99, 103–4, 109, 111, 119–26.

Samway, Patrick H. *Walker Percy: A Life*. Chicago: Loyola University Press, 1999, 300–301.

Schnabel, Eckhard. Personal communication.

Scott, Robert and George W. Gilmore, eds. *Selections from the World's Classics*. Vol. 9. New York: Funk & Wagnalls Co., 1916, 19–21, 54–55.

———. "Thoughts on Religion," in *Selections from the World's Devotional Classics*. Vol. 6. New York: Funk & Wagnall, 1916, 173–74.

———. *The Life of God in the Soul of Man*, in *Selections of the World's Devotional Classics*. Vol. 9. New York: Funk & Wagnalls, 1916, 54.

Simpson, Donald H. Personal communication.

Slaymaker, Olav. Personal communication.

Smith, Rick. Personal communication.

Spilsbury, Paul. Personal communication.

Stapleton, T. *The Life and Illustrious Martyrdom of Sir Thomas More*. London: Burns Oates, 1928, 111, 115.

Stevenson, Gail. Personal communication.

Stowers, Stanley K. *Letter-Writing in Greco-Roman Antiquity*. Louisville: Westminster John Knox Press, 1986, 100–101, 122–25.

Suh, Robin. Personal communication.

Tarrants, Tom. Personal communication.

Tauler, Johannes. *The Sermons and Conferences of Johann Tauler*. Translated by Walter Elliott. Washington D.C.: Apostolic Mission House, 1910.

Telford, John, ed. *The Letters of the Rev. John Wesley*. Vol. 8. London: The Epworth Press, 1792, 264–65.

Temple, F. S., ed. *William Temple, Some Lambeth Letters*. London: Lambeth Palace Library, 1963, 25–27, 40–41, 113–14, 135–38, 148, 158–59.

St. Theophan the Recluse. *The Spiritual Life: And How to Be Attuned to It*. Translated by Alexandra Dockham. Wildwood, CA: St. Xenia Skete Press, 1995, 149–50, 227–29.

Toews, John B. *Czars, Soviets & Mennonites*. Newton, KS: Faith and Life Press, 2004, 157–58.

Torrance, Alan. Personal communication.

Tyndale, William. *The Fathers of the English Church*. London: John Hatchard, 1807, 351–52.

van Bruggen, June. Personal communications.

van Eeghan, Ernst. Personal communication.

Venn, Henry. *The Life and a Selection of Letters of the late Rev. Henry Venn*. London: John Hatchard, 1836, 538–39.

Voillaume, Rene. *Brothers of Men: Letters to the Petit-Freres*. Edited by Lancelot Sheppard. London: Darton, Longman and Todd, 1966, 132–36, 190–91, 206–207.

von Hugel, Friedrich. *Letters from Baron von Hugel to a Niece*. Chicago: Regnery Press, 1955, 21–22, 137.

von Moltke, Helmuth James. *Letters to Freya, 1939–1945*. Edited and translated by Beate Ruhm von Oppen. New York: Vintage Books, 1995, 407–12.

Wallace Jr., Charles, ed. *Susanna Wesley: The Complete Writings.* New York: Oxford University Press, 1997, 41–48, 79–81, 164–167.

Walls, Andrew. Personal communication.

Walter of Hilton. *Towards a Perfect Love: The Spiritual Counsel of Walter Hilton.* Translated by David L. Jeffrey. Portland: Multnomah, 1985, 8–12.

Waltke, Bruce. Personal communication.

Watts, Rikk. Personal communication.

Weil, Simone. *Waiting for God.* Translated by Emma Crafurd. New York: Putnam, 1950, 23, 26–27.

Wesley, John. "Letters," in *The Works of John Wesley.* Vol. 25. Oxford: Clarendon Press, 1980, 382–85.

Wesley, Susanna. *Samuel Wesley Jr. Letter Book.* Manchester: Methodist Archives, 9–34.

— — —. *The Life of the Rev. John Wesley, A.M.* London: Paramore, 1792, 241–44.

Whyte, Alexander. *Santa Teresa: An Appreciation.* Edinburgh: Oliphant, Anderson and Ferrier, 1897, 78.

William of St. Thierry. *The Enigma of Faith.* Translated by John D. Anderson. Washington, D.C.: Consortium Press, 1973, 35, 37–38, 91–92.

Wycliffe, John. *Writings of John Wycliffe.* Philadelphia: Presbyterian Board of Publications, 1842, 48.

Zlotnik, Michael. Personal communications.

Additional copies of *Letters of Faith through the Seasons Vol. 1*
are available wherever good books are sold.

෨ා૭ଓ

If you have enjoyed this book, or if it has had an impact on your life,
we would like to hear from you.

Please contact us at:

HONOR BOOKS
Cook Communications Ministries, Dept. 201
4050 Lee Vance View
Colorado Springs, CO 80918

Or visit our Web site:
www.cookministries.com

HONOR HB BOOKS

Inspiration and Motivation for the Seasons of Life